$\mathcal{P}$*hilosophy*

Illinois Central College
Learning Resources Center

GAYLORD

$\mathcal{P}$hilosophy
at $33\frac{1}{3}$ rpm

Themes of Classic Rock Music

James F. Harris

I.C.C. LIBRARY

Open Court

Chicago and La Salle, Illinois

OPEN COURT and the above logo are registered in the U.S. Patent and Trademark Office.

© 1993 by Open Court Publishing Company

First printing 1993

Printed and bound in the United States of America.

Library of Congress Cataloging-in-Publication Data

Harris, James F. (James Franklin). 1941–
    Philosophy at 33 1/3 rpm : themes of classic rock music / James F. Harris.
      p.   cm.
    Includes bibliographical references (p.) and index.
    ISBN 0-8126-9240-3.—ISBN 0-8126-9241-1 (pbk.)
    1. Rock music—1961–1970—Themes, motives, Literary, 2. Music—Philosophy and aesthetics.   I. Title.
ML3532.H33 1993
782.42166—dc20   93-6390
                                CIP
                                MN

Rock is dead. . . . Long live rock. . . .

Pete Townshend

Contents

Preface

Rock music has received very little attention and practically no respect from the self-appointed guardians of American culture. For the most part, rock music is simply ignored in discussions and serious treatments of important elements of American culture. Perhaps these "serious" critics still suppose that 1960s rock music is the peculiar product of a bunch of drug-crazed hippies, and certainly the prevalent use of drugs by "rock stars" and the drug-related deaths of major rock figures including Jimi Hendrix, Brian Jones, Janis Joplin, and Jim Morrison have not helped. It is difficult for many people to get past the "excesses" and the outrageousness of much of rock music to be able to evaluate it soberly. For whatever reasons, rock music has been taken seriously only by a clearly identifiable sub-culture of critics and writers whose territory is limited to popular culture or, more specifically, just to rock music itself. These include the various writers and editors for *Rolling Stone* and other music magazines, and the writers who have written books specifically about rock music. However, these reviews, articles, and books about rock music have focused, almost exclusively, upon the aesthetic values which are internal to rock music, as a genre, or upon the social or political significance of rock music.

Now the social and political significance of rock music should not be minimized, and I will, indeed, have some things to say about these aspects of rock. But this book breaks new ground by concentrating on a facet of rock music which has received far too little attention: the intellectual themes, preoccupations, and even arguments, to be found in the lyrics of rock songs. One of the immediately striking features of classic rock, contrasted with popular music before and since, is its conscious and literal concern with big ideological issues. In an attempt to begin an explanation of rock's aesthetic, literary, and philosophical importance, I will compare classic rock with other products of both "high" and popular culture.

I will show how the rock music from this period represents

not only a major cultural departure but a fundamental philosophical departure from the popular music which came before it and provided it with its roots. By analyzing the lyrics of classic rock, we will see how many rock musicians of this period reacted to the political and social upheaval of the time by turning to and borrowing from classical philosophy, theology, literature, and poetry to shape the questions that they were asking and the pronouncements that they were making. And, by doing so, these song writers and performers were able to make serious comments on the human condition in much the same way as classic literature, drama, and opera are able to do. I will show explicitly how the lyrics of numerous different rock compositions can be understood as general, thematic expressions of these different classic philosophical theories. I will also show how these same themes were recurring in other media of popular culture during the 1960s—especially novels, movies, and "pop" psychology, sociology, and philosophy books.

There are always many ways to interpret a creative work, and what I offer here is one set of categories for making some sense of classic rock music. There are others. For example, I have very little to say about racial and sexual stereotypes or "personae" in rock music, and these are important themes to be examined. My main motive is to provide the material and the impetus to encourage serious, intellectual discussion of rock music, and if I provoke disagreement and dissent, I will have done that. So this is not a book of right answers. Rather than comparing different songs on a completely individual, *ad hoc* basis, at least we will have a framework with some categories into which we can fit songs and which we can use to analyze them and compare them. The particular categories which I have chosen are those of alienation, friendship, community, hedonism, *carpe diem*, self-assertion, judgment, and redemption. Each one of these categories has several sub-categories as well, and these are sometimes mutually supportive and complementary so that they tend to form a cohesive grid for interpreting rock music; however, there are also sometimes conflicts between the different categories— suggesting that we still have not arrived at any definitive and exhaustive set of categories to impose upon rock music. And perhaps we never shall.

I do not try to be exhaustive in this book—either in terms of the categories which I suggest or in terms of the songs I use to illustrate these categories. I must leave some work for you, the reader. I hope to pique your interest so that you will begin to think of additional categories or additional songs to illustrate those categories.

This is not another book about rock 'n' roll trivia. I admit that knowing things such as that the Beatles were originally named Johnny and the Moondogs or that Stu Sutcliffe, who died of a brain hemorrhage, was the original bass player for the Beatles can be interesting. Knowing that Carl Perkins recorded "Blue Suede Shoes" before Elvis Presley did and that Perkins's version actually reached a higher place on the charts (Number Two in March 1956) can be "cool" or "neat", as well as enabling you to win $10,000 on Jeopardy someday, or at least a tee-shirt from some radio call-in quiz show. However, there are no simple, neat, quick answers to the questions I want to ask about the philosophical themes in classic rock music just as there were no simple, neat, quick answers to the questions which the musicians themselves and the other people in the 1960s were asking. We can join the intellectual and moral quest together, but we are likely to find a long and winding road with many branches, and the way is not clearly marked.

This is also not a book which contains a lot of biographical information and personal trivia about the lives of the musicians. While I understand the fascination which ordinary people have with the lives of "the rich and famous", it is not a fascination with which I am particularly sympathetic. I hope that this book is several levels above such interests. We may sometimes find it interesting to examine what musicians have to say about their music, but usually we will find it more rewarding to look at what the music has to say about its musicians—as well as what it has to say about the rest of us.

I certainly do not intend to offer a single, definitive, "correct" interpretation of rock music (except in very unusual individual cases). What I offer is *one* possible way of understanding *some* rock music, and although this may seem a modest claim, my approach can be valuable for gaining some understanding of the importance of rock music and giving it its rightful place in discussions of popular culture. Some rock music, of course, is little more than entertainment, and, like all forms of entertainment, some of it is good, some of it is not so good, and some of it is just plain garbage. What I am suggesting is a fresh way of understanding many of the compositions of classic rock music as culturally important and intellectually engaging. I don't expect everyone to agree with the particular selections I have chosen to discuss in each chapter of the book. I've written about the groups and compositions which I know best, but this does not mean that they are the "right" ones. If, while you are reading a chapter, you begin to think of other groups or compositions which illustrate the particular theme or theory better for you than the ones which I have chosen, or if you think of different philosophical themes from the ones which I have chosen, then *Philosophy at 33⅓ rpm* will have been successful. This is exactly what I would like to happen because then you are considering rock music as a medium for serious, intellectual thought.

As I approach the analyses and interpretations of the various "texts" we find in the lyrics of classic rock music, I will "unpack" the general, serious philosophical themes which we find there. It is sometimes said that you can quote the Bible to prove anything, which illustrates something of the difficulty of trying to provide a clear and consistent exegesis of any particular text. With *Philosophy at 33⅓ rpm*, we have the added difficulty of having no standard, commonly-agreed-upon text and no standard body of literature to point the way or to react against in attempting to provide exegeses of rock compositions. Perhaps the analyses of the songs of classic rock music which I provide in this book will begin to build that body of literature and will prove to be the beginning of a new genre of serious writing about rock music.

I focus in this book upon the versions of songs which appeared on LP albums—music at 33⅓ rpm. I have not always identified the dates of the first releases of songs as singles. I have tried to give the dates of the releases of albums to aid the reader who might want to locate a particular album, although a particular song might well now be available from more than one source—particularly from more recent "best of" albums and CD's for different artists. Understanding and making my way through the bureaucratic labyrinth of the music publishing business has been very complicated and time-consuming. While many other authors seem to completely ignore the problem of getting permissions to quote songs, I have made every effort to identify and gain permission from those who control the rights to the lyrics of the published songs used in this book. In some cases, there are two or even three different publishers who control different percentages of songs. There are several other songs which I would have liked to quote briefly in the book, but in some cases I was unable to gain the necessary permissions, and in others the requested fees were prohibitively high. I have taken the lyrics from authoritative printed sources—the album liner notes where nothing better was available—and my quotations retain whatever grammatical irregularities may be in the original.

I am grateful to those people who have read earlier versions of this book, made very helpful suggestions, and corrected what would have been embarrassing errors, including Jim Goggin, Tom Hale, George Harris, Trey Harris, Allen Knapp, John Levy, Edward Roberts, and Peggy Young. I thank the Band Box, Williamsburg, Virginia, for its co-operaion. I also appreciate the support, sage advice, and invaluable editorial assistance of David Ramsay Steele of Open Court. Finally, I would like to thank those friends whose encouragement and confidence made this project both possible and enjoyable, especially Peggy.

Acknowledgements for Permissions

"Someday" by James Pankow and Robert Lamm. Copyright © 1969 Lamminations Music, Moose Music, and Aurelius Music. Used by permission of CPP/Belwin, Inc., Miami, Florida. International Copyright secured. Made in U.S.A. All rights reserved.

"Someday Never Comes", composed by J.C. Fogerty, published by Wenana Music Co.

"Stranger in a Strange Land". Lyrics and music by Leon Russell and Don Preston. © 1971 Irving Music, Inc. (BMI). All rights reserved. International Copyright secured.

"State of the Union" by Robert Lamm. Copyright © 1972 Lamminations and Big Elk Music (ASCAP). Used by permission of CPP/Belwin, Inc., Miami, Florida. International Copyright secured. Made in U.S.A. All rights reserved.

"Take Me to the Mardi Gras" Copyright © 1973 Paul Simon.

"(Let Me Be Your) Teddy Bear". Words and music by Kal Mann and Bernie Lowe. Copyright © 1957 by Gladys Music, Inc. Copyright renewed and assigned to Gladys Music (administered by Williamson Music). International Copyright secured. All rights reserved.

"White Rabbit" by Grace Slick. Copyright © 1967 Irving Music, Inc., c/o Rondor Music International. Used by permission of CPP/Belwin, Inc., Miami, Florida. International Copyright secured. Made in U.S.A. All rights reserved.

"Why Don't We Do It in the Road". Words and music by John Lennon and Paul McCartney © 1968 by Northern Songs Limited. All rights controlled and administered by MCA Music Publishing, a division of MCA Inc., New York, New York 10019. Under license from ATV Music. Used by permission. All rights reserved.

"Won't Get Fooled Again". Words and music by Pete Townshend. Copyright © 1971 Fabulous Music Ltd.

"Yakety Yak". Words and music by Jerry Leiber and Mike Stoller. Copyright © 1958 by Tiger Music, Inc. Copyright renewed. All rights assigned to Chappell and Co. (Intersong Music, Publisher), Quintet Music, Inc., and Bienstock Publishing Co. All rights administered by Chappell and Co. International copyright secured. All rights reserved.

"You've Got a Friend" by Carole King. © 1971 Colgems-EMI Music Inc. All rights reserved. Used by permission.

1

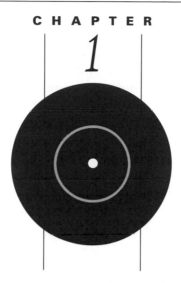

A Long, Strange Trip: From Rock 'n' Roll to Rock Music

The first vinyl discs, the 78s, represented a significant techno-logical advancement over the original voice coils for recording sound. The quality of the sound reproduction as well as the ease and efficiency of operation of the Victrolas were greatly im-proved. However, as significant as these developments were technologically, they had little or no impact upon the kind of music which was being produced. This was the period which saw the continuation of the music of Tin Pan Alley. The major vocalists were Bing Crosby, Frank Sinatra, Perry Como, Patti Page, Rosemary Clooney, and the Andrews Sisters. The music they sang came from the pens of George Gershwin, Irving Berlin, and Cole Porter, and the bands were led by Benny Goodman, Tommy Dorsey, and Count Basie. The introduction of the vinyl disc did not affect the *kind* of popular music being produced. During the 1930s and 1940s, American popular music was almost completely uniformly structured in the same way in which it had been previously—16-bar form, with four-bar phrasing and a rhythm which accented the dominating first and third beats. So, popular musicians kept producing the same kind of music which had been around for several decades, in the same musical form, and because of the vinyl disc, the rest of us could hear the reproduction of the music better and more conveniently—at 78 rpm.

45 rpm

Next in the early 1950s, came the 45s, and again, the development of the smaller and lighter (and cheaper!) 45s represented a significant technological advance over the old 78s. Smaller and easier to operate reproduction systems, to become known as "hi-fi's", could even be operated by teenagers and taken very easily almost anywhere, anytime, as a self-contained unit—to a sockhop, sleep-over, or teentown. When you arrived at a party in the mid-1950s, people would ask you not only if you had brought your records, but if you had brought your hi-fi as well. This was music and a format for music made for bobbie-sox and bluejeans—easy, casual, straight-ahead, what-you-see-is-what-you-get music.

The 45s format quickly came to dominate the recording industry and both reflected and reinforced the *kind* of popular music which was being produced—early rock 'n' roll. Since producing Top 40 songs and "singles" became the financial driving force of the recording industry, these were the kind of compositions which characterized the music of the 1950s— short songs which could fit on a 45 and into AM radio play time, just two minutes, give or take a few seconds. So, we got bubble-gum smacking, finger-snapping, foot-patting, and hip-swaying music, and it was, undeniably the hard, driving, pulsating beat and rhythm of this music with its obvious sexual tension which gave it its appeal.

Early rock 'n' roll, from the early and mid-1950s, represented a remarkable departure from the popular music of Tin

Pan Alley[1] as well as everything else which had come before it in popular music. Rock 'n' roll used the twelve-bar phrase structure of black rhythm and blues (4 + 4 + 2 + 2) with the very simple chord progressions of blues music (simple, three-chord melodies). There is no "development" of the chords towards a big ending for the song as was characteristic of Tin Pan Alley. The same three chords are just repeated over and over again. And, most importantly, the rhythm of rock 'n' roll accented the second and fourth beats, the *off* beats—pa-BOOM! pa-BOOM![2] This is what gave rock 'n' roll its pulsating BEAT and made it so impossible for young people to stand or sit still while listening to it. And the tempo of the beat was fast—much faster than anything typical of earlier Tin Pan Alley songs. The repetition of the same three chords, the emphasis on the off-beat, and the fast tempo provided early rock 'n' roll music with its sense of urgency and energy.

Awopbopaloobopalopbamboom
For the most part, the lyrics were irrelevant. Think of the hottest performers and the hottest songs of the 1950s: Certainly, Elvis Presley earned his title of "King of rock 'n' roll" in the 1950s with such Top 40 hits as "Heartbreak Hotel" (1956), "Hound Dog" (1956), "Don't Be Cruel" (1956), "All Shook Up" (1957), "Teddy Bear" (1957), "Jailhouse Rock" (1957), "Don't" (1958), "Hard Headed Woman" (1958), and "A Hunk of Love" (1959)—all Number One hits.[3] There was Little Richard and "Tutti-Frutti" (1956), "Long Tall Sally" (1956), "Lucille" (1957), and "Good Golly, Miss Molly" (1958).[4] Other early hits which have now become widely regarded "standards" from the 1950s include Bill Haley and the Comets with "Rock around the Clock" (1955), The Platters with "The Great Pretender" (1956) and "Smoke Gets in Your Eyes" (1959), The Everly Brothers with "Wake Up Little Susie" (1957) and "All I Have To Do Is Dream" (1958), Danny & The Juniors with "At The Hop" (1958), Buddy Holly with "That'll Be the Day" (1957) and "Peggy Sue" (1958), and Chuck Berry with "Maybelline" (1955) and "Johnny B. Goode" (1958).[5]

Now think of the memorable lines from the lyrics of some of these songs. "You ain't nothing but a hound dog, crying all the time." "I'm in love, huh, I'm all shook up." "Awopbopaloobopalopbamboom, Tutti Frutti, all a rootie." "One, two, three o'clock, four o'clock, rock." "Wake up, little Susie, we've got to go home." "Let's go to the hop, oh baby, let's go to the hop." "Go, go, go, Johnny, go. Go, go, go, Johnny, go. Go, Johnny B. Goode."

These memorable lines are memorable just because they are so completely insignificant. The lyrics are, at best, superficial and shallow, and, at worst, silly and meaningless. It is the beat which is important, and you can substitute almost any words or sounds for the original lyrics without losing very much. If you also throw in all of the doo-wops, grunts, huh's, yells and screams and other unique sounds—the vocal equivalents of whistles and cowbells—which characterized these monster Top 40 hits, you gain more of an appreciation of the insignificance of the lyrics for these songs.

Masterpiece Theater and "Tutti-Frutti"

I remember a cartoon strip which I saw some years ago by Doug Marlette, the creator of "Kudzu." In the strip a parrot is watching a television production of "Masterpiece Theater" with Alistair Cooke. The program is the third and final episode of a three-part series focusing upon the dramatization of that "immortal classic", "Tutti Frutti" by Little Richard. Marlette has the voice of Cooke summarize the first two parts which were broadcast earlier:

> In Part One we met the carefree, young protagonist. As luck would have it, he "has a gal named Sue" who, as he so charmingly puts it, "knows just what to do!"

The voice from the set continues,

> In Part Two we learned he has another more fitful, turbulent relationship . . . with a "Gal name' Daisy" who "almost drive' him crazy. . . ." It seems "she know' how to love" him "yes,

indeed," but as he laments, "Boy, you don't know what she do to me!"

The satire upon Masterpiece Theater and rock 'n' roll continues with the analysis of the meaning of thc lyrics:

> What is the meaning of the seemingly magical incantation, "Tutti Fruitti, all-a-rootie"? Is it invoked to relieve the stress of romance gone awry? Tonight we shall see in the fateful *coup de grâce* resolving the torturous conflicts arising from our hero's infidelities and now . . . Little Richard's "Tutti Frutti" . . .

The strip then ends with an explosive, "a-bop-bop-aloo-bop! a-bop-bam-boom!" and the famous sign-off, "For 'Masterpiece Theater' I'm Alistair Cooke . . . Good night!" Marlette's irony points up the lack of any serious content to the lyrics of early rock 'n' roll. There is precious little of intellectual interest in any of these songs.

There were also the specialty/comic songs which became Number One hits in the 1950s. These include "The Ballad of Davy Crockett," by Bill Hayes (1955),[6] "The Green Door" by Jim Lowe (1956), "Witch Doctor" by David Seville (1958), "The Purple People Eater" by Sheb Wooley (1958), "The Chipmunk Song" by the Chipmunks (1959), and "The Battle of New Orleans" by Johnny Horton (1959).[7]

There is nothing meaningful, hidden or otherwise, about the lyrics of these songs. Learning the lyrics to these songs was something of a challenge, like being able to get through a tongue-twister ("it was a one-eyed, one-horned, flying purple people eater"), but few people were actually up to the challenge. These simple, funny songs are simply simple and funny with lyrics which tell a simple, funny story in an innocent fashion. There is not a scintilla of satire, iota of irony, or measure of metaphor to be found anywhere in these lyrics. There isn't much scope for plumbing depths of meaning by philosophical analysis. There's not a lot of heavy thinking going on here. (And, for those of you who are wondering, "Itsy Bitsy Teenie Weenie Yellow Polkadot Bikini" by Brian Hyland appeared in 1960.)

Remember those serious adult songs you first learned as a

kid, songs that you had to sing in school assemblies or church, songs like "Bringing in the Cheese" and "The Church is One Foundation"? As we learned many of those songs, we invariably got some of the words wrong and continued to get them wrong well into young adulthood. And when we finally figured out what the adults had really been saying (it is "amber waves of grain," stupid, not "Aunt Bea has a pain"), we were embarrassed or mildly amused at ourselves because we did not realize at the time that we were getting it wrong. Well, one of the interesting things about the lyrics from these early rock 'n' roll Top 40 hits from the 1950s is that those of us who tried to sing along could never get all of the words right, we knew at the time that we weren't getting the words right, and it really didn't matter very much whether we got them right or not. We made some kind of audible but indistinguishable sound and kept right on going. Not getting the words right was inconsequential.

And the Beat Goes On

Getting *the beat* right was the really important thing. This is why early rock 'n' roll can be "canned" and turned into "easy listening," elevator music. You can either use the original versions and simply turn down the volume until the music fades into the background or you can use special, Mantovani-style arrangements, with no lyrics, and with a lot of violins (and no drums) to soften the beat until it fades into the background. This is exactly the technique which was used to produce the safe, sanitized, and more socially acceptable "covers" of early rock 'n' roll songs by established, white pop singers, such as Pat Boone's covers of Little Richard's "Tutti-Frutti" and "Long Tall Sally" in 1956. Originally a practice which started in the early 1950s to deal with the threat of "cross-over" songs from the rhythm and blues and country charts,[8] these covers of the original songs kept the same lyrics but re-orchestrated the music with arrangements which turned the raw, driving beat and the fast tempo of the originals into the familiar, mellow, and non-threatening style of white popular music. In other words, although the lyrics remained the same, the "safe" covers changed the medium by changing the beat, and thereby, they changed the message. If there is a period of rock music about which Marshall McLuhan's famous dictum "the medium is the message" (from his book *Understanding Media*) is really obvious, it is this early period of rock 'n' roll. When the beat is lost, the message is lost.

In early rock 'n' roll then we have a medium with no message distinguishable from the medium itself. It was the medium which was anti-social, irreverent, and a threat to the dominant culture. In this regard, rock 'n' roll as a new, powerful and still-developing medium was like an empty vessel waiting to be filled. The social and political consciousness and the personal and political alienation which were to be caused by the momentous and tragic events of the 1960s were to provide the *content* for the empty vessel—*messages* for the medium. Rock music was on its way. In this sense, rock music can be understood as a development of and a progression from early rock 'n' roll.

So, one way to understand Don McLean's now well-known claim about "the day the music died" in "American Pie" is to use the event of the deaths of Buddy Holly, The Big Bopper, and Richie Valens, as watershed events marking the end of a certain period of a certain kind of music. "The day the music died", when the plane with those three early rock 'n' roll stars fatally crashed in February, 1959, and the closing of the decade of the 1950s might well have signaled the end of the 50s era and early rock 'n' roll in which the music itself was the message. However, this end was just a new beginning in American popular music, and what was just beginning was, in many ways, not only significantly different from but also a significant development of what had ended.

What a Long, Strange Trip It's Been
The development of rock music has been, as the Grateful Dead claim, "a long, strange trip", and the beginning of the trip, in

the 1950s, was one of the strangest parts. Now don't get me wrong. I *like* this music. I *enjoy* this music. It is an important part not only of the history and development of rock music but of the history and development of American culture. It is an important part of who I am, and it is a part of what we are today as a country. It was loud and raucous and, sometimes, downright outrageous.

The blending of different music traditions into early rock 'n' roll, including black rhythm and blues, white folk and country and western, and southern gospel was iconclastic for the stilted status quo in American pop music at the time, and it was prophetic of things yet to come. Thus, neither popular music nor we will ever be the same because of Top 40, 1950s music at 45 rpm. It is *important* music, but it is not *serious* music. And it was important music, at the time, exactly because it was not serious. By being so completely non-serious and at the same time so raucous, happy and sensuous, it was a threat to everything represented by the adult world—maturity, responsibility, respectability and decorum. Rock 'n' roll at 45 rpm is good times music, and it hardly ever gets serious at all, except for an occasional lost love.

For parents and other serious adults, early rock 'n' roll music, the musicians, and the teenagers were like a loud, rowdy, and obnoxious bunch of kids throwing a non-stop party—laughing and joking—in an otherwise, nice, quiet, respectable, serious neighborhood. The kids were having too much fun at their own private party, and the adults were not invited—besides, the adults were too uptight to allow themselves to respond to the beat of the music and they had to get up and go to work in the morning. The very fact that the kids were having too much fun was disrespectful and threatening to the adult world.

By the end of the decade or thereabouts, things were about to change. Now I don't mean that the changes took place on the stroke of mid-night as 1959 turned into 1960. Strictly, "The Sixties" is a misnomer. It denotes the period from roughly the early-to-mid-1960s to the early-to-mid-1970s. (This isn't unusual. It's often said that the nineteenth century ended with the outbreak of war in 1914.) The Sixties began with the Cuban Missile Crisis in October 1962 and ended with the resignation of Richard Nixon in August 1974. An enormous amount of history took place in this short period. It took a little while for the cumulative effect of the world-shattering events of the early 1960s to begin to be felt in our culture and in rock music. The early music of the Beatles ("Love Me Do", "I Want to Hold Your Hand", "She Loves You", "Can't Buy Me Love", "A Hard Day's Night", and "I Feel Fine"—all Number One hits of 1964) represented no great departure, in their lyrics from the music of the late 1950s. Think of the memorable lyrics from these early Beatles hits: "Oh, please say to me you'll let me be your man and please say to me you'll let me hold your hand." "She loves you yeah, yeah, yeah. She loves you yeah, yeah, yeah." "Can't buy me love, ev'rybody tells me so. Can't buy me love, no, no, no, no." "I'm in love with her and I feel fine." These songs are all continuations of the feel-good, happy-times of early rock 'n' roll of the 1950s. This music is still not *serious* music even though it is usually identified as *rock* music instead of rock 'n' roll.

It took Bob Dylan and his switch from straight, acoustic folk music to an electric, amplified format to initiate the new dawn in rock music. After his performance at the 1965 Newport Folk Festival with electric instruments and his combination of folk lyrics with hard rock music on "Like a Rolling Stone" (which reached Number Two on the Top 40 charts in 1965) from the *Highway 61 Revisited* album,[9] rock music was never the same.[10] The naive, serendipitous good-times 1950s had given way to the thoughtful, introspective, tumultuous Sixties, and music at 45 rpm had given way to music at $33\frac{1}{3}$ rpm.

$33\frac{1}{3}$ rpm

Just in time for the 1960s, we got $33\frac{1}{3}$ rpm and long-playing albums (LPs) and stereo-sound. Even though LPs had first been introduced by RCA Victor in the 1930s and even though Columbia Records released several LPs in the 1940s, these were for the most part classical and semi-classical recordings. This was a time when the recording equipment and technology had temporarily out-distanced playback equipment and technology in the recording industry. So, even though the recordings were available, the equipment for people to play them was not widely available, and the equipment was very expensive. In the early 1960s, albums, recorded at $33\frac{1}{3}$ rpm, became the standard of the industry and the new recording format for the fledgling new medium of rock music.

Curiously, when you think about it, although stereo sound represented a major technological advancement over high-fidelity sound, there were several features about music on LP's and at $33\frac{1}{3}$ rpm which were not exactly user-friendly. The LP albums were larger and more cumbersome to handle and, at the same time, required more careful handling and greater maintenance in order to produce the superb stereo sound without hisses, bips, and pops. And LP's were more expensive. All of these are reasons why, during the 1950s, teen music was on 45s and only adult, serious, mainstream popular music and classical music was on LP's. Upon reflection, the "stereo systems" of the 1960s, made up of separate "components", for playing music at $33\frac{1}{3}$ rpm, were (by comparison to the nice, compact, portable hi-fi's of the 1950s) gigantic, unwieldy, and unsightly, with wires and connectors running all over the place to the different components.

However, unlike the technology in either the 78 format or the 45, music at $33\frac{1}{3}$ rpm and the introduction of LP's also opened the door of opportunity for a different form of artistic expression by composers of popular music, in a way which is unparalleled in the history of recorded sound, by anything before or since. The opportunity for narration and composition must have seemed limitless. Suddenly, the composers of popular music, both the writers of lyrics and music, who had operated under the restriction of "scrunching" their creations into the limitations imposed by the format of 45 rpm, were faced with the challenge and opportunity of producing compositions which were six, eight, or ten minutes long, or even longer.

LP's

Performing popular musicians were faced with the opportunity, for the first time in the history of the recording industry, to perform extended instrumental passages and elaborate riffs in the same manner in which jazz musicians had been doing all along in live jam sessions and the manner in which classical virtuosos had been doing all along with the cadenzas which they added to classical compositions. Of course there still had to be the "singles" for the Top 40, AM play, but the LP format gave the musicians the opportunity to include other non-Top 40 music on the album. The singles supported and "carried" the other songs which did not have to fit into the Top 40 format. Album covers also provided the opportunity for graphics, lyrics, and liner notes to accompany the music in a manner which had previously been reserved only for "serious", classical music. The creative artists had wonderful new worlds to explore. LP's and music at $33\frac{1}{3}$ rpm provided a technological boost to popular music, but also an artistic and creative impact. A new day in American popular music was dawning.[11] The creative opportunities offered by the LP albums combined with the technological advances in communication and mass distribution of the products of the industry (records) provided popular culture with the unique opportunity for the creation and general, mass distribution of rock music simultaneously with the events which were influencing that music. Both musicians and fans were thus able to "feed off of" events in and with rock music in a fashion which was then new and unique. The new technology of LP's, combined with the cultural and political energy of The Sixties, provided us with what we now call 'classic' rock music—music at $33\frac{1}{3}$ rpm.

CD's

The technology of the digital Compact Disc is a monumental advance over previous formats of recording and reproducing sound. In terms of the clarity and authenticity of the reproduction of the original sound, as well as the ease of operation and

maintenance, CD's represent the single most significant im-
provements ever in sound recording technology. However, the
CD format does not provide any increased opportunities for the
creative musician—in terms of composition or of performance.
Indeed, the first and most important CD releases by recording
companies and the first and most important CD purchases by
rock music fans were "classic" rock LP albums remastered for
CD. These classic rock albums still represent a significant share
of the CD market. In contrast with LP's in the 1960s, digital
CD technology did not generate a new genre of popular music
in the 1980s which is, in any way, uniquely defining of the
1980s. There is no genre of music which we might identify as
"CD Music" comparable to "music at $33\frac{1}{3}$ rpm".

The Sixties

We use decades as a way of identifying and clustering entire
musical and cultural epochs. Think, for example, of the rich and
full images which are now associated with the use of the phrase
"The Sixties". These are images which identify a period of
time, a culture, and a generation. We can do the same thing
through a similar kind of process, with different images, equally
rich and full, for "The Fifties" and "The Forties". It is
interesting to wonder whether we will ever be able to do the
same thing for "The Seventies" or especially "The Eighties", or
whether these decades were so culturally and musically vacu-
ous that they defy any such identification. There is, no doubt,
something very special about the designation of "The Sixties"
—both to those people who lived through them and were
permanently etched by them intellectually, culturally, morally,
and musically and to those people who did not (but wish that
they had).

The Sixties was a unique period in American history.[12] Now,
in one sense, such a claim is totally trivial because every
individual period of time is unique in some fashion or other; so,
obviously, we need to explore why The Sixties were unique and
so important. There were a number of momentous political and

historical events in the 1960s which invariably impacted upon and helped shape the people, the culture and the music.

Suppose I were to challenge you, "Name the most important decade in American history (and, of course, explain and defend your answer)." There is no single "correct" answer. This is simply a really effective (and intellectually stimulating) way to learn your history and to learn to appreciate the compelling nature of the events which define different ages and which have brought us to where we are today. Let us say, for the sake of discussion, that we consider the periods 1776–86, 1860–70, 1912–22, 1935–45, and 1962–74. Let's not be too rigid and legalistic. We can give ourselves a little flexibility so that we can extend the periods a year or two in either direction for the sake of the argument.

Now a really good case can be made for regarding each of these periods of American history as the most important. 1776–86 saw the stabilization of a young country under very difficult circumstances and the framing and adoption of the Constitution. The United States really became a country during this period. 1860–70 saw the secession of the southern states from the Union, the Civil War, the assassination of Abraham Lincoln, and Reconstruction. 1912–22 saw World War I, the Lost Generation, and the League of Nations. 1935–45 saw what was perhaps an unparalleled menace of world domination in World War II, the beginning of the Nuclear Age, and the United Nations.

What do we say about 1962–74? Thinking about the most significant events which happened during this period will eventually help us to understand their influence upon the rock music which was produced at that time. When we begin to chronicle the events from this period, there are two obvious and important things to observe: 1. the sheer number of major, defining events of the period, and 2. the overwhelmingly negative character of those major events.

As I list these events, even after giving the process a great deal of thought, the fact that I will probably leave out some event that you will think is really important is itself a strong indication of the significant number of such events. My list includes the following: the Bay of Pigs, the Cuban Missile Crisis, the assassination of John Kennedy, the Poor People's March, the Civil Rights Movement, the Civil Rights Act of 1964, the Watts riots, the Vietnam War, the Detroit riots, the assassination of Martin Luther King, Jr., the assassination of Robert Kennedy, the anti-Vietnam War movement, the 1968 National Democratic Convention, the bombing of Cambodia, Kent State, the resignation of Spiro Agnew, Watergate, and the resignation of Richard Nixon. The personal and political effect of the cumulative weight of such extraordinary events was tremendous —and I could easily double the list.[13] And however we might judge the relative importance of these different periods of American history, it is undeniable, and I think that most people would agree, that the period of The Sixties was a defining historical moment in the life of our country. We should also expect, then, that these events would help to determine the popular culture which the period produced, and we will soon see exactly how that happened with classic rock music.

Ideological Motifs of The Sixties

Before beginning our philosophical analysis of classic rock music, it is important to have some understanding of the period which produced it. During discussions of classic rock music from the Sixties, probably one of the questions most often asked by young people today of those of us who experienced and survived the Sixties is, "What were The Sixties really like?"[14]

There are seven different characteristics which I take as defining of The Sixties. Collectively, as a cluster, I believe that these characteristics uniquely characterize The Sixties or at least give a complete enough picture of the period that readers can understand something of what it was like to have lived through it.

1. A feeling of shared victimization. Think of the different events which I mentioned earlier—especially the tragic deaths of John Kennedy, Martin Luther King, Jr., and Robert Kennedy. There was the strong, compelling feeling among the younger,

college-age "kids" of The Sixties that these were all things done by "them" to "us". Consider also the Vietnam War, the lottery for the draft, the brutality of the 1968 National Democratic Convention and the murders at Kent State. All of these different events served to solidify the feeling that the adults of society and "The Establishment" were doing these things to persecute *us*. It was Herbert Hoover who first said, "Older men declare war. But it is youth who must fight and die," but *this* generation identified with Phil Ochs as he sang in "I Ain't Marching Anymore": "It's always the old to lead us to the war, always the young to die." This feeling of being persecuted by adults, more than anything else, I think, gave the feeling of generational solidarity to the younger people in The Sixties. When The Who sang "My Generation", it was like a religious liturgy which only the young could sing or understand. This view of generation victimization explains why so many of the differences and conflicts among people in the 1960s are to be accounted for solely on the basis of age and is what gave rise to the phrase "the Generation Gap". And, of course, because of the post-World War II "bulge" of the baby-boomers, there were a great deal more of the members of this generation with which the older, dominant society had to deal.

2. A feeling of community. The feeling of shared persecution led to a feeling of community—"we've got to stick together, man." And the music, either recorded or in live concert, was a way of cementing that community—similar to the practice of singing hymns or reciting liturgies in church by the religious faithful. Most important about this sense of community, I think, was the fact that this feeling was forced upon those who felt abused, persecuted, and disenfranchised by society—blacks, hippies, and college students—activists and non-activists alike. It was not simply an artificial choice to feel identified with a certain group of other people. This is the reason, I think, that such a feeling of community has rarely been duplicated since those times.[15] It is difficult to imagine people feeling persecuted or left out by society and "The Establishment" or having a deep-seated need for community when they drive their BMW's and Porsches to rock concerts as yuppies did

in the 1980s—especially when the Porsches and BMW's are *theirs* and not their parents.

3. A feeling of self-importance and having something to say. The music of the 1950s, early rock 'n' roll, fit into a classic pattern of psychological avoidance or escapism. Neither the lyrics nor the music had "messages", and they were not confrontational. By the mid-1960s, this was changing drastically, and a new pattern was emerging—both culturally and in the music. Musicians began saying, "Well, we've got something to say, and, like it or not, here it is. And you'd better listen to it because 'the times they are a changin''."

4. A rejection of the received wisdom of older generations and a feeling of finding one's own way. The musicians of classic rock from the mid-1960s to the mid-1970s (and those who listened to it) were not only hesitant and suspicious of the older generation and what it had to offer; the younger generation held the adults responsible for the violence and for generally "screwing up" the world. The mayhem which erupted in American society in the early and mid-1960s resulted in a mixture of feelings of contempt, suspicion, and fear of adult society and its establishments, institutions, and authorities. This suspicion and fear meant a rejection of the prosperity, consumerism, and worship of security which had characterized The Fifties. For many members of the younger generation, these feelings translated into a refusal to accept the authority and legitimacy of the government, the family, organized religion, or the police. The search for new values included, for different people, excursions into new and radical political beliefs, drugs, "Eastern religions", and radically divergent lifestyles.

Perhaps there is no more poignant example in popular culture which illustrates this rejection of the sage advice and the dominant values of the older generation than the scene from the 1967 Mike Nichols movie, "The Graduate". The new classic anti-hero, Benjamin Braddock, struggles with his self-identity and the meaning of life, as he approaches his 21st birthday. He worries about his future and wants it "to be different". The adults in his life are useless during this process. His father and mother dote on him. The best, most sage advice he's offered by an adult friend of the family, Mr. McGuire, is "plastics". This one-word pronouncement is somehow supposed to be a meaningful and significant revelation for Mr. McGuire. It rings hollow and meaningless for Benjamin. What could represent a more empty and unrewarding way to spend one's life—without meaning or personal fulfillment?, Benjamin must think. This was a chord to which many younger people in The Sixties were highly responsive.[16] Since we live in a world today which is highly plastic and disposable, it is difficult to imagine anything like the same response from current generations—not without another cultural revolution. Ironically, the only advice Mr. Robinson has to offer is for Ben to "sow a few wild oats"—which he does, of course, with Mrs. Robinson.

It is also ironic that adults at the time saw a younger generation "out of control" when the younger generation saw a world, a product of the older generation, which was "out of control". "Liberation" meant liberation from the adult culture which was responsible for the disastrous events of the 1960s. It meant finding your own way—your own values and what to do with your life. So, Phil Ochs sings a song of defiance and individual freedom in "I Ain't Marching Anymore", and Cat Stevens echoes (from another great movie about a young man trying to grow up in an absurd, adult world, "Harold and Maude"), "If You Want to Be Free, Be Free". The same theme occurs in many songs such as "Go Where You Want to Go" by the Mamas and the Papas.

5. A sense of mission and quest. There was also the feeling that something must be done about the mess the adults had made of the world. Now exactly what was to be done varied considerably from one group to another. Ken Kesey and cohorts, for example, thought that their mission involved a pursuit of pleasure and enlightenment—mainly through the use of hallucinogenic drugs—and became the Merry Pranksters.[17] Others, of course, saw and found their "mission" in different places—from various kinds of communes to various kinds of political action, to various kinds of alternative lifestyles. The most common sense of mission was vague and not carefully organized or thought out or realistic or practical. There

was simply a desire for "love and peace" and "peace and brotherhood". And even though the answers were not all that clear or generally agreed upon, there was still a very general belief that the answers were "out there" to be discovered and that society had not yet found the best way for people to live together in the most peaceful, productive and self-fulfilling manner possible. The message (or mission) divided the generations since it was not simply a message or mission intended for the young alone, but a message which only the young could understand. As Bob Dylan sings in "Ballad of a Thin Man," "Something is happening here, but you don't know what it is, do you, Mr. Jones?"

6. A sense of empowerment. Compared to the 1950s, the children of The Sixties believed that they could make a difference. Even though they were outcasts of society and targets for The Establishment, there was still the feeling that what individuals and groups of individuals do really mattered. And when the groups gathered together, whether at a demonstration or a concert, there was a general feeling of the empowerment of the group to do great things—to change the world by bringing about world peace and brotherhood. In this way, I think, the anti-Vietnam war movement learned from the Civil Rights Movement. All you have to do is "sing along (with feeling)", Arlo Guthrie tells us in "Alice's Restaurant" (1967), "if you want to end war and stuff, you have to sing loud." As Country Joe McDonald chides the crowd at Woodstock in the middle of the song, "I-Feel-Like-I'm-Fixing-to-Die-Rag,"

> Listen, people, I don't know how you ever expect to stop the war if you can't sing any better than that. There's 300,000 of you fuckers out there. I want you to start singing! Come on!

7. A sense of a moral imperative. Perhaps it sounds strange to claim that the activists, hippies, flower children, and other creatures of the 1960s felt a sense of moral superiority. After all, viewed by straight society and "The Establishment", the protestors, members of communes, and even rock musicians and their followers flouted conventions and laws with illegal protests, drugs and "free" sex. But there was a feeling among

the young people of the 1960s that they were *right,* and a feeling that they were morally superior to the adults who were running the world. Moral worthiness was viewed from the perspective of a relative and comparative judgment—we don't murder our leaders, napalm innocent people, and lie to the people the way adults do. The bitter sarcasm aimed at the hypocrisy of the adult world and "The Establishment" appeared in many folk songs at the time including such songs as "Are You Bombing With Me Jesus?" by Shurli Grant, "With God on Our Side" by Bob Dylan, "What Did You Learn in School Today?" by Tom Paxton, and "Your Flag Decal Won't Get You into Heaven Anymore" by John Prine. Typical of these songs is the revelation in Grant's song that the pilot of the *Enola Gay,* the plane which dropped the atomic bomb on Hiroshima, clutched a rosary in his hand on the flight. With sarcastic naivety, Paxton narrates a story of what children learn in school including that the government is always right and that war is "not so bad".

This was a difficult and tumultuous time—a time when America lost its innocence and struggled with trying to go on without that lost innocence. We ought to expect to find—in the popular culture generally and in rock music particularly—expressions of those classic philosophical, theological and literary themes to which people turned in such difficult times, and that is exactly what we do find. Ironically, then, we find a situation where the prophets of a new popular culture turn to the themes and theories of the past and use them in order to express themselves and to make their case against the past and the present culture.

Name the Best

There is an intellectual parlor game which I frequently play with some good friends. It's a serious, intellectual drinking game called "Name the Best" (close variations and permutations are "Name the Most Important" and "Name the Greatest"). The game is played by one person asking another to Name the Best one of something of a particular kind, for example: "Name the Best Second baseman of all time" or "Name the Best American novel ever written." Of course, the particular answer given is simply a prelude to the intellectual debate which follows, say, comparing William Faulkner's *Light in August* and John Steinbeck's *Grapes of Wrath* (and there will always be those who defend Herman Melville's *Moby-Dick*). The subjects available for inquiry are, of course, endless and depend solely upon the knowledge and intellectual abilities of the players. For example, think of "What is the most important *single* event of the twentieth century? Of all of human history? Who is the most important philosopher to have ever lived? The most important person? What is the most important single discovery of science? What is the greatest single athletic achievement of the twentieth century?" In each case, of course, different people will have different answers, and the pleasure in the game is to be found in the intellectual conversation where each person explains and defends his or her own choice.

When we turn our attention to rock music, then playing the game of "Name the Best" offers an opportunity to open up new insights into our understanding of the music. And when I play this game with other people, I never fail to learn something and to be continually impressed and fascinated with the subtlety and complexity of rock music. Think of "Name the Best rock album," and "Name the Best single rock composition." And are the answers to "Name the Best rock group of all time" and "Name the Most Important rock group" the same or different? How about "Name the Best single line from the lyrics of any rock song" or "Name the Best single guitar riff performed 'live' "? There are many permutations, and you can probably think of more than I can, but again, the most important part of the game is having to answer the "Why?" and defending our choices. Asking certain kinds of serious questions about rock music and exploring the reasons for the possible different answers will hopefully encourage us to think about rock music in a more serious manner, and exploring some of the connections and comparisons between rock music and "intellectually serious and respectable" philosophical works will open various new ways for people to think about rock music as an important and neglected part of their popular culture.

Name the Worst

"Name the Best" also has another somewhat perverse but entertaining variation called "Name the Worst." We sometimes see examples of this variation in lists such as the list of "worst dressed people" or the worst movies of a particular year. How about a list of the ten worst rock songs of all time? This may be a little difficult because the competition is so keen, and one thing which might make agreement more difficult is that, fortunately, many really bad songs do not get widely known. In one Bad Song Survey conducted by Dave Barry, a syndicated newspaper columnist, "MacArthur Park" by Richard Harris (no relation to the author) was an easy winner.[18] My own contenders would be "She's Having My Baby" by Paul Anka and "My Ding-A-Ling" by Chuck Berry (both of which reached the Number One position on the Top 40 charts). But, one person's ceiling is another person's floor, and my candidates for the worst songs may be your candidates for the best ones, which is exactly what makes this such an interesting and challenging enterprise.

Creatures of Culture

In the past few years, the world in which we live has undergone what are perhaps the most dramatic and pervasive peaceful changes in human history. These changes have affected not only the republics and the peoples of the former Soviet Union and the countries and peoples of eastern Europe but the entire world as well. The confusion, conflict, and strife which have followed these changes are understood by many people as evidence of the importance of political order, structure, and stability for the peaceful commerce of human affairs. However, these same conflicts are also indicative of a basis upon which people relate to each other, both peacefully and belligerently, which is more fundamental than politics and government. This most fundamental level of human association is what scholars call "culture", and while there are many definitions of 'culture', the basic notion involves some pattern of thought, values, and behavior which provides a unifying and identifying structure for the institutions and people of a society. In this sense then, culture is more basic than government, and government is a product of culture.

When we think of a culture, we think of the values and beliefs, the social customs and institutions, the language and ideas, the patterns of behavior relating to other people, nature and other animals, and the things produced through human skills, creative talents, and labor. Within the context provided by culture, we are able to ask the most important and fundamental questions about ourselves and our world. What is the origin of the universe? What is the origin of human beings? Who am I? Why am I? How shall I live my life?

It is culture which allows us to identify and make sense of talking about different "peoples". Think, for example, of your understanding of such diverse peoples as the ancient Greeks, Native Americans, Zulus, Australian aboriginals, and contemporary Americans. The basis of our understanding and identification of other people and ourselves must go beyond mere physical appearance, including racial features, to a more fundamental understanding of "a way of life"—a culture.

The English word 'culture' comes to us from the Latin 'cultura' which means 'cultivation' or 'tending' with a particular connection to its agricultural meaning, as in the "cultivation" of the soil through farming to produce a particular crop. Consequently, when we talk about "human culture", it is very easy to think of it as the "cultivation" of the human mind through education and "acculturation" to produce a person with a particular cultural heritage and identity.

Culture of Creatures
Somewhat neglected, by contrast, has been the relationship by which we *produce* culture. After all, culture is *human culture.* It

is not just what distinguishes one people from another; it is what distinguishes us together, as a species, *Homo sapiens,* from other species.[19] When NASA launched the Voyager spacecraft, the first human-made object to leave our solar system, items representing human culture were selected to be placed aboard. The idea is to provide some material evidence which would allow intelligent aliens who might someday intercept the spacecraft to determine something about the nature of human beings. It is interesting to note here that the popular music selected included Chuck Berry's "Johnny B. Goode". Well, things could have been worse—at least it wasn't "My Ding-A-Ling". After all, "Johnny B. Goode" never got higher than Number Eight (1958) while "My Ding-A-Ling" reached Number One in 1972.

The production of culture by a people is the *projection* of their most important and fundamental beliefs and values; it thus serves as a *reflection* to themselves and others of what it is that makes them the people that they are. As human beings, we are not creatures helplessly, mindlessly, and indelibly formed by culture. We do inherit our culture, and it undoubtedly shapes us, but we also shape it, a mutual process of interactive influence. Cultures do change, and at different times and in different places different cultures change more or less slowly or rapidly. Except under the most sudden, complete, and radical conditions which might be the result of disease, natural disasters, or war, cultural changes are brought about through the use of some part of the existing culture. We use part of our cultural inheritance in our attempts to change other parts. In one sense then, there is really very little under the sun which is new.

The lyrics of classic rock music demonstrate how the people who attempted to change their culture in the 1960s used different parts of what was their shared cultural inheritance in their attempts.[20] Many social critics and historians regard The Sixties as a radical departure from the mainstream of American history and culture. In demonstrating the cultural indebtedness of the Sixties and the music which they produced, I hope to demonstrate how many of the themes and "messages" which we now associate with The Sixties were not as radical and as "far out" as people have imagined. In other words, much of the "culture" of the 1960s, including the social and political upheavals as well as the rock music, can be understood in terms of inherited cultural themes and categories.

High and Popular Culture

The apparent incongruity of the juxtaposition of 'philosophy' and 'rock music' is evidence of how we have become accustomed to the ways in which we divide and evaluate our culture. It is now a somewhat familiar and common practice to think of certain parts of our culture as "high"—meaning that such parts and products of our culture are both more important and to be valued more highly than other parts. This "high" culture is thought to be, at the same time, beyond the appreciation (and perhaps the understanding) of most "common" people. Contrasted with "high" culture, we have, not "low" culture, which is too pejorative, but "folk" or "popular" culture—the culture of the masses. As paradigms of high culture, we have opera, "classical" music, the "fine" arts, "serious" literature, and, perhaps "the highest of the high", philosophy. These examples of high culture are now usually performed and experienced in places physically separated from ordinary life (and consequently from ordinary people) such as opera houses, concert halls, museums, and college and universities. By contrast, popular culture is all around us in our ordinary, daily lives. We get it in the supermarkets, on television, in magazines, on radios, and, of course, from our stereos.

The difference between "high" and "popular" culture is illustrated with great irony in a line from Paul Simon's song, "A Simple Desultory Philippic": "When you say 'Dylan', he thinks you're talking about Dylan Thomas, whoever he was. The man ain't got no culture." There have been some explicit attempts to infuse "high" culture into the popular culture medium of rock music by producing rock covers of classical compositions. *Switched on Bach* by Walter Murphy and the Big Apple Band hit Number One in 1976, and Emerson, Lake, and Palmer produced an album length cover of Mussorgsky's "Pictures at an

Exhibition" in 1972. There were also cultural "cross-over" concerts such as Rick Wakeman's performance of "Journey to the Center of the Earth" with the London Symphony Orchestra in the Royal Festival Hall in London in 1974.

Philosophy and Popular Culture

As a consequence of the differences between "high" culture and popular culture and between the "fine" arts and popular art as I have described them, popular culture, for the most part, has been routinely dismissed by critics and scholars as a purveyor of serious intellectual thought. When serious scholars have sought the reflection of those fundamental cultural features which make us the people that we are, they have, for the most part, not looked to popular culture for that reflection.

Such an attitude toward popular culture has been particularly dominant in philosophy—perhaps because of the very dominant influence of Plato on Western philosophy. In one of his major dialogues, *The Republic*, in which he characterizes his understanding of the ideal state in which philosophers are to be kings (after all, he thought, it makes good sense—doesn't it?—for those who are the wisest to rule) Plato completely bans poets (and artists generally) from his ideal state because of what he regards as their pernicious influence upon the intellect. Since ordinary physical objects which we become aware of through our senses are themselves copies of the perfect Forms or Ideas, and since poets, sculptors, and other artists produce copies of those copies, then they are twice removed from genuine knowledge, Plato thought.

Even in the twentieth century, serious philosophical inquiry concerning the arts and philosophical theorizing about the arts has not yet recaptured its lost sense of respectability. Aesthetics is still considered, in most academic philosophy departments at colleges and universities, one of the "soft" areas of philosophy, and treatments of philosophy and popular culture have not yet reached the level of general respectability among "serious" philosophers.

Philosophy and Rock Music

Most people are anti-intellectuals when it comes to music. This is especially true of popular music and even more so of rock. People might admit or even recognize some intellectual themes in classical music, but what does philosophy have to do with *rock* music? And what do rock musicians have in common with philosophers? Aren't philosophers eccentric and impractical, locked away in their ivory towers just "thinking" about all kinds of abstract and abstruse things? True, we are not likely to find elaborate, highly sophisticated and complicated philosophical systems and theories expressed by or explained in rock music or other kinds of popular culture. In all likelihood, nothing will ever replace written prose for the purpose of developing and explaining such complicated systems and theories. We are not, therefore, likely to find a budding Aristotle or Kant among popular novelists or rock musicians. When I talk about philosophy and rock music, I am talking about very general thematic influences which philosophy and, in some cases, theology have had on rock music. Most of this influence is to be found in the lyrics so I will be doing some fairly detailed analyses of those lyrics—what theologians call an "exegesis" of the text.

Even when we find such general themes expressed, we are not likely to find detailed arguments for those claims, whatever they may be, for a couple of reasons: First, the medium itself does not lend itself to elaborate explanation and argumentation. After all, we don't find systematic expositions of theory in high art either—in the songs of Schubert, Wolf, or Richard Strauss, for example—but no one therefore concludes that these works have no place in intellectual history. Second, even though in many cases the impact of different philosophical, theological, and literary influences upon rock musicians might have been immediate and direct and hence, consciously a part of composition, in other cases, the influence is more vague and diffuse, and not necessarily known to the composer. This ought not to seem very strange. We know that we are all continually influenced by all kinds of factors in our culture which we are not consciously aware of at the time, and these influences have their impact upon much of our behavior, including, perhaps especially, our creative behavior.

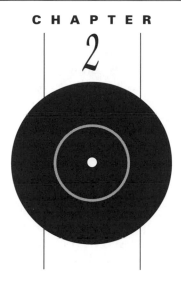

2

Stranger in a Strange Land:
Rock Music and Alienation

More has been written about the alienation of The Sixties than about all other characteristics of that decade combined; so it seems appropriate to begin our examination of the major philosophical themes of classic rock with an examination of the expression of alienation in the 1960s. One of the most common and useful ploys of philosophers as they begin any philosophical investigation or analysis is the process of making distinctions. By analyzing the alienation of youth in The Sixties, we can make distinctions both about how the alienation of that generation of youth differed from the alienation of previous generations and among different kinds of alienation felt in the 1960s.

This process will provide us with a better understanding of how much of classic rock music serves as an expression of those different kinds of alienation. We will then be in a position to understand better such well-known songs as "Father and Son" by Cat Stevens, "Levon" by Elton John, "The Pretender", by Jackson Browne, and "Respect", by Otis Redding as well as such albums as *Who's Next* by The Who and *Dark Side of the Moon* by Pink Floyd.

Alienation of the Sixties

Although much has been written about the alienation of The Sixties, no one has captured all of the varieties of alienation which we will find expressed in rock music. Surely, there have been other periods in Western history characterized by generational alienation, and, in many ways, the student protests in France and Germany in the 1960s were more radical and violent than the protests in the United States. The social unrest and violence which accompanied the rise of labor unions in the United States certainly equaled anything from the 1960s. We might even say that every generation must go through some period of alienation and adjustment—some anger and loss of innocence—on its journey into adulthood. However, the alienation of The Sixties generation was different—both in form and content—than any previous period in American history. Let us look at the reasons why.

A Crisis in Culture

One of the main reasons the alienation of The Sixties was different was its magnitude and scope. Compared to a political revolution, the student protests in Europe, or the movement to establish labor unions, the protests and alienation of the Sixties produced *a cultural crisis*. The target of the dissent and the cause of the alienation was not simply the government or the universities or management. The scope of the rejection and alienation ran across the entire fabric of American culture—including the received political, social, personal, religious, economic, and moral views of the dominant culture. The general, inclusive nature of the alienation left no Archimedean point to provide a foothold or beginning point for leverage against the dominant culture. So, much of the alienation and anger and rebellion seemed pointless or aimless since it was so general and unfocused.

The crisis in American culture in the 1960s can easily be seen in the intensity and scope of the youth rebellion of that generation, but it must be open to question (and the subject of a more elaborate, scholarly study by someone else) just how much the cultural crisis and the alienation of The Sixties were causally related. A good case can be made that American culture was headed for a crisis anyway, and young people in the 1960s—the activists, the hippies, the flower children, the counter-culturalists, the commune dwellers—were simply the first people to realize this and act upon it. Numerous scholarly and popular books which were produced during the Sixties or became popular at the time were understood and interpreted as describing, predicting, or satirizing the crisis in one form or another—including *Growing Up Absurd,* by Paul Goodman; *Silent Spring,* by Rachel Carson; *The Population Bomb,* by Paul Erlich; *Catch-22,* by Joseph Heller; *The Catcher in the Rye,* by J. D. Salinger; *Understanding Media,* by Marshall McLuhan; *The Secular City,* by Harvey Cox; *One-Dimensional Man,* by Herbert Marcuse; *Nineteen Eighty-Four,* by George Orwell, *The Hidden Persuaders,* by Vance Packard, *The Affluent Society,* by John Kenneth Galbraith, and a whole host of existentialist novels— just to name a few.

Such words and descriptions as 'post-industrial', 'technocracy', and 'secularization' were adopted and popularized by social critics to describe American culture, and the April 8th, 1966, cover of *Time* magazine was emblazoned with the question, "Is God Dead?" The New Left, including Students for a Democratic Society (SDS), became an important source of social and political criticism.[1] Arguably, American culture was in deep trouble in the 1960s even without the impact of civil rights and Vietnam. The combined effect was of a culture which was "coming apart". Indeed, Allen J. Matusow appropriately entitles his book on The Sixties *The Unraveling of America*.[2]

Alienation in Personal Relationships

One of the areas in which alienation was felt most acutely in The Sixties was in the area of personal relationships—including familial relationships, love relationships, and friendships. With the advent of popular psychology and "self-help" books, the great American public turned its attention upon "relationships" in the 1960s in a way which was previously unequaled. Self-examination and psychological examination of self and others became the order of the day.

We might have expected, perhaps, that such relationships would be the subject of popular fiction; however, we now find that these relationships become one of the main themes to be found in classic rock music as well. Personal relationships are frequently depicted as the source of a particular kind of alienation. Personal alienation is alienation which results from the failure of a personal relationship or the betrayal by another person. Such failures and betrayals occur frequently enough to suggest a particular view of human nature which is frail and fickle (while perhaps not being really corrupt) and which explains why such relationships are limited and inevitably, or nearly inevitably, lead to disappointment, alienation, and loneliness.

Parent-Child Alienation

The alienation which frequently results from familial relationships is episodic: it occurs at certain periods in a person's life and is caused by or directed toward another individual or group of individuals (such as parents or children). In other words, such alienation is not alienation from society at large or people in general, and it is not aimed at the political, social or religious systems or authorities.

An explicit and illustrative example of a song which describes parent and child alienation is "Father and Son" by Cat
Stevens from his *Tea for the Tillerman* album (1971)—a song
which was also used in the movie "Revolution". In this song,
Stevens has the father and son carry on a conversation with each
other as the father tries to convince the son not to leave home to
go to fight in "the revolution". The father and son argue with
each other in voices which range from angry and frustrated to
tortured and anguished as each tries to somehow reach the
other so the other will understand. The song begins with the
father giving the son a parental lecture about life, and the father
sings to the son in a very controlled and mature voice:

> *It's not time to make a change*
> *Just relax, take it easy.*
> *You're still young, that's your*
>   *fault, there's so much you have to know.*
> *Find a girl, settle down.*
> *If you want you can marry.*
> *Look at me, I am old but I'm happy.*

Now the father doesn't sound all that unreasonable. He seems
to care about his son and to be sympathetic and concerned
about his son's decision and well-being. And the father continues to give advice by telling his son how he understands since he
went through very similar periods of difficulty when he was a
young man.

> *I was once like you are now, and I know*
> *That it's not easy to be calm when you've found*
> *Something going on, but take your time,*
> *Think a lot, why think of everything you've got,*
> *For you will still be here tomorrow*
> *But your dreams may not.*

Be careful. Take it easy. Go slow. Be home before midnight.
Don't forget your lunch. Drive carefully. All caring and loving
parents worry about the safety of their children. And eventually
every child must go his or her own way and make his or her

own way in a cold and sometimes dangerous world. So the son replies in a voice which is obviously more agitated and excited, and up-tempo and up-volume,

> How can I try to explain
> 'Cause when I do he turns away again?
> It's always been the same, same old story.
> From the moment I could talk, I was ordered to listen.
> Now there's a way and I know that I have to go.
> Away, I know, I have to go.

In the movie, the son is singing of leaving to join the revolution, but the particulars don't seem to be that important to the conflict which is taking place. The conflict might have been generated as easily by the son's decision to join the army or resist the draft, to go to college or drop out of college, to marry or not to marry, or to join a commune or a monastery. The important point is that under certain circumstances a parent and child come to complete loggerheads—where a child insists upon taking a certain course of action and the parent disagrees and refuses to permit the child to do it or to support the child in the decision. Such situations, and such conversations, occurred quite frequently in the 1960s.

In the next verse, as the argument continues, Cat Stevens cleverly has the father and son talking to each other at the same time (the same way in which many such conversations actually take place). While the father cautions, "It's not time to make a change, just sit down take it slowly . . .", the son is singing to the father, "Away away away, I know I have to make this decision alone—no." And, at the end of the song, the son is singing, ". . . now there's a way, and I know that I have to go away, I know I have to go" while the father is pleading, "Stay stay stay, why must you go and make this decision alone?" The father and son talk *at* each other while neither listens to the other, and presumably, the son leaves while the father pleads with him to stay—a circumstance which might be common in any generation but which was particularly poignant during The Sixties.

Although it is episodic and caused by and aimed at some

particular individual, parent/child alienation is also frequently regarded as a universal condition of human nature, and, as such, it is a very common theme in serious literature. We know from the plays of Sophocles that serious parent-child conflict dates back to the fifth century B.C. in ancient Greece. In *Oedipus Rex* (King Oedipus) Sophocles tells how Oedipus killed his father, Laius, and married his mother. Sigmund Freud is responsible for our current common use of the phrase "Oedipus Complex" to capture the seriousness of the conflict between father and son. "The End" by the Doors is a deliberate and explicit portrayal of the Freudian Oedipus Complex: In this very troubling song about a very troubled person (and sung by a very troubled person), Jim Morrison sings about what is supposedly the commonplace desire of the song's protagonist to "kill" his father and "fuck" his mother (lines which are sanitized in the most easily-available recorded version).

Sophocles also gives equal treatment to women. In *Antigone,* he tells the story of how Antigone (Oedipus's daughter) is sentenced to death by her uncle, King Creon of Thebes, because she deliberately disobeys him and buries her brother, Polynice. In the 1960s, one of the most commonly read books which treats the same theme was *Brothers Karamazov* by the nineteenth-century Russian novelist, Fyodor Dostoevsky, in which Fyodor Karamazov is murdered by one of his sons (but which one?). And one of the best-known examples from twentieth-century American literature of a novel which focuses on such alienation is J.D. Salinger's *The Catcher in the Rye.*

Given the almost universal character of the parent-child conflict in world literature and given the ways in which parent and child alienation and estrangement were accentuated in American society during The Sixties, it should come as no surprise to find that this theme occurs very commonly in classic rock. And the theme is as dramatically and tragically illustrated as it is in *Oedipus Rex, Antigone,* and *The Brothers Karamazov.*

For example, in John Lennon and Paul McCartney's "She's Leaving Home" from *Sgt. Pepper's Lonely Hearts Club Band* (1967), the daughter runs away from home by sneaking out in the wee hours. So we, the audience, are left to hear the story behind the girl's leaving from the parents who sing about the child. In their typical fashion, Lennon and McCartney use a minimum of words to paint an elaborate picture for us. The line "She's leaving home after living alone for so many years" gives us a pretty good idea of what the relationship between daughter and parents has been like. Upon discovering that her daughter is gone and after reading the letter which she left, the mother cries and says to her husband,

> *Daddy our baby's gone.*
> *Why would she treat us so thoughtlessly?*
> *How could she do this to me?*

Such a completely egocentric reaction from the mother gives us a clear picture of exactly why the daughter has left to try and find or make some life for herself. The pitiful, self-serving, and ironic chorus which the parents sing confirms that they are only thinking of their own selfish interests:

> *She (We never thought of ourselves)*
> *Is leaving (Never a thought for ourselves)*
> *Home (We struggled all of our lives to get by).*

The final tragedy is driven home by the complete inability of the parents to recognize any responsibility or blame for their daughter's leaving. "What did we do that was wrong?" they ask. We cannot be very optimistic about any reconciliation for this family, but neither are we starry-eyed about the daughter's future without the parents.

A similar kind of parent-child estrangement is told by a very different kind of story in Bernie Taupin and Elton John's "Levon" from the *Madman Across the Water* album (1971). Levon is a very wealthy man who "wears his war wound like a crown", "likes his money", and makes so much of it that he spends his days "counting [his money] in a garage by the motorway." Levon is "a good man" and "in tradition with the family plan", and his "family business thrives."

Levon's son is named Jesus, and Taupin's choice of this name for the son can be a source for fertile speculation. Is the juxtaposition of the names "Levon" and "Jesus" supposed to borrow from and also bring to mind the juxtaposition of Judaism and Christianity? Is Levon's concern with money a crude stereotyping of Jews, in the tradition of Shakespeare's *The Merchant of Venice?* If we adopt such an interpretation, we certainly get a rich understanding of the conflict between Levon and Jesus. But even without such an interpretation, just the use of the name "Jesus" for the son and the description which Taupin gives us of Jesus are enough to provide a really clear picture of the nature of the relationship between Levon and Jesus. The "family business" which is thriving and making Levon so rich is the business of selling "cartoon balloons". Cartoon balloons represent the family business, success, and wealth for Levon, but what is Jesus's reaction to the family business and cartoon balloons? He simply "blows up balloons all day" and "sits on the porch swing watching them fly."

Taupin's choice of the cartoon balloon business is a particularly provocative one. There are at least two different ways of interpreting the significance of "the cartoon balloon" business. We can take it literally and very straightforwardly. In this case, the father, Levon, really does spend his time manufacturing cartoon balloons. Or we can understand "cartoon balloons" to mean the speech or thought "bubbles" which occur in cartoon strips. In this case, Levon's business and success is dependent, metaphorically, upon comic characters. In *either* case, Jesus wants none of it. It had to be *cartoon* balloons! And it had to be the *family* business! What more of a silly, ridiculous way can there be, Jesus thinks, to spend one's life. For Jesus, this is a life without substance or meaning! Jesus wants none of Levon, his war wound, his money, the family tradition, or especially, his cartoon balloons. Jesus "wants to go to Venus." He wants to blow up a balloon and sail away on it "while Levon, Levon slowly dies." The only good Jesus might see in Levon's balloons is a means of escape from Levon. It was another Jesus who told the parable of a wealthy man who gains great wealth but loses his soul. "Fool. This night your soul is required of you; and the things you have prepared, whose will they be?"[3]

Perhaps one of the better-known songs which illustrates this theme of parent and child alienation is Harry Chapin's "Cat's in the Cradle" from *Verities and Balderdash* (1974). This cleverly written, ironic and poignant song describes the relationship between father and son from the time of the son's birth to the time when the son is middle-aged and the father is growing old. From the time the son can talk, he says, "I'm gonna be like you, Dad. I'm gonna be like you." And as the son grows older, he says, "When you coming home, Dad?" and "Thanks for the ball, Dad, come on let's play." And, each time, the father replies, "Not today. I've got a lot to do." "I don't know when, but we'll get together then. You know we'll have a good time then." The father is too busy to spend time with his son—too busy earning a living, paying the bills, or being successful. But the son still wants to be just like his dad, "I'm gonna be like him, yeah. You know I'm gonna be like him." When the son comes home from college and the father wants to sit and talk, the son replies, "What I'd really like, dad, is to borrow the car keys. See you later. Can I have them, please?" Then as the father retires and the son moves away from home, the father seeks the kind of time and contact with his son which he was earlier too busy to give. But, alas, the son sings, "You see the new job's a hassle and the kids have the flu" as the father laments, "When you coming home, son?" And, in the end, the father finally realizes that the son had indeed "grown up just like me. My boy was just like me."

Romantic Love and Alienation

The theme of romantic love has been so common to practically every period of human history that the question becomes what makes the theme of romantic love any different in The Sixties than it has been during any other period. Well, there are two aspects concerning romantic love which are important for understanding the importance of such relationships to popular culture in general and to classic rock music in particular. If there was any single characteristic which was used more frequently in the 1960s to describe romantic relationships (or increased emphasis upon a particular characteristic), it was an emphasis upon male-female alienation. Now, of course, the battle of the sexes has been waged since the dawn of time, but the kind of alienation which is frequently described in the literature and music of The Sixties is both more deeply seated and more general than the usual conflicts between men and women. The alienation is more of a fear of a fundamentally monotonous and boring existence with another person. Although novelists and songwriters seldom footnote the influences which bring them to write what they write, it is possible to identify two different sources for the development of this kind of attitude toward romantic relationships. One possible source was the silly and superficial depictions of romantic life from television shows of The Fifties, including such shows as "I Love Lucy" and "Father Knows Best". Another source was the increasing influence and popularity of existentialist novels and other books which were being read in the 1960s, works by such writers as Albert Camus, Jean-Paul Sartre, Franz Kafka, and Hermann Hesse. There are more varied and conflicting depictions of romantic relationships and their advantages and disadvantages to be found in rock music than of any other topic.

Dangling Conversation

Paul Simon's "Dangling Conversation" from *Parsley, Sage, Rosemary, and Thyme* (1966) captures, in a very dramatic fashion, the silent desperation of those people who are involved in many romantic relationships, including many marriages, from which there seems to be no escape. In this song, we find a portrait painted of a relationship in which people have grown apart and in which they now relate to each other only in the most superficial and habitual ways. They talk only of quasi-intellectual matters such as "Can analysis be worthwhile? Is the theater really dead?" They are "verses out of rhythm, couplets out of rhyme." Ironically, in a relationship which has no love or beauty, they look for it in the poetry of Emily Dickinson and Robert Frost, "lost in the dangling conversation." These people sound more like colleagues in a debating society than they do lovers. There is very little to suggest any emotion or *passion* in this relationship.

So, Paul Simon's "Dangling Conversation" tells us of the losses in a relationship which is over-intellectualized and emotionally superficial. Certainly during the 1960s and into the 1970s there was a lot of attention given to "relationships", and a whole new mass market was opened for popular psychology, including everything from "women's" magazines in grocery stores to *Psychology Today*. Talking about feelings, "opening up", and "sharing" became the buzz words for characterizing intimate and meaningful relationships. On the other hand, Carly Simon warns of the pain and losses which result from too much sharing and too much honesty in "We Have No Secrets" from *No Secrets* (1972). "We tell each other everything, about the lovers in our past, and why they didn't last." But, even though the two lovers might know each other better, there are, perhaps, some things which are better left unsaid and some things which are better left unknown.

> *Sometimes I wish,*
> *Often I wish*
> *I never knew*
> *Some of those secrets of yours.*

Donald and Lydia

Although properly regarded as more of a country/folk song than a rock song, "Donald and Lydia" by John Prine from the album *John Prine* (1972) paints a captivating picture and tells a compelling story about the alienation which results from the highly romanticized and glamorized notions of sex and love generated by Hollywood. Donald and Lydia are two lonely and unattractive social misfits, two losers in the game of life, for whom the idealized notions of love and romance will never be fulfilled. Prine describes Lydia as a fat woman who works as a cashier in a penny arcade and reads "romance magazines", the closest she will ever come to romance. Donald, Prine tells us, is a young PFC in the army who lies in his bunk, stares at the ceiling and fantasizes about romance. In the last verse, Donald and Lydia make love. "They made love in the mountains. They made love in the streams. They made love in the valleys." But, of course, it is all fantasy. They never get closer than ten miles apart, and the only love they make is what they make "in their dreams".

Late for the Sky

Jackson Browne's song "Late for the Sky", from *Late for the Sky* (1974), is a song about trying to understand what has gone wrong in a relationship when it is about to end. He sings of "trying to understand how our lives had led us there" when we come "close to the end of the feeling we have known." The underlying problem is this failed relationship is the result of the inability of each to understand the other person. When the singer looks into the eyes of his beloved, he is surprised to find that "there was no one I'd ever known." The lyrics struggle with the age-old problem of how to be oneself in a love relationship while trying to meet someone else's expectations of what one should be. "You never knew what I loved in you. I don't know what you loved in me—maybe the picture of somebody you were hoping I might be." So the years have gone by while each person has tried to be something different in order to satisfy the other person. One of the closing laments is: "How long have I been dreaming I could make it right if I closed my eyes and tried with all my might to be the one you need?"

Social Alienation

By "Social Alienation," I mean the kind of alienation which results from one's position in life and society, determined by one's class, race, sex, occupation, and social or economic status. We find in both the rock music and the popular literature of The Sixties abundant expressions of anger, contempt, and frustration concerning existing social conditions. It is characteristic of such alienation that a person who regards himself or herself as victimized directs the anger and frustration at society at large or at some perceived dominant group of society. Social alienation is another example of the general, perceived view of the world where "they" are doing this to "us"—a view which is naturally socially disruptive and divisive. Songs with themes of social alienation are unlikely ever to be heard on Muzak or turned into elevator or shopping-mall music since both the music and the lyrics are so completely disturbing. These are not the kind of songs to put people in the mood to spend their money happily.

Hollis Brown

Bob Dylan's "Ballad of Hollis Brown" from the album *The Times They Are a Changin'* (1964) is particularly compelling because the alienation and despair of Hollis Brown result from failure and poverty (in the dust bowl during the depression). Dylan's lyrics capture a complete and terrifying scenario for us, and, in this case, the single guitar accompaniment, with a strong, driving, and monotonous beat, pushes the song toward its inevitable climax. The repetition of the first line of each verse magnifies this captivating monotony. This is a song which demands careful and serious listening and is very disturbing which is why you are not likely to hear it as background music while in an elevator or a dentist office.

Hollis Brown is a desperate, failed figure who is forgotten by society. He lives "outside of town with his wife and five children." He cannot find work or money, and his desperation grows as the rats eat the family's flour and disease kills the horse, a reference to the plight of Job depicted in the Old Testament story. His prayers are unanswered, and he has no friends. He desperately wonders: "Is there anyone who knows? Is there anyone who cares?"

The tempo and the volume begin to build to push the audience along with Hollis Brown toward the terrible climax of the song. As Hollis Brown buys the shells for his shotgun, and as his "eyes fix on the shotgun", we know what is going to happen, and we want the song to stop. But we cannot stop the song, and we cannot stop Hollis Brown or help him. It is too late, and we are impotent. Then "seven shots ring out," and "there's seven people dead on a South Dakota farm."

In the last verse, in typical laconic Dylan fashion, he is able to suggest the inevitable cyclical nature of human poverty and despair simply by saying "there's seven new people born." And as the monotonous and driving guitar accompaniment begins again, we are faced with the harsh realization of the recurrence of the tragedies and despair brought about by poverty.

A Day in the Life

Such tragic unhappiness with one's position in life is not limited, of course, to the poor. In Lennon and McCartney's "A Day In the Life" from *Sgt. Pepper's Lonely Hearts Club Band* (1967) the "lucky man" who "blew his mind out in a car" was someone who had "made the grade" and was famous and maybe even a member of "the House of Lords". Lennon and McCartney suggest that such events are inevitable and even routine since they enter into *our* lives as part of the news we read or hear as we rush to get out of the house in the mornings—"Found my coat and grabbed my hat. Made the bus in seconds flat." After all, this is simply, "A Day in the Life", and life goes on. Juxtaposed against the routine of daily living is death. The extreme dissonance and the rising crescendo in the disturbing instrumental passage at the end of the song demands resolution which comes in the form of the final and lasting organ chord—in much the same way, we might imagine, that death resolves the tension of an unhappy life.

Paul Simon's "Richard Cory" from *Sounds of Silence* (1966) is similar. The lyrics were inspired by and adapted from the poem "Richard Cory" by American poet Edwin Arlington Robinson (1869–1935). Robinson's poetry generally conveys his defense of "naturalism" and expresses his condemnation of the ravages of modern industrialized society within peoples' lives. Simon's song continues Robinson's general theme by relating the story of a very successful and wealthy man who owned "half of the town". He was "a banker's only child" and "had everything a man could want—power, wealth, and style." He had his picture in the papers and parties on his yacht, but with a suddenness which catches us unprepared, Simon sings: "Richard Cory went home last night and put a bullet in his head."[4]

Other songs which illustrate this theme and are worth listening to very carefully include "Eleanor Rigby" by the Beatles, "Only a Pawn in Their Game" by Bob Dylan, and "Lonely People" by America.

Marx and Capitalism

The Sixties were also a time when many people were freer to experiment with the social and political philosophy of Karl Marx (1818–1883) and his criticisms of capitalist economics. The publication and general availability of Marx's earlier writings with a greater emphasis upon such themes as alienation also had an important impact. After all, as Don McLean, tells us in "American Pie" from the album *American Pie* (1971), even "Lennon read a book on Marx."[5] In the 1960s and 1970s in America, such books as *The Sane Society* by Erich Fromm, *Technics and Civilization* by Lewis Mumford, *The Pursuit of Happiness* by Robert M. MacIver, and *One-Dimensional Man* by Herbert Marcuse were responsible for popularizing Marxist criticisms of capitalism. And because of the emergence of the New Left, there was a larger and more knowledgeable group of broadly Marxist activists who were no longer tied to slavish apology for the Soviet Union and its "official" brand of Marxism. Lennon certainly wasn't the only person reading a book on Marx.

Marx's indictments of capitalism were many, but specifically important here are his criticisms of the kinds of alienation capitalism produces among the populace—problems with which we are still struggling, the collapse of the Soviet Union and worldwide communism notwithstanding. Among the fatal flaws of capitalism which Marx identified are the continual and massive accumulation of wealth which results in the oppression of the masses. The essential ways in which modern, industrialized capitalist societies are structured, he thought, are bound to produce alienation in the workers. This alienation both originates in and is manifested in several different ways. Human beings, under capitalist economic systems, become alienated from nature, other human beings, their act of labor, the products of their labor, and ultimately, from themselves. But, if the value of things (including a person's labor and value to society) is determined by money and wages, then, Marx thought, several things are bound to happen. We will then begin to look at nature simply as a source for supplying resources and materials for manufacturing. We will then have no interest in and see no value in our jobs (frequently, mindless jobs involving endless repetition) except as a source of getting money (wages) to buy *things*. Competition with our fellow human beings for wealth and things results in alienation from them (the other members of our own species). Finally, since modern, capitalist societies do not provide people with authentic sources of happiness and satisfaction, we become alienated from ourselves —we lose meaning in and for our lives.

Another ideology which impacted upon the political climate of The Sixties was the elevation of social consciousness resulting from Third Worldism. The idea that the poverty of much of the world was the responsibility of the rich, Western countries became very popular, and many people adopted a kind of Robin Hood attitude toward the concentration of wealth in Western European countries and in the United States and Canada.

Romanticism

Such criticisms of capitalism need not be based upon Marxist philosophy. Indeed, such themes, critical of modern industrialized living, characterized the period of literature known as Romanticism at the beginning of the nineteenth century. The romantic English poets William Wordsworth and Samuel Taylor Coleridge made claims (very similar to those of Marx) about the adverse effects of industrialization and mechanization upon the human spirit and upon human happiness at the beginning of the nineteenth century—before Marx was even born. Indeed, Wordsworth's immortalization in 1807 in "The World Is Too Much With Us" of the evil consequences for us of "getting [things] and spending [money]" is still something which most school children read (the fortunate ones, anyway):

The world is too much with us; late and soon,
Getting and spending, we lay waste our powers:
Little we see in Nature that is ours;
We have given our hearts away, a sordid boon!

The Romantic Movement included such writers as Robert Burns in Scotland, Jean-Jacques Rousseau in France, Johann Wolfgang von Goethe in Germany, and, in America, William Cullen Bryant, James Fenimore Cooper, and Edgar Allan Poe. These writers, in a reaction to what has become known as The Age of Reason, during which the human intellect and cognitive powers were thought to dominate human affairs, stressed the importance of emotions and sentiments. They resisted what they regarded as an overly industrialized and commercial world and encouraged a return to a more "natural", primitive, simple, and pastoral kind of existence. Their poems and novels draw upon "unrealistic" themes—fantasies and dreams—folklore and myth—fairy tales and legends. Their "classicist" critics, who accorded a high value to human reason, and in the arts looked for harmony, form, balance, and structure, regarded the romantics as impractical and unrealistic and their fanciful works as dangerous.

Both classic rock and popular literature from the 1960s embody many of the themes of Romanticism. We can easily see the influence of Romanticism upon The Sixties by looking at the criticisms of modern, post-industrial, technological capitalism embodied in many classic rock compositions. The influence of Romanticism upon The Sixties was so great that the period could justifiably be called the Age of Neo-Romanticism.

Big, Yellow Taxi

A song which dramatically illustrates the impact of money and profit on our relationship to nature is Joni Mitchell's "Big Yellow Taxi", from the album *Ladies of the Canyon* (1970), written at a time when environmentalists in California were trying to save redwood trees from loggers and developers. Ronald Reagan was governor of California and was reported as saying, "If you've seen one redwood, you've seen them all"—a remark which ought to have warned American voters of the extent of Reagan's environmental commitments. With the ever-expanding threat of the ugly specter of urban sprawl, one might think that we will eventually be faced with the need for a "tree museum". Such a museum might well be the only place our descendants might be able to find trees if we don't protect the environment, Mitchell suggests. At some point in the future, a family might load into the family "space vehicle" and go to the Museum of Trees on a Sunday afternoon for a special outing for the kids. The trees pay the price for much of what we call "progress".

At a time when words such as 'environment' and 'ecology' were just beginning to creep into our vocabulary and into the public's consciousness, Mitchell cleverly captured the now familiar conflict between environmentalists and developers. Just what we need: another shopping mall with nice little boutiques and swinging night clubs—something for everybody. And, of course, there must be room for everybody to park their automobiles, so "they" (the ubiquitous, alien "they" again) had to pave the paradise which was already there to create a parking lot. Paradise for a parking lot! What a bargain! Won't we ever learn and get it right? Mitchell is not very encouraging about learning from our mistakes. Whether it's the loss of precious woodland or the loss of a very special love in our lives, it seems that it's part of human nature that we just don't appreciate the value of something special until its gone, and then it's too late.

Money and Property

Pink Floyd's "Money" (written by Roger Waters) from *Dark Side of the Moon* (1973)[6] focuses upon the alienation which results from trying to find happiness by accumulating money and the things which it can buy. "Get a good job with more pay and your OK." The very definition of a "good job" is simply one with a higher salary. And if we "grab that cash with both hands", we'll be able to buy a "new car", "caviar", or maybe even a "football team". And "Don't give me any of that do goody good bullshit . . . And I think I need a Lear Jet." The words of Wordsworth and Jesus should echo here: "Getting and spending, we lay waste our powers", and "For what will it profit a man if he gains the whole world and forfeits his life?"[7]

These same motifs of Romanticism—the rejection of the products of an overly commercialized society and the return to nature—are the dominant themes of the song "Signs", written by Les Emerson, which reached Number Three in 1971. This was the only hit from the only album, *Good-byes and Butterflies* (1971), by The Five Man Electrical Band, a Canadian group. The signs, of course, are everywhere—the ubiquitous reminder of the overly-structured, overly-regulated, overly-suppressive influence of "society".

> *And the sign said, "Long-haired, freaky people need not apply"*
> *So I tucked my hair up under my hat, and I went in to ask him, "Why?"*
> *He said, "You look like a fine, upstanding young man. I think you'll do."*
> *So I took off my hat. I said, "Imagine that—me working for you."*

The signs say, "Do this. Don't do that." "Can't you read the sign?" The suggestion is that there is little opportunity for individual diversity and individuality. The signs also alienate us from nature.

> *And the sign said, "Anybody caught trespassing will be shot on sight."*
> *So I jumped on the fence and yelled at the house, "Hey, what gives you the right*
> *To put up a fence to keep me out or to keep Mother Nature in?*

If God was here, he'd tell you to your face, 'Man, you're some kind of sinner.' "

If we understand 'man' in the last line generally and generically, then we have a good expression of a very common general theme of Romanticism. It could easily be a final line of a poem by Burns, Coleridge, or Wordsworth.

Where Do the Children Play?

"Where do the Children Play?" by Cat Stevens continues these same themes. In this song, from the *Tea for the Tillerman* album (1971) there is some recognition of the advantages of the products and conveniences provided by a post-industrial, technological society. "We've come a long way," Stevens admits, and we can "switch on summer from a slot machine" or "take a ride on a cosmic train." We can now get all kinds of things—almost anything we want. "Yes, get what you want to, if you want, 'cause you can get anything." But, of course, there is a high price to be paid for such products, conveniences, and pleasures. The recurring refrain and lament is "where d' the' ch'ldr'n play?"—a line which captures very nicely the suggestion that what we have sacrificed for a technological society is something that is in our basic natures, and our innocence, and our future. There is also the suspicion that the price will even get higher. In lines reminiscent of Big Brother from George Orwell's *Nineteen Eighty-Four,* Cat Stevens asks: "Will you make us laugh, will you make us cry, will you tell us when to live, will you tell us when to die?" By the end of the song, there is little doubt that the price tag of living in "modern society" is too high.

The Pretender

Although it slightly stretches the limit of the time-period which I have imposed upon myself, Jackson Browne's song "The Pretender" from *The Pretender* album (1976) illustrates this theme. In "The Pretender", Browne describes the life of a man who has bought the American dream and tried to buy the golden ring of happiness by getting a house in the suburbs and a station wagon. The Pretender has surrendered his dreams to "the things that money can buy," and his job is just a means to those ends, and each morning, he must "get up and do it again."

> *I'm going to rent myself a house*
> *In the shade of the freeway*
> *I'm going to pack my lunch in the morning*
> *And go to work each day.*
>
> . . . . . .
>
> *I want to know what became of the changes*
> *We waited for love to bring*
>
> . . . . . .
>
> *Caught between the longing for love*
> *And the struggle for the legal tender*
>
> . . . . . .
>
> *I'm going to be a happy idiot*
> *And struggle for the legal tender*
> *Where the ads take aim and lay their claim*
> *To the heart and soul of the spender*
> *And believe in whatever may lie*
> *In those things that money can buy*
> *Though true love could have been a contender*
> *Are you there?*
> *Say a prayer for the pretender*
> *Who started out so young and strong*
> *Only to surrender.*

It's Alright, Ma

Other powerful songs contain this same theme of alienation from material possessions. Bob Dylan wrote several. The strongest, as well as the most moving, is "It's Alright, Ma, I'm Only Bleeding." Dylan's raspy voice drips with venom as he attacks the commercial world of getting and spending:

As human gods aim for their mark
Make everything from toy guns that spark
To flesh-colored Christs that glow in the dark.
. . . .
For them that must obey authority
That they do not respect in any degree
Who despise their jobs, their destinies
Speak jealously of them who are free
Do what they do just to be
Nothing more than something they invest in.
. . . .
Money doesn't talk, it swears
Obscenity, who really cares?

Shangri-la

"Shangri-la" by the Kinks from their album *Arthur (or the Decline and Fall of the British Empire)* (1969) is another song which is perhaps somewhat lesser known but which continues the satirical, stinging attack upon consumerism and the value of acquiring material possessions. "Shangri-la" is the paradise of suburbia where we get our rewards for "working so hard", including the car which we have dreamed of, indoor plumbing, a TV set, and a radio. We can put on our slippers and sit by the fire in our rocking chair. Underneath the facade of happiness is the nagging realization that we are really captives in Shangri-la and can't leave, and along with the other residents of Shangri-la, who live in houses which all look the same and who drive cars which all look the same, we have to go to work to pay the mortgage and the gas bills and the water bills and the payments on the car. In the end, the Kinks sing, "Life ain't so happy in your little Shangri-la." (The original Shangri-la was the fictitious paradise on earth, in the high mountains just beyond the border of British India.)

Perhaps a good way to try and understand the changes which took place in American society in the 1960s, as well as the differences between early rock 'n' roll and classic rock, is simply by comparing the schmaltzy Number One hit, "The Great Pretender" by the Platters (1955) with Jackson Browne's cynical, sarcastic "The Pretender" (1976). To focus upon the differences in the themes regarding wealth and possessions between The Sixties and the "me first" Eighties, compare George Harrison's "Living in the Material World" with Madonna's "Material Girl".

Sexual Alienation

There has been much dispute about the role of women as depicted in classic rock. Some feminists have rightly criticized the status of women in early stages of the music industry and the anti-Vietnam war movement. Much of the current wave of feminism can be traced to the 1960s. The comparatively liberated position of women in our society today is as much the result of the social revolution of the 1960s as the liberated position of blacks is the result of the Civil Rights Movement. The changes in the roles of women brought about by World War II were largely reversed during the 1950s. Thus, the changes in the roles of women initiated during the cultural and social war of The Sixties constituted an important episode in the continued struggle for sexual equality and are major factors which have contributed to bringing us to where we are today.

Several songs from classic rock focused directly upon the plight of women, but no song from this period is more angry and explicit on this subject than "Woman is the Nigger of the World" by John Lennon and Yoko Ono from the album *Some Time in New York City* (1972).[8] The lines from this song could easily be made into a liturgy for contemporary feminists.

> *We make her paint her face and dance.*
> *If she won't be slave, we say that she don't love us.*
> *If she's real we say she trying to be a man.*
> *While putting her down we pretend she's above us.*
> . . . .
> . . . .
> *We insult her every day on TV*

And wonder why she has no guts or confidence
When she's young we kill her will to be free
While telling her not to be so smart
We put her down for being so dumb.

. . . .

. . . .

We make her paint her face and dance.
We make her paint her face and dance.

Lennon and Ono implore us to "think about it" and "do something about it."

Racial Alienation

There are also songs which express alienation resulting from racial prejudice. Buffy Sainte-Marie, a Cree Indian from Saskatchewan, Canada, carried the banner for Native Americans with "Now that the Buffalo's Gone" and "My Country 'Tis of Thy People You're Dying". In the latter, exceptionally moving song, Sainte-Marie's strong and proud voice tells how Uncle Sam "won the West" by trading smallpox-infected blankets to the Indians for land. She sings: "The tribes were wiped out and the history books censored." The proud eagles which symbolized America, she says, were never anything but "carrion crows" which stole the eggs from the nests of wrens, wrought ruin upon a civilization, and even robbed the graves of the dead. Even the use of imagery of animals and nature carries through on the theme of the wanton destruction and violence to nature which accompanied the "settlement" of the West.

Hands on our hearts, we salute you your victory.
Choke on your blue, white, and scarlet hypocrisy.

There were several other songs from this period about the plight of Native Americans. "Indian Sunset" (written by Elton John and Bernie Taupin) from Elton John's *Madman Across the Water* album (1971) is a song which also captures the loss of the culture of the American Indians. "Indian Reservation", by Paul

Revere and the Raiders, hit Number One in 1971. Michael Murphy entered the charts with "Renegade" in 1976, and Styx's "Renegade" climbed to Number One in 1979.

"Living for the City" by Stevie Wonder from *Innervisions* (1973) chronicles, in almost prophetic fashion, the ways in which urban life threatens the health, dignity and very lives of blacks in American cities. Wonder tells of a black family in which the boy is unemployed and unable to find a job because he is black. The boy's father and mother work long hours at menial jobs and manage to earn just enough for the family to survive in the city. The title of the song comes from the image of the demands of urban or inner city living upon the lives of the poor who live there and cannot escape the cycle of poverty and unemployment. The city demands its share of each person's life, and the share which is required is so great that all of a poor black family's combined efforts is just enough to satisfy the demands of the city. The imagery developed here uses the city to replace the demanding nobles and landowners who, at different times in history, placed such heavy demands upon serfs and tenants. For urban blacks, Wonder tells us, "the city" takes on a life of its own and almost like some pagan deity requiring human sacrifice, demands the lives of those "Living for the City".

Another song about the plight of blacks in America is Aretha Franklin's version of "Respect", which reached Number One in 1967. This song, written and recorded earlier by Otis Redding, captures the theme of "black is beautiful" and depicts the difficulties which minorities face when the dominant culture sets the standards for physical beauty and social acceptability.

Political Alienation

One of the more common themes of classic rock is suspicion towards and mistrust of political and legal authority, and when most people talk about the alienation of the 1960s, they most often have political alienation in mind. This same political alienation was also a common theme in other forms of popular culture of the period including many books and movies. Sometimes it is difficult to separate political alienation from social alienation or from alienation with respect to the military. President Dwight Eisenhower's concerns about the relationship between "the military-industrial complex" and the government were certainly legitimate in the sense that, by the mid-1960s, many people had difficulty distinguishing the two. George Orwell's *Nineteen Eighty-Four*, Joseph Heller's *Catch-22*, and Ken Kesey's *One Flew Over the Cuckoo's Nest* both echoed and amplified the political disenchantment of the 1960s.

Conspiracy theories, not just about the political assassinations, but about government, business, and the military, abounded among the members of the radical left, student demonstrators, activists, and hippies. This is hardly astonishing: the entire duration of the cold war, from the end of World War II, had been a period where the government and military had adopted secrecy and deception as major components of their *modus operandi*. No doubt a case can be made that such cloak-and-dagger secrecy was necessary, but it took a heavy toll on the trust and confidence of the populace. The government and military certainly had their conspiracy theories as well— such as, in foreign policy, the myths of monolithic, "worldwide" communism and the domino theory and, in domestic affairs, the myths of communist conspiracy and "outside agitators".

The election of 1964, which pitted incumbent Lyndon Johnson against "hawk" Barry Goldwater, along with the incidents which immediately preceded and followed it, could serve as a good case study of the suspicion and divisiveness which would eventually erupt into the major confrontations of the 1968 Democratic Convention in Chicago and the various marches on Washington, D.C.[9]

The Credibility Gap

No other single event of the 1960s, at the same time historically momentous, was more of a lightning rod for mistrust of the government and the military than the Gulf of Tonkin incident of August 1964. According to military sources and the Johnson administration, two American warships, the *Maddox* and the *Turner Joy*, were attacked by North Vietnamese torpedo boats. Reactions were swift and decisive. Johnson ordered a retaliatory attack against North Vietnam, the first of many, and Congress overwhelming passed the Gulf of Tonkin Resolution which the Johnson administration described as a "functional equivalent of war."[10] It was this resolution which gave Johnson practically unlimited powers in waging the undeclared war in Vietnam. It also allowed Johnson to respond to Goldwater's accusation of being "soft" on communism and the war in Vietnam. Johnson, the hawk on Vietnam, had been hatched, and what was to become known as "the credibility gap" had been created.[11]

Suspicion concerning the reported events of the Gulf of Tonkin "incident" were almost immediate and widespread. Most of the details of the event, as they were reported to Congress, were either greatly exaggerated or simply, blatantly false.[12] But Johnson and the military did not back down, and, as a result, many of those who later opposed the war in Vietnam came to feel as if they had been duped. They came to believe that the government's original policy towards Vietnam and consequently, the war itself was based upon a lie. Trust and confidence in the government eroded, and the credibility gap widened. Big Brother was alive and well and had set up camp in Washington, D.C.

From the initial reservations about the report of the Warren Commission concerning the death of John Kennedy at the beginning of this period to the break-in at offices of the National Democratic Committee in the Watergate, the intense suspicion and mistrust of the government by what was initially a tiny minority of activists and radicals continued to grow. After Watergate, the conspiracy theories of the radicals gained enormously in credibility. Theories which had been off-the-wall rapidly became respectable and even conventional.

Much of this is now "ancient history". The importance of these events for our purposes here is to help us understand both the intensity and the pervasiveness of the sense of betrayal which was felt at the time by so many people. In the minds of many, within a few short years, the embodiment of everything good and noble of King Arthur's Camelot in the Kennedy administration had come crashing down and had been replaced by the deception and evil of Machiavelli's *The Prince* in the Nixon administration.

The Social Contract

The philosophical context within which the attitudes of 1960s political activists towards the relationship between government and individuals was generated was a libertarian, social contract tradition whose roots go back to John Locke (1632–1704), Jean-Jacques Rousseau (1712–1778) and Thomas Jefferson (1743–1826).

John Locke was an English philosopher whose *Two Treatises of Civil Government* were a monumental step in the development of modern, democratic government. Locke argued against, and even ridiculed, the notion of "the Divine right of Kings", according to which certain people were thought to be directly descended from Adam and thus to possess a unique God-given authority to rule over other human beings. Locke maintained that in an original "state of nature" (before civil government existed) all human beings were equal and were guided to behave properly by the "law of nature" which is "writ in the hearts of all mankind". Because of prejudices and the inclinations of a few individuals towards selfishness and greed, it becomes necessary, Locke thought, for people, by common agreement (a social contract), to form a government to protect the rights—particularly the property rights—of everyone. This is a contract among free and equal individuals, and from this contract, a government is born. The government becomes obligated to protect the people and provide certain services and the people become obligated to support and provide for the government. Such a view of the limited and voluntary nature of the origin of civil government is what first gave rise to the philosophical notion of the "rights" of an individual.

Jean-Jacques Rousseau developed a similar theory to explain the philosophical justification of government in *The Social*

Contract.[13] Rousseau's version of the social contract theory is based upon his view of human nature, according to which human beings are basically good, and government derives its authority over individuals through the same kind of social contract as Locke described. If human beings are basically good and have certain personal rights—"inalienable rights" which cannot justifiably be taken away from them—then a view of government restrained within certain limitations is a natural consequence. Government is understood as a creation of the people in order to serve the needs of the people. This is the philosophical framework which gives force to Abraham Lincoln's famed remarks, in his Gettysburg Address, concerning a "government of the people, by the people, for the people."

Locke's theory of the social contract and Rousseau's theory of human nature provided the philosophical basis which helped to generate both the American Revolution and the subsequent French Revolution. The influence of both Locke and Rousseau upon Thomas Jefferson and the Declaration of Independence was very significant. Jefferson inherited Locke's attack upon the notion of "the Divine right of Kings" and Locke's idea that government is the result of a voluntary agreement among the governed. Such an understanding of the nature of government also leads to a minimalist view of the nature of government— the view that we should only have as much government as is absolutely necessary. The rights of individuals must be protected—property rights and personal, individual rights, and liberties such as freedom of religion and of the press. If the people themselves are to have the power to govern, then all human beings must be regarded as capable of governing; so human nature must be regarded as inherently good.

The libertarian social contract theory of the nature of the origin of government and its authority over the individual thus creates the context within which a government is obligated to the individual and within which the government is limited in its authority over the individual. It is this view of government which gave rise in the 1950s and 1960s to the notion of "civil rights". Much of the political controversy and much of the political alienation of the 1960s can be understood as being generated by disagreements over the conflict between individual autonomy and state authority. Individual FREEDOM is one of the strongest and most prevalent themes we find in classic rock music. As the number one hit by the Rascals said in 1968, the "People [Have] Got To be Free".

Love It or Leave It

Determining exactly where to draw the line in limiting the authority of the state or granting the freedom of the individual is a difficult matter, and this was one of the most important issues which separated the political activists and the members of "The Establishment". Those who favor granting the state more authority over the individual will not find much philosophical kinship with Locke, Rousseau, or Jefferson. Another philosophical theory for justifying government authority which might be juxtaposed against the theories of Locke, Rousseau, and Jefferson for comparison (and which was quite influential in The Sixties) is the form of the social contract theory which can be traced to Thomas Hobbes (1588–1679). According to the view which Hobbes developed in his *Leviathan*, human beings are basically evil and the "state of nature" is really a state of war of everyone against everyone else where only the strong survive. Government is necessary, on this view, to save human beings from each other and from lives which would otherwise naturally be "solitary, poor, nasty, brutish, and short". Such a conception of human nature gives rise to a view of government where political and legal authority is valuable *per se*—in and of itself, regardless of its nature or content, and the limitations upon government authority are much less restrictive, with very little or no concern about individual freedom and rights. The result is that the philosophical basis for an individual's questioning or challenging the state are undermined, and individuals who persist in such actions are viewed as "bad" or "evil" simply because they are a threat to stability and order. In The Sixties, the commonly repeated slogans which captured this view of the nature of the relationship between individuals and the state included, "Love it or leave it" and "My country, right or wrong."

Waist Deep in the Big Muddy

"I Ain't Marching Anymore" by Phil Ochs from the album of the same name (1965) and "Waist Deep in the Big Muddy" by Pete Seeger from the album *Waist Deep in the Big Muddy and Other Love Songs* (1967) both became theme songs of the anti-Vietnam War movement. Seeger was invited to sing "Waist Deep in the Big Muddy" on "The Smothers Brothers Comedy Hour" only to have his performance censored by the network executives. The storm of controversy and the public outrage which followed ensured that Seeger was eventually allowed to return to the show to sing the song. This single incident is illustrative of the powerful political influence of the arts generally and of music in particular. "We're waist-deep in the Big Muddy, and the Big Fool says, 'Push on.'"

The Whole World Is Watching

The 1968 National Democratic Convention in Chicago spawned the group Chicago which used actual recording of the chanting of the protestors, "the whole world is watching, the whole world is watching" (from August 29th 1968) as a prologue to the song, "Someday", on Chicago's first album, *Chicago Transit Authority* (1969). (The group was first named Chicago Transit Authority, but changed its name to Chicago after the release of this album.) Chicago uses the actual demonstration in Chicago as a metaphor for life in America in the late 1960s. "Would you look around you now and tell me what you see? Faces full of hate and doubt. . . ." The alienation and suspicion and fear which divided the world into "us" and "them" in The Sixties are recurrent here. "You'd better run, you know. The end is getting near." You'd better run "as *they* try to get you" because *"they'd* love to burn you." Putting the oppression and suppression of the Chicago police, the National Guard, and the government on display for the whole world to see, the chant, "the whole world is watching, the whole world is watching" is repeated again in the middle of the song.

The injustices and excesses of "the system" are also captured by Chicago in the ironic song, "State of the Union" from the same album. In this song, the singer is involved in criticizing the state but talking about ways to "fix it." When a voice says, "Tear the system down." The singer argues with the voice—defending the system—but, in doing so, uses "a word which was quite nasty." The singer is arrested and taken away to jail for using "coarse language", and the voice is left to end the song with "Tear the system down. Tear it down, down to the ground." You just can't win for losing, the song seems to say, and *"they"* (the police, the government, the army, the system) will "get" you eventually.

Revolution or Evolution?

Notice that the singer in "State of the Union" does not advocate revolution. A major misconception, both of the political protests of the time and of the music, is that they generally involved the rejection of all political authority and embraced revolution or anarchy. Certainly there were extremist groups, radical fringes of the protests, who were what could correctly be called revolutionists or anarchists, but you will find very few expressions of such radicalism in rock music. One of the few is "Volunteers" (written by Paul Kantner and Marty Balin) by Jefferson Airplane from the album of the same name (1969). "Look what's happening down in the streets. Got a revolution. Got to revolution." And the cry goes out to the Volunteers of America to join in the revolution: "Pick up the cry. Hey, now its time for you and me. Got a revolution. Got to revolution."[14] Even if we take the lyrics at face value, however, they are still open to different interpretations. The song doesn't explicitly advocate a violent, armed revolt. Indeed, the line, "Hey, I'm dancing down the streets," suggests that the "revolution" is a peaceful one.

It is common to find the explicit rejection of violent revolution in various compositions from classic rock music. For example, listen carefully to the Beatles song "Revolution 1" by Lennon and McCartney from the album *The Beatles* (1968) (known as "The White Album"). All of the hoopla and misinterpretations concerning the song "Back in the U.S.S.R." notwithstanding (from the same album), the Beatles sing that "we all want to change the world"; however, "when you talk about destruction, you can count me out." And "if you go around carrying pictures of Chairman Mao, you ain't going to make it with anyone anyhow." And, in "Lost in a Lost World" (by Mike Pinder) from *Seventh Sojourn* (1971) by The Moody Blues, the lines explicitly say: "Revolution never won. It's just another form of gun."

Won't Get Fooled Again

Another explicit rejection of revolution comes from The Who's album, *Who's Next* (1971)[15] in their song, "Won't Get Fooled Again" (written by Pete Townshend). The album cover is a clever depiction of the rejection of authority, and I am amazed at the number of people who have absolutely "no clue" what the picture on the cover is about when they look at it. In the center of the picture is a large monolith, the symbol of higher intelligence and authority (and god, perhaps?) from "2001, A Space Odyssey", the monstrously popular movie from 1968.[16] The members of The Who have obviously just finished urinating on the monolith because the streaks are clearly visible. The Who are turning away and zipping up the flies on their pants. The title of the album, "Who's Next?" invites all of us to treat authority in a similar fashion. This album is an expression of the message displayed on one of the most common and provocative buttons of the period which simply said: "Question Authority."[17]

"Won't Get Fooled Again" begins with a loud, monotonous,

oppressive line from the synthesiser, repeated over and over again, which represents life under the oppression of the government. The lyrics begin with a description of the revolution, accompanied by light, "happy" riffs on the guitar, and some really up-beat, snappy drum beats, which symbolize the revolution.

> *There'll be fighting in the street*
> *With our children at our feet*
> *And the morals that we worshipped*
> *Will be gone*

Followed by the chorus:

> *I'll tip my hat to the new constitution*
> *Take a bow for the new revolution*
> *Started free with the change all around*
> *Pick up my guitar and play, just like yesterday*
> *Then I'll get on my knees and pray,*
> *"We don't get fooled again."*

In the song, the revolution does, in fact, succeed. The guitar and drums battle the synthesiser and finally win, but you can still hear the synthesiser faintly in the background.

Now many people who might have listened to this song superficially might think at this point that this is really a song advocating and encouraging political revolution. The "message" of the song, however, is directed at all political authority, and, just as clearly as the Beatles had done, The Who are saying that revolution is not the answer. After the revolution, Townshend tells us, "the men who spurred us on sit in judgment of all wrong", and

> *The world looks just the same*
> *History ain't changed*
> *'Cause the banners they all go*
> *In the next war*

Things after the revolution are no better. "Nothing in the street looks any different to me." Political revolution is like baseball— you can't tell the players without a scorecard. One political authority is no better than another. In a reference missed by many Americans, Townshend says, "The parting on the left is now the parting on the right." In British English, a "parting" means a "part" in a hairstyle. So political styles change, and those who used to be one side are now the other side.

During the musical interlude while the revolution is going on, there is a lot of strong guitar and drum music—the revolution is at its peak and things seem really groovy. But by the end of the song the synthesiser begins to come back in again. The synthesiser gets stronger and louder, repeating, in a long solo, the same monotonous and dominant theme with which the song begins. A drum solo represents the death thrash of the revolution, followed by a terrible, soul-rending death scream, and the final words of the song are "Meet the new boss. Same as the old boss." As Walt Kelly, creator of the comic strip "Pogo" put it, "We have met the enemy and he is us."

Among other songs on the theme of political alienation which deserve careful consideration and serious listening: "Street-Fighting Man" by the Rolling Stones; "Ohio" by Crosby, Stills, Nash, and Young; and "For What it's Worth" by Buffalo Springfield.

Existential Alienation
In the cases of personal, sexual, racial, social, and political alienation, the alienation originates out of a person's distinctive circumstances in life or because of particular reasons. Such alienation is also directed towards particular circumstances or specific individuals thought to be responsible for those circumstances. Existential alienation does not arise out a person's particular circumstances in life; rather, it arises from what we might call "the human condition". Such alienation is universal: it is an alienation in which all human beings share, and it is simply our "humanness" which is responsible for this "condition". Existential alienation is thus more of a vague sense of unhappiness, or as Søren Kierkegaard described it, a "gnawing dread". Existential *"Angst"* is not directed at or caused by

some particular individual or group of individuals or some particular set of circumstances which make a person feel oppressed or unhappy. It is a dread which is directed against all of a person's existence, everything and everybody in a person's life. The way in which *Angst* is usually used by existentialist writers is to describe a general, vague sense of alienation and despair *which takes no particular object.* In other words, *Angst* is simply alienation or despair *in general* rather than alienation from a particular individual or group of individuals.

As a philosophical movement, existentialism is usually traced to the writers and thinkers on the European continent following World War II—although existentialism also owes a very strong philosophical debt to some nineteenth-century writers, especially the German philosopher, Friedrich Nietzsche (1844–1900) and the Danish philosopher, Søren Kierkegaard (1813–1855).

Although there are many differences among these existentialist thinkers, there are common elements of existentialist thought. The human condition in which we all find ourselves is one, according to the existentialists, in which we are forced to make momentous decisions or choices about how we will live our lives. These choices are momentous because they affect not only our own lives but the welfare and lives of other people. Moreover, traditional philosophy and religion which have been thought to provide different systems of answers or guidelines for making these choices are worthless. There are no "objective" values or answers. In the end, when it comes right down to it, each of us must make our choices alone. The individual is the sole authority for what is right and wrong, and ultimately, only the individual can possibly give meaning to his or her own life. What you do is entirely up to you. We are thus "condemned to be free" since we, and we alone (*individually,* not collectively) are responsible for how we live our lives.

The realization that each of us is pitted against and is at the mercy of such overwhelming forces as society, other people, fate or luck, and, above all else, death is the source of human angst. Those who refuse to recognize this condition and embrace instead some kind of religion, philosophy, or moral code, in the belief that they can thus elude individual responsibility and individual vulnerability, are deceiving themselves. Only the person who realizes the human condition and his or her own existential plight is able to live a life of *authentic existence*. These various themes of dread, alienated *existence* from society, the absence of objective values, death, suicide, and authentic versus inauthentic existence recur commonly in such existentialist novels as *The Stranger, The Plague,* and *The Fall* by Camus, *The Trial* by Kafka, *Steppenwolf* and *Narcissus and Goldmund* by Hesse, *Nausea* by Sartre, and Sartre's play, *No Exit.*

Stranger in a Strange Land

These same existentialist themes recur in various forms in popular culture from The Sixties, particularly science fiction and yes, in rock music. For example, one of the most popular and best known science fiction novels from this period and perhaps of any period, *Stranger in a Strange Land* (1961) by Robert Heinlein, focuses very clearly upon many of the same issues involving the nature and value of human existence. The song of the same title by Leon Russell and Don Preston from the album, *Leon Russell and the Shelter People* (1971) uses the vague imagery of Jesus on earth as a way of contrasting an existence which is pure and innocent (and perhaps divine) with human existence.

> *How many days has it been since I was born*
> *How many days until I die?*
> . . . .
> *He's a stranger in a strange land*
> *Just a stranger in a strange land*

The notion that literally from the moment of our birth we are destined to die and the image of being a "Stranger in a Strange Land" are compelling existentialist themes. However, other parts of this song are less existentialist sounding since Russell and Preston entertain the hope of our learning "to love each other."

The Moody Blues strike a similar note in "Lost in a Lost World" (written by Mike Pinder) from their *Seventh Sojourn* album (1972) (yes, this was their seventh album).[18] The Moody Blues sing of being "Lost in a Lost World", and of people everywhere "searching" and "looking for an answer" but in the end any serious existential philosopher would say that this song is evidence of "inauthentic existence" because Pinder holds out the hope that "love will find them in the end."

Looking for ultimate answers, according to the existentialists, is like looking for a black cat in a dark basement at night, when the cat really isn't there. It's an absurd quest, and there's no reason to expect that we will someday find what we seek. Until our deaths, each of us is swept along by forces which are beyond control so we live all of our lives as helpless victims of our human condition. This situation is captured very graphically by Paul Simon in "Patterns" from the album *Parsley, Sage, Rosemary, and Thyme* (1966).

> *From the moment of my birth*
> *To the instant of my death*
> *There are patterns I must follow*
> *Just as I must breathe each breath*
> *Like a rat in a maze*
> *The path before me lies*
> *And the pattern never alters*
> *Until the rat dies.*

We are doomed to follow patterns all of our lives, Simon says. Furthermore, "like the color of my skin or the day that I grow old" these are patterns "which can scarcely be controlled."

Either/Or

Perhaps one of the most poignant representations of the absurdity of human life described by the existentialists is "Sammy's Song" by David Bromberg from his first album, *David Bromberg* (1972). In this song, Bromberg tells the story of Sammy, a young boy of 16, who is on the verge of becoming a man. His uncle who is trying to help Sammy takes him to a brothel "somewhere in the South of Spain" for his first sexual experience. The woman Sammy selects speaks only Spanish and Sammy speaks none, but somehow, they understand each other—supposedly in some basically human way which is more fundamental than language. As the two are about to have sex, Sammy insists that the woman remove all of her clothes even though she does not want to, and when she does, she reveals a body which is horribly scarred from a terrible accident.

This situation is typical of the kind of situations frequently described by existentialist writers. Life cannot be so carefully planned as to eliminate events which suddenly happen to us in such a way that we are forced to deal with them completely on our own and in such a manner that all of the things that we might have believed up to that moment are of no use to us at all. Imagine the overwhelming nature of such a situation for a 16-year-old boy who started out the day simply "for a ride", to have a good time, and "to see the sights". Suddenly and unexpectedly, life has imposed itself upon Sammy's consciousness in a way which nothing could have prepared him to handle.

According to many existentialists, the real test of the nature of our existence comes with such situations which *force* necessary, momentous and irrevocable *choices* upon us. In several of his writings, including *Either/Or*, Søren Kierkegaard especially emphasizes the importance of such choices in determining whether our existence is authentic or not. In "Fear and Trembling", he uses the familiar story from the Bible, of God commanding Abraham to kill his beloved son, Isaac, as a sacrifice. Think of the fateful yet inscrutable quality of such a situation! Think of being faced with such a momentous decision! This is the kind of ordeal which makes us or breaks us, Kierkegaard thinks. Such dilemmas come completely by surprise, and we must face them utterly alone.

This is the kind of situation in which Sammy finds himself in Bromberg's song. What is Sammy to do? What would you do? Well, in a way Sammy freaks out. "His eyes are wide. His brain is numb." He can't think. His intellect is not going to help him here. He must act on some level which is more basic and fundamental than human reason. He is "moved by some far distant mind" as he "sees himself outside his body and his brain" as he tenderly kisses and caresses her as they make love "to silence screaming in his skull." Later, when he's back at the hotel, Sammy tries to "heal himself", but "without the grace of tears or sickness", he simply "shakes and shakes some more." There is no deliverance, and there is no help. Sammy has had to deal with this frightful situation completely on his own and by himself, and by doing so, in existentialist terms, he has become a man by living an authentic existence. His life will never be the same. This is another song which you are not likely ever to hear as "canned" background music in a mall or elevator, except in a Monty Python or Saturday Night Live skit.

Among other classic rock songs which depict the crises of existence caused by the absurd and overwhelming predicaments life surprisingly forces upon us is "Locomotive Breath", by Jethro Tull. It tells the story of a man who discovers his "woman" in bed with his best friend. This is a far cry from the kind of "love story" or erotic tableau depicted in Tin Pan Alley ballads or in early rock 'n' roll songs.

Death Is a Dancer

There are many songs which might be used to illustrate the importance of facing the reality of one's own mortality. "Facing the reality of one's own mortality" means facing one's inevitable death in an existential way—not just intellectually. For example, think of the old syllogism:

> All humans are mortal.
> I am a human.
> Therefore, I am mortal.

Any reasonable person can examine the truth of the premises of this syllogism, understand the logic involved, and then *reason* his or her way to the conclusion. This is a purely logical or intellectual way to understand that each of us is mortal. However, this is quite different from the position of a person who, because of circumstances beyond his or her control, is existentially faced with his or her own immediate death.

A powerful song which illustrates this theme extremely well is Jackson Browne's "For a Dancer" from his *Late for the Sky* album (1974). Prompted by the death of a friend, Browne uses the metaphor of life as a dance to focus upon the nature of death. Prominent in Brown's lyrics is our inability to fully understand death.

> *I don't know what happens when people die*
> *Can't seem to grasp it as hard as I try*
> *It's like a song I can hear playing*
> *Right in my ear that I can't sing*
> *I can't help listening.*

The dance of life and death is a dance we learn from others, and, in this sense, it is the human dance.

> *Just do the steps that you've been shown*
> *By everyone you've ever known*
> *Until the dance becomes your very own.*

In the end, however, we must all dance our own dance, and die our own deaths. As Browne says poetically, "In the end, there is one dance you'll do alone." Until then, the best that we can do is simply keep on with the dance.

> *Into a dancer you have grown*
> *From a seed somebody else has thrown*
> *Go ahead and throw*
> *Some seeds of your own*
> *And somewhere between the time you arrive*
> *And the time you go*
> *May lie a reason you were alive. . . .*

This last really beautiful verse turns us all into dancers and holds out the possibility of a reason for our own existence and for human existence. It appears that Browne has "copped out" and fallen back into an "inauthentic existence", as Leon Russell did in "Stranger in a Strange Land" and as The Moody Blues did in "Lost in a Lost World", by countenancing the promise of some sort of meaningful understanding of death. However, Browne bravely adds as the last line of the song, "But you'll never know." In other words, even if there is some meaning to your life, you'll never know what it is. As dancers then we are each in the position of K. in Franz Kafka's novel, *The Trial.* K. struggles to defend himself against the accusations that he has committed some crime. He never knows what crime he's accused of or how to defend himself or even who the judge is. K. hopes for any sign that someone cares about or even knows of his plight. As he is about to be executed, a window opens, and K. thinks for a brief moment that he is finally about to get some answers—a reprieve perhaps or at least some explanation. Maybe it was the judge or someone trying to help or someone who simply cared, but then his executioner plunges the knife and he dies. If there were some reason for his life and death, he never knew, and the dance is over.

The Divided Self
When existential alienation leaves a person unable to cope with life, either suicide or madness results. Existentialist psychiatrists have suggested that some forms of what we call "mental illness" are much closer to "authentic existence" than what we call mental health. R.D. Laing was a Scottish existentialist psychiatrist known for his fascinating and controversial work involving schizophrenia. In his books, *The Politics of Experience* and *The Divided Self,* read by everyone in the 1960s, or at least by everyone who ever read a book, Laing maintains that our human aloneness and our fear of death cause us to form *groups* for some kind of security, groups such as families, clubs, society, and nations. From these groups, we learn to "process" our experience in terms which are created by and controlled by the groups, and "normal" (mentally healthy) people are those who process their experiences in the ways which they have learned in the groups and which are approved by the groups. Schizophrenics are those people who do not, for whatever reason, process their experience in socially acceptable ways.

Usually, Laing argues, it is because such people do not have normal defenses which allow them to protect what we would call their "private thoughts" from other people. They feel "transparent" and vulnerable as if other people can "read their thoughts".

As a protective mechanism, so-called schizophrenics develop what Laing calls an "inner self" which is radically private. This inner self is regarded by a schizophrenic as removed from his or her own body: such a person feels as if there is no special connection between the inner self and his or her own body. One's own body is regarded as simply another object in the world. The life of the inner self is removed from reality and deals only with objects of fantasy.

However, such people still have to operate in the real world, and to do this, schizophrenics develop what Laing and other existentialist writers call a "false self". Through the false self, a person is able to communicate with other people and otherwise operate in an objective, real world. All of sense experience is experience of the false self. This false self is simply a mirror which gives a reflection of socially acceptable behavior and is usually very compliant with the orders, rules, expectations, and needs and wants expressed by other people. As such, the false self is an example of an unintegrated self, an inauthentic existence. A schizophrenic with an inner self and a false self firmly in place will see "herself outside herself": the actions of the false self are experienced as artificial, controlled and "unreal". Society calls such individuals "mad" or "crazy" because they do not process experience the way most people do. But Laing poses the inevitable question of which is which and who is who and who gets to decide which is which and who is who.

The Dark Side of the Moon

It is common to describe a person who has a second, evil nature or a double life as having a "dark side;" however, in these cases, the second, dark side of the person is as publicly accessible, in theory, as the normal side. Indeed, such people are "exposed" by having someone catch them at their "dark", sordid behavior. The dark side of a schizophrenic is never "exposed" because by its very nature it is inaccessible to other people.

As far as I know, Mark Twain was the first person to employ the metaphor of the dark side of the moon to capture the notion of the private, inner self which is not seen or otherwise known by other people. In *Pudd'nhead Wilson's New Calendar* (1894), Twain says, "Everyone is a moon and has a dark side which he never shows to anybody." It is difficult to imagine a more appropriate metaphor to capture Laing's notions of the inner self and the false self. The light side of the moon is, of course, only a reflection of the light from the sun while the synchronization of the rotation of the earth and the moon ensures that the far side of the moon continually faces away from earth and is hence always dark.

Since its inception, the British group Pink Floyd has regularly infused themes from philosophy, literature, and poetry into its music. For example, both the title and the general theme of its first album, *Piper at the Gates of Dawn* (1967), comes from a poem by the English poet, William Blake (1757–1827), who explored, in his poems, the "spiritual" part of human nature which "transcends" the physical world. Their later album *Animals* (1977) is an obvious development of social themes from George Orwell's *Animal Farm*.

Pink Floyd's best album, and one of the best albums ever made, is *Dark Side of the Moon* (1973). The album cover of *Dark Side of the Moon* is certainly one of the most visibly recognizable and familiar album covers ever produced, but again, I have been amazed that so few people have ever thought about the importance of its symbolism. As the album is opened, on the outside of the cover we see a straight, narrow band of white light (with no apparent source) which stretches between two prisms. When the light hits the prisms on either side, and when it emerges from the opposite, unseen side of the prisms, it is refracted into the colors of the spectrum, and as the album cover is opened, we see that these colors continue on the inside of the album with a green band which fluctuates and deviates from the straight path of the other colors. This ingenious graphic ought not to go unappreciated. The cover is a depiction of the metaphor of the dark side of the moon and the existentialist theory of schizophrenia which it symbolizes. In other words, what we have is a graphic representing a metaphor representing a theory representing a private, inaccessible inner self. Thus, we see depicted the false self and inner self, inauthentic and authentic existence.

It is a complete travesty, which somehow seems appropriately ironic, that the graphics from the inside of the original LP album, which represent the diversity, freedom, and autonomy of the radically private inner self are completely omitted in the little folder which comes with the CD. We thus have a self-application to the album of one of the general themes of the album, "Got to keep the loonies on the path." By eliminating the graphics from the inside of the album, the publishers have performed a graphic lobotomy on the "loonies" and upon us, the audience. Can young listeners who have never seen the original album cover ever completely understand or appreciate the significance of this music? Will they ever have the chance?

Since *Dark Side of the Moon* is a "concept album" with a general theme, it would be easy to analyze each song from the album at great length and in great detail. However, it seems that it would be a valuable and interesting enterprise to have you, the reader and serious music listener, do some of this yourself; so I will simply give what I think are a few clues for understanding some of the different songs. The general theme of the album is, of course, mental illness—but with a definite slant toward Laing's view of schizophrenia. Some prelude to this theme can be found in the song "If" by Roger Waters from *Atom Heart Mother* (1970). It is also surely no mere coincidence that Syd Barrett, a member of Pink Floyd until 1968, had repeated bouts with behavior disorders, and possibly mental illness, caused by hallucinatory drugs. His erratic behavior while a member of Pink Floyd is well-documented. He now lives in seclusion and was reportedly institutionalized briefly after leaving the group.

Time

The beginning of the album should give us all the clues we need to understand its general theme. The first audible sounds are those of an identifying heartbeat, symbolic of the most primitive and persistent connection of the private, inner self to the "real" world. The first intelligible words following the identifying heartbeat are, "I've always been mad", followed by maniacal laughter. In "Time", our senses are bombarded by the loud jangle of clocks and bells as the cold, harsh and hectic external world of reality impinges upon the quiet, inner self. If you listen very carefully, you'll hear the heartbeat very cleverly mixed with the up-tempo, staccato percussion passage carrying the pace of a fast life. The lyrics of "Time" tell us of how time is simply a way of measuring the beginning and end of human life.

> *The sun is the same in the relative way,*
> *But you're older,*
> *Shorter of breath*
> *And one day closer to death.*

In the end,

> *The time is gone, the song is over.*
> *Thought I'd something more to say. . . .*

Us and Them

"Us and Them" attacks any notion of objective truth. Those in authority (such as "the General") decide "which is which and who is who," but really, "it's [simply] a battle of words." "Brain Damage" explicitly continues the theme from Ken Kesey's 1962 novel, *One Flew Over the Cuckoo's Nest*. The battle for the control of the mind is waged in Kesey's novel by the lone individual, Murphy, against Big Nurse and all of the powerful resources and authority of society and "the system" which she represents. In the song, the same struggle is waged between the singer, the lone individual and "you", meaning *us*, the listeners, society at large. "The lunatic" starts out in the song "on the grass". Then, the lunatic moves to "the hall". Then, "the lunatics" are in "my hall". Finally, the lunatic is "in my head". And we, responsible members of society that we are, "help" the lunatic by "treating" him—most radically, by a frontal lobotomy.

> *You raise the blade, you make the change*
> *You re-arrange me 'till I'm sane.*

> *You lock the door*
> *And throw away the key*
> *There's someone in my head but it's not me.*

The final cut on the album, "Eclipse", lists those experiences which are the result of our sensory experience of the world along with all of those experiences which are the result of our physical bodies being in the world, i.e. all of the things which we buy and save and otherwise have ("Money") along with everything that is "now", "gone", or "to come" ("Time"). All of these things are, of course, experiences of what Laing calls the "false self", and all of them, all things and all time, are eclipsed when the sun is "eclipsed by the moon"—which brings us back to the dark side of the moon. In the end, the only connection with reality is the heartbeat, and then . . . AND THEN . . . , even that fades away. And the last intelligible words spoken on the recorded version are, "Now there's no dark side of the moon really. Matter of fact, it's all dark."

Tommy

Although in many ways it is a category unto itself, much of Pete Townshend's and The Who's rock opera *Tommy* (1969) can be understood as embodying a very similar theme of mental illness.[19] Tommy's life in the opera, up to the point where he undergoes the "Miracle Cure", parallels life on the dark side of the moon. Tommy is traumatized as a child, and withdraws into his private, inner self, where he has very little contact with the "real" world. What follows for Tommy is a life of abuse from those in the real world, including, specifically, abuse by "Uncle

Ernie". In the popular "Pinball Wizard", Tommy, as "the deaf, dumb, and blind kid", has minimal contact with the external world and plays only by "sense of smell" and "by intuition", a suggestion that there are perhaps more direct (and more real?) ways of experiencing "reality". This is an interesting image. Just think about it! The image of a person who is deaf, dumb, and blind playing a pinball machine is, on the surface, amusing, but, if we think about it more seriously, weightier epistemological questions begin to surface. How could "intuition" enable him to play? Does he even know that he is playing? Does he know that he is winning? That he gets "the replay"? *How* could he? He always wins, so it seems that somehow he must know. But how? The answers to such questions are only to be found on the dark side of the moon.

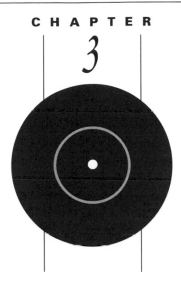

Bridge over Troubled Water:
The Greening of Rock Music

A Positive Side to the Sixties

It would be a mistake to think that The Sixties had nothing positive to offer or nothing to propose or suggest for ways of changing society and the people in it. Many people, both those who are old enough to remember The Sixties and those who are not, tend to have a very myopic and negative view of those times. "Nothing but a bunch of criticism and protest" is a common reaction. "All they wanted to do was tear things down." However, there were many positive features of The Sixties, and to ignore these aspects is to miss much of what has had lasting importance and what resulted in what I will call "the greening of rock music".

We can best understand these positive attitudes as responses to the various forms of alienation of The Sixties. This alienation prompted people to ask fundamental questions of themselves and each other: Who am I? Why are we (humans) here? How shall I live my life? What are my responsibilities to my fellow human beings? These basic philosophical questions were exactly the kinds of issues which philosophers have considered since the time of Socrates. Different answers which people explored were responsible for many of the best songs of classic rock. These are songs about friendships, community, and plans for social living (utopias), themes widely explored in both the literature and the music of The Sixties. Songs about friendship produced during this period are among the most lasting and timeless songs ever produced in American popular music. Included in this group of songs of friendship and community are such songs as "You've Got a Friend" by Carole King, "Bridge Over Troubled Water" by Simon and Garfunkel, "Lean on Me" by Bill Withers, "He Ain't Heavy, He's My Brother" by the Hollies, "Come Together" by the Beatles, "Imagine" by John Lennon, "We Can Be Together" by Jefferson Airplane, and "Woodstock" by Joni Mitchell. As we shall see, there are many others.

The alienation which resulted from personal relationships was understood, not as an inevitable result of a corrupt and sinful human nature, but rather as the results of particular circumstances existing in the society. The Neo-Romanticism which was so influential and so frequently expressed in the songs is associated with a view of human nature whereby human beings are regarded as basically good. One possible response to all of the alienation, which was regarded as being the product of society, government and "them", was obviously some form of personal relationship. However, equally obviously, personal relationships within the normal framework and structure imposed by society for such relationships would not do, so we ought to expect some kind of radical departure from societal norms for personal relationships. This is a theme which we shall find recurring frequently as we examine the various kinds of responses to alienation which were explored and which found expression in the culture and the music of The Sixties. In the themes of *carpe diem*, self-assertion, and individualism, we also find the conspicuous and prevalent need to "go outside" the normal societal boundaries for the expression of these themes. The established social and political institutions, including organized religion, failed to supply adequate answers, in the eyes of many of those in The Sixties asking fundamental questions about the meaning of human life.

Friendship

One of the answers expressed in many classic rock songs is friendship. Many of these songs are testimonials or "anthems" to "real", "authentic" friendships (or personal relationships). These are relationships which are not structured or constricted by a person's occupation or professional life nor are they the result of other socially structured patterns for relating to other people. These relationships are represented as genuine friendships—based upon the values and affections of the "real" people involved; they are "person to person". These friendships also represent the highest form of human relationships—more intimate and permanent than romantic relationships. As a result of the promise of a better, more meaningful life and hopeful existence deriving from such authentic friendships, we have one aspect of the "greening of rock music".

Surprisingly, philosophers have had very little to say about friendship in recent centuries, perhaps because "The Philosopher", Aristotle, treated the notion of friendship so thoroughly. Aristotle distinguished three different kinds of friendship: one is based on utility, one is based on pleasure, and one is based simply on the people involved.[1] In the first two kinds of friendship, people do not love each other "for themselves" but simply for the sake of some good or pleasure which the other person is able to provide. In the third kind of "perfect friendship", the love for the other person is directed at the other person *qua* person and is not based upon what the other person can do for me. Such friendships are permanent and quite rare, according to Aristotle.[2]

Aristotle's "perfect friendship" is the kind of friendship described in Proverbs where the writer says, "There is a friend that sticketh closer than a brother" (Proverbs 18:24). This is the kind of friendship which some philosophers, especially Aristotle, considered the most important and valuable kind of human relationship, which endures and sustains a person when all else and everyone else fails. The kind of friendship which we find expressed in many of the songs of classic rock is Aristotle's "perfect friendship"—a relationship which is "closer than a brother" or a lover. This is also the kind of relationship which theologian Martin Buber described in *I and Thou*, which becomes possible between people when they are able to relate to each other in the "fullness of their beings". The model for such relationships, Buber thought, is the "personal encounter" which a religious believer has with God. In The Sixties, for the many who had rejected any form of organized religion, they sought such a relationship with each other and not with God.

You've Got a Friend

Among the many songs which might be chosen to illustrate the theme of friendship, some of the choices seem rather obvious because of the strong and explicit expression of the theme of friendship in the songs and because of the initial popularity of the songs. Carole King's anthem to friendship, "You've Got a Friend", is from her album *Tapestry* (1971), one of the most popular albums of classic rock and also one of the biggest selling albums of all time. The lyrics are familiar to most people since both King's version and James Taylor's remain popular and receive a lot of play time on FM radio stations across the country.[3]

Although there are definite hints of some romance involved between the friends described in this song, the main thrust of the nature of the friendship is definitely not romantic. Indeed, the kind of friendship expressed in the lyrics is the kind which is considered to be more fundamental than romantic or familial relationships. I get the very strong feeling that even if there is a romantic or sexual relationship between the "friends" in this song, the friendship would withstand the end of the romantic or sexual involvement. For example, we can imagine, years later, that one of the friends is sick or at the end of another romantic relationship and needs the solace and comfort of the other friend. The anger and hostility which so frequently results from the end of a marriage or romantic involvement would prevent a future friendship between the individuals, but, in the case of the friends in King's song, we know that the friends are going to remain friends no matter what happens.

> *When you're down and troubled*
> *And you need some loving care*
> *And nothing, nothing is going right*
> . . . . .
> *You've got a friend.*

Such a friendship is constant and provides security, comfort and support in all seasons—"winter, spring, summer, or fall." And such a very special friendship supersedes other relationships. After all, only people who are really close to you in some special way are capable of hurting you or deserting you or taking your soul as King describes in the last verse:

> *Ain't it good to know that you've got a friend*
> *When people can be so cold*
> *They'll hurt you, and desert you*
> *And take your soul if you let them.*

But in the midst of crisis or hardship or heartbreak, when other people hurt you and desert you, "you've got a friend."

Bridge Over Troubled Water
The same qualities of such special friendships are also captured in "Bridge Over Troubled Water" by Paul Simon from the

Simon and Garfunkel album *Bridge Over Troubled Water* (1970).

> *When you're weary, feeling small,*
> *When tears are in your eyes.*
> *I will dry them all;*
> *I'm on your side. When times get rough*
> *And friends just can't be found,*
> *Like a bridge over troubled water*
> *I will lay me down.*

Simon also emphasizes the constancy and steadfastness of such friendship by promising to "take your part"—no matter what —"when you're down and out", or "when you're on the street", or "when evening falls so hard", or "when darkness comes and pain is all around". The redeeming quality of friendship is actually present in "Bridge Over Troubled Water" because by the last verse, the person to whom the song is being sung is finally over the difficult period, and the song takes on a quality of celebration for the good fortune of a friend.

> *Your time has come to shine.*
> *All your dreams are on their way.*

So, things are going to turn out all right, it seems, but if they don't and "if you need a friend, I'm sailing right behind." As with "You've Got a Friend", I feel strongly that, even though this might be a love relationship, the friendship is more fundamental and more enduring than the romance. Even if these two lovers part and go their separate ways, their friendship will survive.

Radical Friendships
The friendships represented in these songs are very personal, one-to-one relationships. These are not friendships *based upon* some familial relationship although they might certainly be

friendships between family members. These friendships are also not based upon membership in some other group or the result of some commitment to a shared ideology or religious beliefs. They are radically personal; the relationship and the commitment is to the person, individually. Such relationships are radical in that they might challenge existing social or political obligations or violate socially accepted norms for relationships. Sex, race, social status, class, political or religious beliefs, or other characteristics which a person might have do not affect these friendships. Such "radically personal" friendships are based simply upon a commitment to the individual person, and they are thus the most basic and fundamental kind of relationship.

Famous figures in history and literature have debated and differed over the value of such relationships, and the differences reflect the different views of human nature and human relationships which have prevailed at different times. The dominant theme in America, since her beginning, has certainly been to honor "God and country" before friends, especially in The Fifties. When E.M. Forster said "if I had to choose between betraying my country and betraying my friend, I hope that I should have the guts to betray my country",[4] he was expressing what would have been decidedly a minority position in The Fifties.

Lean on Me

It is a sign of the nature of the times which produced this music that so many of the very popular and well-known songs of classic rock are, in the best tradition of the romantic poets, "Odes to Friendship"—friendship in the tradition of Aristotle's "perfect friendship". In addition to those which I have discussed above, think of "Lean on Me" by Bill Withers (1972) and "He Ain't Heavy, He's My Brother" by the Hollies (1970). The Hollies, of course, use the familiar metaphor of life as a "long, long road". And the road has "many a winding turn . . . from which there is no return." As we travel this road of life "which leads us to who knows where," we must help others along the way. He's my brother, and "his welfare is my concern." Both the theme and the imagery are quite similar in "Lean on Me".

> *If there is a load*
> *You have to bear*
> *That you can't carry*
> *I'm right up the road*
> *I'll share your load*
> *If you'll just call me.*

"I'm strong, strong enough to carry him," the Hollies sing, but, as Withers reminds us, even though we might be the strong ones now, all of that might change later, and we may be the ones who need help. "We all need somebody to lean on."

> *Lean on me*
> *When you're not strong*
> *I'll be your friend*
> *I'll help you carry on*
> *For it won't be long*
> *Till I'm gonna need*
> *Somebody to lean on.*

There are many other excellent songs which could be used to express this theme of friendship. For example, you might listen to "Friends" by Elton John and Bernie Taupin from the album of the same title (1971) which is a soundtrack of the movie of the same title. "Old Friends" by Paul Simon from *Bookends* (1968) by Simon and Garfunkel captures the importance of friendship for those growing old and "sharing the same fear" of death. This song emphasizes the permanence and enduring nature of friendship. When you're old and have come to the end of your life and finally face death, it is "old friends" who are most important.

There are many other songs which contain similar themes of friendship and these deserve some careful attention. For example, listen to "Stand By Me" by Ben E. King, a song which has had many covers, including one by John Lennon, and "Reach Out I'll Be There" by the Four Tops.

Secularization

Several factors contributed to the emphasis on friendship in The Sixties. One of these was the increased "secularization" of American culture—the loss of the kind of spirituality and sense of "other-worldliness" which many forms of religious belief provide.

In 1965, Harvey Cox published a book called *The Secular City* in which he described both the plight of and opportunities for human existence in a completely secularized world.[5] The two dominant features of modern urban living are *anonymity* and *mobility*, according to Cox,[6] and these two features are responsible for both "the terror and delight of human freedom"[7] for people in "the secular city". What Cox calls the terror of human freedom is the massive weight of responsibility which comes with the realization that you and I are ultimately responsible for ourselves and for each other. The responsibility for human welfare and destiny is forced upon us not just by a few "weird" existentialist philosophers or a handful of "radical" priests and theologians but by "the whole character of urban-secular civilization."

Traditional theology, dependent upon the characterization of a deity which allows us to vitiate or even escape our responsibility for our fellow human beings, must be abandoned. We must no longer look to god, or the *Bible*, or the church for answers. We look to ourselves and each other. This freedom and responsibility are the blessing and the curse of being a modern person in a modern, secularized world.[8]

So modern, secularized human beings must take control of their lives and make them meaningful themselves. We must face our existence and our future without god, without religion or any other system of beliefs which provides an objective meaning and set of values for human existence. One possible form of an answer to the question of the meaningfulness of human existence and one possible refuge from the terror of facing an existence alone is *other people*. If god is dead, we either face our lives and future alone or together. Human relationships thus provide the opportunity for recapturing something of the special, "holy" nature of the lost relationship with god.

Honest to God

In *Honest to God,* another very popular book in the 1960s, Anglican Bishop John A.T. Robinson suggests that we must eliminate the "other worldliness" of religion and capture the religious notion of "the holy" by focusing upon "the depth" of ordinary, common experiences which can reveal the fundamental importance of love.[9] In terms of human relationships, this means that we can reintroduce the lost sense of "the holy" into our completely secular lives by seizing upon "ordinary" human relationships and making them special, we can elevate these ordinary human relationships and use them to replace the loss sense of the sacred and the holy which has resulted from modern secularization. In other words, we can replace our lost, special relationship with god by special, love-relationships with other people.

This whole debate surrounding the theological impact of modern secular living did not take place behind the sheltered, cloistered, ivy-covered walls of universities and divinity schools. This was an issue which was very much in the public domain—in both explicit and implicit ways. Explicitly, *Time* ran a feature, cover story on August 8th, 1966, asking "Is God Dead?" The appearance of the story in the major news magazine of the day is good evidence of just how widespread the tension was between secularized spirituality and organized religion.

Both *The Secular City* and *Honest to God* were books which largely repeated and popularized arguments propounded earlier by less accessible writers. *The Secular City* leaned heavily on Max Weber, David Riesman, Paul Tillich, and William Barrett (author of *Irrational Man*), while *Honest to God* popularized views long familiar to theologians, from the works of Dietrich Bonhoeffer and other writers. *The Secular City* and *Honest to God* can lay no claim to great originality, but they served as conduits for these ideas to reach the broad ranks of literate Americans and the media. Only a few rock musicians ever read Weber or Bonhoeffer, but anyone who conducted a serious argument with someone who had read *Time* magazine was affected by these ideas.

The Peace Corps offered the opportunity for young Americans to demonstrate their commitment and their feelings of responsibility for their fellow human beings in a manner and on a scale which was unprecedented in American history. Its enormous appeal and success is evidence of the need which tens of thousands of young Americans felt to "help their fellow man" in ways which were not being provided by "the church" and organized religion.[10] Peace corps volunteers were interested in saving lives and helping to provide a better quality of life for others—not in "saving souls". The inversion of the priorities of traditional Christian theology is thus completed. It is human life and *this* life which is important and not some future, eternal spiritual life. What is left is something like the moral teachings of Jesus of doing good "unto the least of these" but without the theology:

> *For I was hungry and you gave me food,*
> *I was thirsty and you gave me drink,*
> *I was a stranger and you welcomed me.*
> *I was naked and you clothed me,*
> *I was sick and you visited me,*
> *I was in prison and you came to me.*[11]

These words of Jesus provide the basis for the imperative which many people felt in The Sixties to help other people but without any of the accompanying theology. For example, in "Fly Like an Eagle" by Steve Miller, from the Steve Miller Band's *Fly Like an Eagle* album (1976), we hear the words of Jesus repeated: "Feed the children who don't have a bite to eat" and help those "who don't have shoes on their feet."

The Death of God

Philosophically, the secularization of modern, twentieth-century American can be traced, in part, to the nineteenth-century German philosopher, Friedrich Nietzsche. Nietzsche was the first to answer the age-old philosophical puzzle about the relationship between humans and god by proclaiming:

"God is dead." In *Thus Spake Zarathrustra,* Nietzsche says "God is dead" (Prologue), and in *The Gay Science,* he adds, "God remains dead. And we have killed him" (Chapter 125). The death of god serves as a cornerstone in Nietzsche's theory of *"der Übermensch,"* the superman (or "overman"). The individual, who is left alone without god, must become a law unto himself by rising above "the herd" mentality and morality. Alone in a world without objective values, the individual must *create* whatever value there is in life. Now exactly what Nietzsche meant by such claims is still a matter of some philosophical dispute. He has been interpreted in many different ways and paid homage to even by such diverse figures as Nazis, nihilists, and Christian theologians.

The combination of Nietzsche's philosophy and Christian theology must seem very strange for those who know the history of philosophy, since Nietzsche has enjoyed a following mainly among secular-minded socialists and anarchists. Exactly how these two different philosophical traditions managed to be brought together is a strange and rather circuitous story. The combination of Nietzsche with any form of Christian theology is very odd, because Nietzsche was uncompromisingly and unrelentingly hostile to Christianity. He called it a "slave's religion" which embodies a slave mentality and a slave's morality. Nietzsche thought that the historic development of Christianity among Jews during the time of the Roman Empire, when Jews were slaves, had determined *the content* of both Christian theology and moral teachings. The promise of a heaven or a paradise after death allows a believer to accept and rationalize many undesirable features of this life, such as poverty and social and political injustices, including slavery. A theology based upon an eschatology where the just will be rewarded and the unjust punished by a god at some unknown and far-distant time is a theology, Nietzsche thought, for the weak—for those in an oppressed position with no means or hope of changing it. A morality based upon such teachings as "turn the other cheek", "do good to them that . . . persecute you", and "love your enemies", is a "herd morality" for the weak person. Such a morality serves the practical purpose of keeping the person (the slave) alive and, at the same time, offers the person the psychological and personal solace of the promise of some future reward "in heaven". The net result is to keep people happy and contented with their lot here on earth and to suppress the individual who is unhappy and wants to change that lot. For Nietzsche, the only course of action for a person who wants to lead an authentic existence is to overcome or transcend such beliefs.

Christian Atheism

From the first century in Rome to the 1960s in America much had changed. So far as the social and political climate is concerned, Christianity had become the dominant religion in this country, the doctrine of separation of church and state notwithstanding. While the abolition of slavery and religious persecution made life easier and more socially and politically just for religious believers, Christian theologians had long worried about a too-close connection between established political authority and Christianity. The fundamental question concerns the extent to which the basic theological beliefs and moral teachings of Christianity are compatible with a comfortable, secure, and even luxurious life.

In the 1960s, this conflict between a spiritual, religious life and a secular one had become the dominant theme of several popular books by Christian theologians. Although there were many differences among these "Christian atheists", many of them made use of Nietzsche's notion of the death of god. There was a common theme: Like the hobos in Samuel Beckett's *Waiting for Godot,* modern human beings are tired of waiting for god, and it is time for us to realize that waiting is futile. It is time to give up the theological belief in a god who is omnipotent and omnibenevolent, who sustains life with divine love, and who will reward all good and punish all evil on some future judgment day. Perhaps the most important generally shared belief of the contemporary "Christian atheists" stressed the necessity of emphasizing the importance of this "secular" life.

This, of course, amounts to a straightforward reversal of "traditional" Christian theology which de-emphasizes the importance of life here on earth compared to a future, eternal, spiritual life in heaven. How is this still supposed to be a *Christian* theology? Well, if the god of traditional theology is dead, this means that god is not around to solve our problems—either now, by divine intervention, or in the future, in heaven. With this much of Nietzsche, the Christian god-is-dead theologians agreed. But then, what are we to do about this situation? For the atheistic theologians, the answer to this question is to be found in the moral teachings of Jesus, and this is what separates Christianity from Nietzsche. If god is no longer around to take care of the ills of humankind, then only you and I are left to do so. If there is poverty and disease and famine and social and political injustice and war, then it is *your fault and mine.* And, if anything is ever to be done about poverty, disease, injustice and war, then you and I must do it. This is "man come of age". Modern human beings can no longer blame the evils and ills of human existence upon "the will of god" nor can we any longer expect god to eliminate those evils and ills. The Christian morality of "brotherly love" provides a basis and a framework for human beings loving and assuming responsibility for their fellow human beings.

A powerful illustration of using human relationships as a possible response to the death of god is the cover of Grace Slick and Paul Kantner's album *Sunfighter* (1971) which shows a newborn baby, presumably their newborn son named 'God', being held aloft by a pair of hands. God is dead. God is born. Long live god.

The Greening of America
In 1970, Charles Reich wrote a book called *The Greening of America*[12] which became one of the most widely read and widely discussed books about American culture in the early 1970s. Reich's book focused upon both the various forms and causes of alienation which I have discussed at length in the first

two chapters of this book and upon the changes which he (and a lot of other people) thought were then sweeping the country. Reich believed that he saw the beginnings of a "kinder, gentler" nation long before that phrase was adopted by George Bush and turned into an empty campaign slogan. During the 1950s, with the development of the Corporate State in America, people developed a form of consciousness which Reich calls Consciousness II. Echoing the critique of American culture developed by William H. Whyte in *The Organization Man*,[13] Reich explains that Consciousness II is based upon a very pessimistic view of human nature according to which human beings are innately and fundamentally selfish, evil, and corrupt.

Law and Order

This view of human nature can easily be traced, in philosophy, to Thomas Hobbes. As I mentioned earlier, Hobbes described a hypothetical original state of human beings, with no government, which was chaotic and "brutish"—a state of anarchy and "war of all against all". Government and the resulting "law and order" provide a social framework which is necessary, according to Hobbes, for human beings to flourish and be productive and happy by being protected from other people and themselves. Law and order are good, not just because of the particular *content* of the laws but because of the particular content of human nature.

Original Sin

A similar view of human nature is also easily traced, in theology, to "original sin." According to the Western Christian doctrine of original sin, human beings, as a result of the sin of Adam, as reported in *Genesis*, are evil, sinful, and corrupt and in need of divine redemption *by their very nature of being human.* Even the most innocent new-born baby is evil and sinful and needs both God's law and human law to overcome this evil nature.

One of the more popular vehicles for the doctrine of original sin in the 1960s was William Golding's story, *Lord of the Flies*, which tells the story of a stranded group of upper-class English schoolboys who revert to a state of barbarism and savagery. Golding thus provided a rallying point for those who think that the restraints of society and civilization, law and order, are necessary to protect us from ourselves and to keep our basic, evil human nature in check.

Given the doctrine of original sin and its view of human nature, people with what Reich calls Consciousness II strongly identify individual interests with state and corporate interests. As Reich says,

> The Consciousness II man thus adopts, as his *personal* values, the structure of standards and rewards set by his occupation or organization. . . . Thus the individual directs his activities toward such goals as a promotion, a raise in salary, a better office, respect and commendation by his colleagues, a title, [or] "recognition" by his profession.

For such a person, "it's a jungle out there", and life is a continual struggle, full of competition with other people for success and all that comes with it. The character Willy Loman from Arthur Miller's play, *Death of a Salesman,* is the stereotype of a Consciousness II person. In a sense, "the organization man" or "the corporate person" was simply a further application of Charles Erwin Wilson's famous claim that what is good for the country is good for General Motors, and what's good for General Motors is good for the country. Willy Loman might have said that what is good for General Motors and the country is good for me, and what's good for me is good for General Motors and the country.

Such an attitude towards life leads to a certain impoverishment and certain restrictions in life-styles for a Consciousness II person. Reich explains the losses suffered by devotees to the Corporate State in some detail,[14] and I'm not interested in explaining those in great detail here. The various effects upon people and their life-styles parallel very closely the effects of different kinds of alienation discussed at length in the previous chapter.

Consciousness III

Consciousness III people, the people Reich saw in the 1960s and whom he thought would be responsible for a "kinder, gentler" nation, a "greening of America", reject the fundamental bases for Consciousness II. By contrast, people of Consciousness III have a view of human nature which values and glorifies the individual self and maintains a healthy skeptical attitude towards any kind of societal, governmental, or corporate authority. Many people think that The Sixties were devoted solely to such alienation and criticisms—protesting, demonstrating, complaining, "tear the system down"—and, as we have seen, there was an enormous amount of such alienation. But Consciousness III provides us with a framework for understanding the strong themes of friendship and community, which contributed to the positive message of The Sixties.

Part of the price paid by "the organization man" and "the corporate person" of The Fifties was in the area of personal relationships and, particularly, friendships.[15] Social and cultural patterns were understood as structuring and controlling the nature of personal relationships within very narrow limits. A person's social life, including friendships and the relationship with a spouse, was, to a great extent, a function of that person's occupation or professional life or the groups (such as the PTA) to which that person belongs or the suburb in which that person lives. Relationships based upon the "external" values which the individual has adopted from an occupation or from some other group, are decidedly limited. As we have seen, the theme of friendship and the songs which express that theme attribute no instrumental value to friendships. True friendships are intrinsically valuable in and of themselves, and such friendships actually constitute one of the highest values which exists.

Utopias

The next step in the greening of rock music is the progression from songs about individual friendships to songs about utopian community living. I have said earlier that the kinds of friendships which we were considering in the previous section are rare; however, since such friendships are person-to-person relationships, this means that there is something fundamental about people *qua* people which makes community and "the brotherhood of man" both possible and desirable.

Within the tradition of Western philosophy and intellectual thought, there is a very rich tradition of utopian writing and thinking. The possibility of some future, "perfect" state has been an irresistible lure for poets, novelists and philosophers alike. Some utopians have believed and maintained that some sort of "ideal", immaculate form of a human social order is *actually* possible, while others have defended utopian thinking because of the philosophical value of imagining *hypothetical* ideal states. Many people have dismissed utopians as unrealistic dreamers who are somehow "out of touch with reality", but such a harsh, summary judgment seems unfair. Minimally, it seems, for abstract theorizing about human social and political affairs, we must depart from the *actual* conditions which just happen to exist at a certain time and a certain place. Without such abstraction from immediate circumstances, it is difficult to understand how human beings could have managed to improve their lot and engage in social and political reform in any sort of reasonable way—as we have done numerous times in human history—including the American revolution. After all, the actual society in which we now live would have seemed no more than a fantastic dream just a few hundred years ago.

There are many classic rock songs which contain some sort of utopian theme, and some of these songs are among the best remembered and most lasting songs from The Sixties. We will need to examine the themes of such songs as "Come Together" by the Beatles, "Imagine" by John Lennon, "The Lee Shore" by David Crosby, "We Can be Together" by Jefferson Airplane, and, of course, "Woodstock" by Joni Mitchell.

The Search for the Perfect Community

Social and political philosophers from the time of Plato have tried to imagine the ideal way of constructing and regulating social and political affairs as a way of assessing actual states and governments. Economists also regularly do the same thing. If we first imagine what an ideal economy would be like, we are then in a better position to make decisions about what efforts to make to influence the way in which an economy develops. The great religious and moral teachers of the ages, including Jesus, Buddha, and Ghandi, have also provided directives for living which seem idealized and impossible to obtain and maintain on a grand scale for any extended period of time.

The 1960s saw a resurgence of interest in utopian living: there was an emphasis upon and an interest in various new and different ways of establishing and maintaining communities. Although there were certain recurring patterns in these proposals, there were still no carefully scripted or highly structured treatises which provided descriptions of what utopia was to be like. There was nothing comparable to Plato's *The Republic*, but certain general themes characterized widely-accepted notions of the ideal community.

The Shakers

Actual attempts before the 1960s to establish utopian communities have met with various degrees of success. The more successful communities seem to have been organized around some shared ideology with a strong and effective means of central control.[16] For example, in America, one of the most successful experiments with socialist, communal living was that of the members of the United Society of Believers (who have become known as "the Shakers" because of their practice of violent shaking, jumping, dancing, shouting, and speaking in tongues). Started by Ann Lee, who became known as "Mother Ann", as an offshoot from the Quakers, the Shakers believed that the "second coming" of Jesus Christ was "at hand". They established several utopian communities in the United States, and these communities thrived during the period from 1840 to 1860.

The Shaker communities, based upon common property,

pacifism, and complete celibacy, were very successful and resulted in several inventions (such as the clothespin and circular saw) and innovations (Shaker furniture and agriculture techniques). As we now know, "the second coming" did not take place as the Shakers expected, and, by the turn of the century, since the Shakers continued to practice complete celibacy, their experiment in utopian living had ended.

The Failures of the 1960s
Why, it might be asked, were none of the attempts at utopian living in the 1960s particularly successful and long-lived? Even the ones which did survive for any period of time did so only marginally, and none of the various experiments with communal living in the 1960s came close to approaching the success of the Shakers. The answer, I think, is simple and obvious. Successful attempts at communal living have featured a very definite and powerful unifying ideology and a very strong, effective authoritarian structure. The various attempts at utopian living in the 1960s had neither. In The Sixties, there was a dominant theme of rugged individualism—in both the literature and the music, and it is impossible to run a utopian community very effectively when each member is "into doing his or her own thing."

Freedom
"Freedom" is one very common theme found in classic rock lyrics about community. Some contemporary utopians, such as B.F. Skinner in *Walden Two*, embrace what they see as the positive advantages of modern technology in providing the mechanism for social engineering to produce a more controlled but more desirable human existence. However, the utopian themes which we find expressed in classic rock music display a strong aversion to more control and government. In contrast to Skinner, The Sixties romanticized *the individual*, and the utopi-

ans themes from The Sixties favor those utopian thinkers who want less rather than more control in society. Henry David Thoreau (1817–1862) and Ralph Waldo Emerson (1803–1882), the two main figures in what is now known as New England Transcendentalism, emphasized a simple life, free of government control. Thoreau's *Walden: Or Life In the Woods* is, from beginning to end, a celebration of the importance of *the individual,* an importance echoed in Emerson's claim that the less government we have, the better.[17]

Failure to appreciate fully the importance of the theme of individual freedom is responsible, I think, for the fears of so many members of "the establishment" that the activists and the protestors of the 1960s would eventually turn the country into a communist state. Those who did advocate some kind of socialistic state did so in a naive and starry-eyed manner. They thought that somehow we would all naturally and voluntarily want to be together and to share resources and wealth. At the same time, as the result of the very strong theme of individuality and individual freedom, people were encouraged, in Peter Fonda's immortal sage advice from "Easy Rider", to "Do your own thing in your own time." In fact, the elevation of the importance of the individual and individual freedom meant that the amount of centralized control necessary for a communist state or even the amount of centralized control necessary for a minimally socialist state was out of the question. This same tension is responsible for the uneasiness with which any utopian theme was addressed in The Sixties. It appears that those who did promote some utopian themes thought that somehow, in some completely spontaneous and unexplained fashion, we would all just want to come together and that this would happen freely and naturally without the need for any kind of central direction.

Other common themes found in rock songs from the 1960s, equally romantic, are "back to nature" and "return to the land". These themes are borrowed from a very rich tradition which includes such notable figures as Jean-Jacques Rousseau, who thought of human beings as "noble savages" existing in an original state of innocence, uncorrupted by society and government, and Henry David Thoreau, who held that we need to return to the land to live a "simple life", to avoid the ravages of modern society. Two different forms of utopian living have proved attractive to some.[18] One kind of utopia merely provides an escape from what a person considers to be the oppressive society in which he or she lives, without being regarded as providing any sort of realistic design or plan for *actually* changing society. Such escape utopia are mere fantasies, like Puff the Magic Dragon's land of Honah Lee, which allow some release for a person without taking into account the "harsh realities" of actual life. Most of the songs which we will look at are examples of this kind of escapist thinking.

Lewis Mumford calls the second kind of utopia "utopias of reconstruction."[19] These are utopias which include actual "re-constructed" plans for how society ought to be arranged in the future—including new social institutions, new values, and new patterns for human interaction for such activities as owning property, or bearing and educating children. Although some songs might fit into this category of utopias of reconstruction, the actual details of the reconstruction which are provided in the songs are always, of necessity, brief and vague.

There are many wonderful songs which might be used to illustrate the theme of community. There is, of course, "Come Together" by Lennon and McCartney, from the Beatles' album, *Abbey Road* (1969), but, aside from the title line which is repeated frequently in the song, there is little in the lyrics upon which we can base any sophisticated theme of community. We actually get very little here except, "you've got to be free" and "come together".

However, another song by John Lennon is an excellent choice to illustrate the theme of utopian community (in addi-tion to being one of my favorite songs). The song is "Imagine" from Lennon's album of the same title (1971). The very explicit lyrics ask us to "imagine" a world without all of the things which normally separate people. Imagine that there's "no heaven", "no hell", "no countries", "no religion", "no posses-sions," and "nothing to live or die for." This is Lennon's real song about how people can "come together". Only if we give up other priorities can we live "life in peace" as a "brotherhood of man".

God

"Imagine" is also a natural follow up to Lennon's earlier song, "God", from the *John Lennon/Plastic Ono Band* album (1970). In "God", Lennon makes his now well-known declaration that "the dream [of the Beatles] is over." He also lists all of the things in which he no longer believes, the things which fall into the same categories which he suggests in "Imagine" keep us from "peace" and "brotherhood." He says, "I don't believe in . . . Magic . . . I-Ching . . . Bible . . . Tarot . . . Hitler . . . Jesus . . . Kennedy . . . Buddha . . . Mantra . . . Gita . . . Yoga . . . Kings . . . Elvis . . . Zimmerman [Bob Dylan] . . . Beatles." If we managed to somehow come up with a list of all of the various "causes" and "escapes" and "solutions" which were popular during the 60s and 70s, it would be difficult to think of many which are not included or at least symbolized in Lennon's list. As the "dreamweaver," he also was one of those things in which people believed, but, as he now tells us, "the dream is over." Now, he only believes in himself and the redemptive power of a personal relationship. As he concludes, "I just believe in me. Yoko and me."

Jefferson Airplane's "We Can Be Together" by Paul Kantner from *Volunteers* (1969) continues the theme of a call to communal togetherness. Part of what provides the conviction of unity is the awareness of shared victimization which we have found to be one of the defining characteristics of The Sixties. "America", that's to say the "respectable", "up-standing", older "pillars of the community", regard us as "outlaws", Kantner says. "They" see us as "obscene lawless hideous dangerous dirty violent and young." The characteristic of being "young" is treated in this line as being simply another one of those characteristics which makes people personally undesirable and socially unacceptable. As the "forces of chaos and anarchy", people think of the "young" only in terms of threats and fear. But instead of "up against the wall", the Airplane urges, "tear down the walls [that separate us]." So starting "here and now",

> Come on now together
> Get it on together
> Everybody together.

But the only way, we can be together is if we "tear down the walls, tear down the walls." Just "Imagine." And maybe "Someday We'll Be Together", as Diana Ross and the Supremes sang in their Number One hit of 1969.

Out in the Country

Three Dog Night made a successful career out of doing covers of songs written by other people. "Out in the Country," written by non-band members Paul Williams and R. Nichols, from the Three Dog Night album *It Ain't Easy* (1970), is another song with the theme of peaceful, utopian living but with more of an element of escapism. "Out in the Country" also includes the motifs of the importance of the individual and a simple life of "back to nature." This song could well have been adopted as a theme song by Thoreau, and it is obviously just a song of escape:

> Whenever I need to leave it all behind
> Or feel the need to get away
> I find a quiet place
> Far from the human race
> Out in the country.

And, once again, it's "us against them".

> Whenever I feel them closing in on me
> Or need a bit of room to move
> When life becomes too fast
> I find relief at last
> Out in the country.

There are no plans for community included here or any suggestion of why being "out in the country" is rewarding or rejuvenating, and we don't get any plans for utopian living. After all, the lyrics say, "I stand *alone* (my emphasis)." However, there is something of a hint of the theme of an apocalyptic judgment (which I treat in Chapter 6) because the song suggests not just that there is something special about being "out in the country" but that it may not always be here: "Before the breathing air is gone. Before the sun is just a bright spot in the night-time." These lines are certainly suggestive of others with a theme of a coming apocalypse such as "A Hard Rain's Going to Fall" by Bob Dylan, "Before the Deluge" by Jackson Browne, and "Eve of Destruction" by Barry McGuire.

"Leaving it all behind" and escaping is also a theme which is found in other songs. For example, "Baba O'Riley",[20] written by Pete Townshend, from The Who's album, *Who's Next,* is a very similar song to "Out in the Country". "Put out the fire and don't look past my shoulder", The Who sings. We're getting out of here because "the Exodus is here." So, come on, and "let's get together." Townshend wants to leave society and all of its institutions behind—including the military and religion. "I don't need to fight to prove I'm right," he says, and "I don't need to be forgiven." He's fleeing a "teenage wasteland", and he just wants to be "out here in the fields" where he can get his back into his living. The romantic image is of one of a simple life working the land with the honest toil of hands and back.

Woodstock

Joni Mitchell's song, "Woodstock", from *Ladies of the Canyon* (1970) is now remembered as the anthem of the Woodstock Festival of 1969. Mitchell incorporates the now familiar theme from Rousseau, the romantic poets, and Thoreau and the other transcendentalists of the original pure and unspoiled aspect of human nature. Mitchell's reference to a child of God in the song is the same as Rousseau's "noble savage". As such, in the state of nature, we all have a "spark of the divine" in us. Society (especially industrialized, technological society) is responsible for corrupting this basic human goodness, and the only remedy according to both Thoreau and Mitchell is for us to "return to nature"—to get back to the garden, the symbol of innocence and goodness.

While some people have suggested a biblical interpretation of "Woodstock" to me because of the line about "a child of God", the overall impression of the song is much more in line, I think, with a secular, romantic theme. Of course, there is still a very strong spiritual emphasis in Rousseau and the other romantic writers. We all have a "spark of the divine" in us. Indeed, this spark is what accounts for the innocence of the "noble savage" in the state of nature according to Rousseau, and it is this natural innocence and goodness of human beings which allows us the opportunity to "return to nature" as Thoreau directed us to do.

The oppression of the anonymous and ubiquitous "they" is present again when Mitchell sings of being "a cog in something turning", and there's just a hint of the same apocalyptic theme we have just found in "Out in the Country". "The time of man" suggests that something terrible is happening or is about to happen, and the fanciful image of bombers turning into butterflies above the Woodstock Nation exhibits romantic utopianism in its most naive aspect.

To examine the theme of utopia and community and brotherhood further, listen to "Get Together" by the Youngbloods, "Try to Love One Another" by Bill Withers, David Crosby's "The Lee Shore", "Family of Man" by Three Dog Night, Guy Clark's "Gotta Get Off That LA Freeway", and "Our Lady of the Well" and "People of the Sun", both by Jackson Browne. And, for a final exercise to place the themes of friendship and community from the Sixties in perspective, juxtapose some rock 'n' roll songs with some songs from "greened", classic rock music. For example, compare the invitations of the Beach Boys to go on a "Surfin' Safari" or for a ride in a "Little Deuce Coupe" with the invitations of Cat Stevens to ride on the "Peace Train" and Gladys Knight and the Pips to ride on the "Freedom Train".

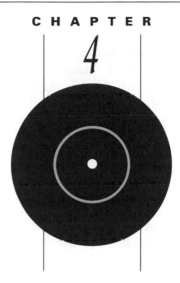

4

Sex and Drugs and Rock 'n' Roll

In addition to being the title of this chapter, "Sex and Drugs and Rock and Roll" is the title of a 1977 release by Ian Dury and the Blockheads, a song written by English rockers Ian Dury and Chaz Jankel. (Traditionally meaning 'nincompoop', 'block-head' became a Sixties term for a person frequently "blocked" or under the influence of drugs.) Although the song failed at the time to make it to the charts, it has continued to enjoy some popularity and is regarded by many casual observers as encapsulating the chief preoccupations of The Sixties.

Actually, much of the period and much of the music (and other popular culture) from the period *was* devoted to sex, drugs, and rock 'n' roll, and we will see in this chapter that there is something philosophically interesting about sex, drugs, and rock 'n' roll. Many of the most memorable songs from The

Sixties are songs which emphasize the enjoyment of the present moment, and we only have to hear the titles of these songs to know what they are about: "But I Might Die Tonight" by Cat Stevens, "Someday Never Comes" by Creedence Clearwater Revival, "Get It While You Can" by Janis Joplin, and "Let's Live for Today" by The Grass Roots.

Sex, Drugs, Rock 'n' Roll, and Philosophy

Although philosophy involves *theorizing* about various matters, the matters about which it theorizes may often be those which are most practical and embedded in our daily lives. For example, philosophers have long been concerned with trying to put together a theory of human nature which will explain and capture such distinctions as the difference between *intentional* and *unintentional* actions and between *free* and *coerced* behavior. It is quite possible to theorize *about* sex, drugs, and music, as philosophers, psychologists, and musicologists have done frequently, without having the theorizing interfere with our actual *experience* of these activities. So we will see that there is indeed an underlying philosophical theme which unites sex, drugs, and rock music as themes of The Sixties and of classic rock. This unifying philosophical theme also allows us to explain what was distinctive about the way in which these interests were treated in rock music.

Hedonism

Much of the popular culture from The Sixties, including the rock music, have been characterized by many people as the result of a rampant hedonism—an uncontrolled indulgence in pleasures of various sorts. We need to examine how the theme of hedonism might be expressed in different ways by various songs from classic rock. Before we can do this, however, we must understand a little bit about the philosophical theory of hedonism.

The English word 'hedonism' is derived from the Greek word for pleasure. In Western philosophy, as a philosophical theory about how and why people ought to act morally, hedonism is usually traced back to the Greek philosopher, Epicurus (341–270 B.C.), and Epicureanism has come to mean, to most people, pursuing a life of pleasure. Basically, hedonism is the belief that pleasure is the only thing which is *intrinsically* worth pursuing. By saying that something is intrinsically worthwhile or desirable, I mean that it is valuable, not because of some utility value it might have for some other purpose or because of some consequences which might follow from it, but simply that it is valuable *in and of itself.*

Although Epicurus did maintain that only a life which is based upon the pursuit of pleasure is worthwhile, there has never been a complete agreement among philosophers about how to interpret this claim. Epicurus said that pleasure is simply the absence of pain in the body and the soul, but this is not very helpful for understanding how to develop a complete moral theory based upon hedonism. Most philosophers have their own interpretations of what "pleasure" really means, and there are many difficult issues about human nature involved here. There are, for example, questions about the varying desirability of different *kinds* of pleasures. Compare a pleasure of a purely sensory nature, say, for example, the pleasure of sipping a single malt Scotch whisky, and an "intellectual" pleasure, say, the pleasure of learning about and coming to understand some new philosophical theory. So there are questions about how to weigh the comparable desirability of pleasures of different types. And most critics agree that Epicurus was interested in the "higher," intellectual pleasures in contrast with the base "pleasures of the flesh." (In everyday usage, a distinction is sometimes maintained between hedonism, as the pursuit of the coarser pleasures, and Epicureanism as preoccupation with refined, civilized, and delicately nuanced pleasures.)

There are also questions about how to weigh and evaluate pleasures of the same type. For example, if we concentrate just on sensual pleasures, some sensual pleasures are intense but last only a short while and may have painful consequences, while other sensuous pleasures may be less intensely pleasurable but last longer and have no known ill-effects. And those intensely pleasurably things may be very difficult to find so they may be relatively rare, while the more moderately intense pleasures may be more easily acquired and therefore more abundant. A hedonist has to weigh the desirability of perhaps missing out on some of the less intense pleasures in order to pursue some of the more intense ones, and the hedonist must calculate his or her chances of actually acquiring whatever pleasure it is that is the object of his or her desire. Consequently, although hedonism initially sounds like a very simple, straightforward philosophical theory, it can actually become an elaborate and difficult task to sort out all of the pertinent problems so that it can be turned into a practical "working theory".

Many philosophers have thought that philosophical hedonism, as a *prescriptive* theory about how people *ought to act,* is based upon *psychological* hedonism, a *descriptive,* scientific theory about human nature. Psychological hedonism maintains that human nature is such that the desire for pleasure and the avoidance of pain are what *actually* motivate human behavior. Even pre-verbal, pre-social and pre-cognitive human infants exhibit behavior which regularly indicates contentment with pleasurable experiences and very clear unhappiness and dissatisfaction with painful experiences. So, psychological hedonism maintains, there must be something about human beings, *just as biological organisms,* which motivates us to behave in the ways that we do. Much of Sigmund Freud's theory of psychoanalysis is based upon a theory of human nature according to which "the pleasure principle" is the main motivation of human behavior.

Adult human beings, the theory goes, are merely a little more complicated with a broader array of different *kinds* of pleasures available to us. As more sophisticated organisms, both emotionally and cognitively, we adults can enjoy and be motivated by the desire of such things as love, friendship, security, or success. According to Herbert Marcuse, one of the most prominent critics of modern, technological society in the 1960s, some of our needs and desires for pleasure are "natural" and "true" (since they are a part of our basic human nature) while others are "social" and "false" since they are superimposed upon the individual by society.[1] If a society is successful in "redefining" the natural needs of the individual into the "false" needs of the society, then the individual internalizes those "false" societal needs and identifies them as his or her own. The individual will then willingly support and participate in and work for that society. Such "control" of the individual was the theme of several prominent works of popular culture in the 1960s, including George Orwell's *Nineteen Eighty-Four*, Stanley Kubrick's "Clockwork Orange", and Paul Simon's song, "Big, Bright Green Pleasure Machine".

Norman O. Brown

Exactly who deserves the honor of having re-introduced hedonism into the mainstream of American thought in the 1960s is open to debate, but one of the leading candidates would have to be Norman O. Brown. His book, *Life Against Death*, first published in 1959, became a major influence upon the counterculture's pursuit of pleasure. Brown explicitly attacked Freud's claim that the instinct for sexual pleasure, Eros, had to be controlled by the Ego and re-directed or "sublimated" into work, careers, and hobbies. Freud concluded that modern human beings are and must be continually frustrated and unhappy since it is necessary for civilization to suppress their fundamental needs for sexual gratification. Gradually, Eros becomes weaker, and Thanatos, the death instinct, becomes stronger, according to Freud.

Brown, on the other hand, argued that Freud was much too pessimistic about people's abilities to achieve sexual gratification. By ending the social repression and attempts at sublimation aimed at controlling the drive for sexual gratification, Brown thought that we could create what he labeled the "Dionysian Ego", an ego in which the unconscious sexual instincts become conscious. Thus, he thought people could liberate Eros from the control of "civilization" and consciously act to satisfy their basic sexual needs. We thus find in Brown's book the underlying anti-Freudian foundation for "free sex" and "love-ins". Brown's revision of Freud's theory is in outline quite similar to Marcuse's, in *Eros and Civilization.*

Carpe Diem

The phrase *'carpe diem'* is Latin and is translated variously as 'seize the day', 'make the most of today', or 'enjoy the present moment'. The origin of this phrase is usually traced to the Roman poet Horace (65–8 B.C.) and the line attributed to him: "Carpe diem, quam minimum credula postero", which means: "Make the most of today and do not trust in tomorrow."[2] Fundamentally, the phrase *carpe diem* captures the part of hedonism which is concerned with making sure that we do not miss whatever pleasures are available today while we are hoping for, planning for, or working for whatever pleasures *might* be available at some time in the future. *Carpe diem* is "the bird in the hand" theory of pleasure, and the life of enjoying the present moment is the life of the grasshopper—not the worker ant.[3]

Why would a person knowingly and deliberately commit to a life devoted to simply enjoying the pleasures of today and refuse to devote whatever time and energy is necessary to plan adequately for the future? Doesn't such behavior ignore the "harsh realities" which we all must face? After all, *someone* must work, pay taxes and the mortgage, buy groceries and clothes, and so forth. Perhaps the most unkind answers to the question why someone would devote themselves to such a life are ignorance, laziness, "raging hormones", or mid-life crises. Certainly, we have all known people for whom any one or more of these different explanations would be accurate.

Perhaps the most plausible and compelling reason though which might give some credence to the notion of *carpe diem* is something like this: It is the very nature of some pleasures, in some circumstances, that if you don't get them now, the chances are you never will. Situations which are dangerous such as war or disease might lead a person to think that the immediate gratification of pleasure is better and even wiser than any gratification which might come later. And it is the very nature of some pleasures themselves that they are fleeting and momentary, regardless of the circumstances! What about the pleasures of youth? Or what about enjoying something like the birth of a child? Miss *that* now, and you will never be able to recapture it.

The fleeting and momentary aspect to pleasure has always been a subject of fascination for poets and has been captured by many different poets in many different ways, including Pierre de Ronsard (1524–1585) in "Sonnets pour Hélène":

> *Live now, believe me, wait not till tomorrow;*
> *Gather the roses of life today.*

Perhaps better known are the lines by Robert Herrick (1591–1674) from "To the Virgins to Make Much of Time":

> *Gather ye rosebuds while ye may*
> *Old Time is still a-flying,*
> *And this same flower that smiles today*
> *Tomorrow will be dying.*

The very ancient saying, "Let us eat, drink, and be merry, for tomorrow we die" is quoted, though not endorsed, several times in the Bible (see Ecclesiastes 8:15; Isaiah 22:13; Luke 12:19; I Corinthians 15:32).

We find the same strong *carpe diem* theme in the literature and the rock music of The Sixties. There are many plausible explanations. The most influential factors were fear of the atomic bomb and the enormous suspicion and insecurity caused by the cold war. This was a generation who, as children, practiced hiding under their school desks in elementary school in order to try and survive a possible nuclear attack and who came to trust nobody (and especially no government) because of the deception and lies of the cold war. America in the early 1960s resembled, in many ways, Western Europe following World War II. The age of innocence was over, and the cultural malaise made the time ripe for the importation of existentialist attitudes. Many young Americans harbored a vague, gnawing existentialist *Angst* and a dread of the future.

But I Might Die Tonight

We will see that there are many songs which feature hedonistic and *carpe diem* themes about the specific topics of sex, drugs, and rock 'n' roll. Yet there are also many songs which confine themselves to the general theme of emphasizing the present moment and forsaking the traditional middle-class deferral of gratification. "But I Might Die Tonight" by Cat Stevens from *Tea for the Tillerman* (1971) is a good example. In this song, a young man resists the advice to "work away, doing just what they all say." He's told to "work hard" and "be wise" and "look ahead" and "be straight" and "think right" in the hope that "one day you'll have a job like mine." Cat Stevens' response to such advice is, "But I might die tonight." Forget about tomorrow; what about today?

Security, success and "the American Dream" require a certain amount of hard work and delayed gratification. *"One day* [but not today or even tomorrow] you'll have a job like mine." To such hope and planning for future happiness, the Moody Blues sing "Never Comes the Day" (written by Justin Hayward) from *On the Threshold of a Dream* (1969). We all just "work away today" and "work away tomorrow" and "never comes the day" for "my love and me". Creedence Clearwater Revival echoes the same sentiment in "Someday Never Comes" by John Fogerty, from the album *Mardi Gras* (1972), the last album released before CCR disbanded. If you think that "someday" you'll finally figure out what life is all about, find some answers to life's important questions, and learn how to be happy, you're in for a real disappointment:

> *Listen, every mother's son*
> *You'd better learn it fast*

You'd better learn it young
'Cause someday never comes.

Get It While You Can

Janis Joplin sings what could easily be the *carpe diem* theme song, "Get It While You Can" from *Pearl* (1971). Another aphorism which captures the same thought and which currently enjoys some degree of popularity is "Eat the dessert first." In "Let's Live for Today", The Grass Roots explicitly sing: "let others plan their future . . . we'll just live for today." And contrary to the attention which Bill Clinton's campaign directed to the song "Don't Stop Thinking 'Bout Tomorrow", by Fleetwood Mac, the much more dominant theme of *carpe diem* is contained in The Grass Roots' advice: "Don't worry 'bout tomorrow. . . . We'll just live for today." As John Lennon said, in his Number One hit of 1974, "Whatever Gets You Through the Night" is all right. And, as Rare Earth sings in "Celebrate" which reached Number Seven in 1971,[4] "I just want to celebrate another day of living."

Somewhat more subtle, but still exhibiting strong *carpe diem* themes are Otis Redding's "The Dock of the Bay", released posthumously in 1968, and John Lennon's "Watching the Wheels" from *Double Fantasy* (with Yoko Ono). It is tragically ironic that these songs by these two great artists were among the very last they produced before their deaths. The songs, although a decade apart, are remarkably similar to each other. Redding's song does not contain what very many people would regard as a recipe for success in twentieth-century America. He is simply "sitting on the dock in the bay" and "watching the tide roll away." And what is he doing while he's sitting on the dock in the bay? Presumably, the same thing that Bob Dylan was doing while "Watching the River Flow". They both could be doing something productive—even if it is writing another song. But they're "wasting time", one of the cardinal sins of anyone hoping to "get ahead" in "the system". After all, as Benjamin Franklin told us, "time is money."

Watching the Wheels

Lennon's "Watching the Wheels", written after the birth of Sean and during the time when Lennon was not recording or performing, uses a different metaphor to paint a very similar picture and convey a very similar message. "He should be working," his friends are telling him. "Especially," we can just imagine someone saying, "given your extraordinary talent."

> *People say I'm lazy*
> *Dreaming my life away.*

When Lennon responds that he's happy just "watching shadows on the wall", people can't believe it. In the recurring refrain, which is so similar to the one in "The Dock of the Bay", Lennon says,

> *I'm just sitting here watching the wheels*
> *Go 'round and 'round. How I love to watch them roll*
> *No longer riding on the merry-go-round*
> *I just had to let it go.*

"But what if everybody had that attitude?" we can imagine Ben Franklin asking. "Time is money, and time's a-wasting."

There are many other songs which focus upon what is happening *now*. For example, "Saturday in the Park," by Chicago, written by Robert Lamm, from *Chicago V* (1972), is ostensibly a song about spending the day in the park, with descriptions of the various activities taking place in the park. However, just a bit of reflection makes one stop and think about how utterly "into" the present moment a person would have to be to notice and enjoy all of the specific things which are described. And why would anybody write a song about them? There doesn't seem to be anything unusual here—"people dancing" and "people laughing" and "a man selling ice cream" and "singing Italian songs". Mac Davis told us that we've got to

"Stop and Smell the Roses" (1974), but the Chicago song is a detailed description of the roses which draws us, the listeners, into the present moment.

There are many other similar songs about the immersion in and the enjoyment of everyday experiences. "Our House" by Crosby, Stills, Nash, and Young is about two people enjoying doing chores around the house—"I'll light the fire while you put the flowers in the vase . . ." "Summer Breeze" by Seals and Crofts from *Summer Breeze* (1972) and "Country Road" by James Taylor from *Sweet Baby James* (1970) are other songs about simply enjoying a nice day. There is no goal-oriented behavior involved in these songs. The present moment is not sacrificed for some future *result* or *goal* which someone is trying to accomplish. The pleasure and satisfaction are in the simple enjoyment of the here and now.

Sex

Throughout the 1950s, the American public struggled with the many changes which were taking place in American life. For many writers and analysts, these changes resulted in the oppression inherent in modern industrialized society and the alienation and loss of identity resulting from a life in which technology seemed to intrude upon every aspect of human existence. "The nuclear age" had made its impact even upon the lives of elementary schoolchildren, as we practiced "bomb drills" by diving under our desks or running to the cloak rooms.

For the most part, people sought and found relief from stress and anxiety "within the system" by adopting the values and goals of the society in which they lived. Thus, "keeping up with the Joneses"—which translated into new and bigger houses, new and bigger cars, new and better washing machines, new clothes, promotions, awards, and public recognition—was the main avenue for seeking happiness and satisfaction for "the organization man" and the "one-dimensional man". However, as instruments for personal happiness and satisfaction, consumerism and success carry a very high price tag. They require "delayed gratification"—planning, saving, dedication, and hard work. They suppress spontaneity and hedonism.

As recreation was becoming an ever more expensive proposition, the difference between recreation and "fun" got wider and wider. Recreational sports began to require more and more specialized and expensive equipment, and spectator sports, which encouraged planned, passive, spectator enjoyment of professionals "playing" some "game" became more removed from the lives of ordinary people and, again, more and more expensive and less and less spontaneous. "Let's get together at my house next Sunday and have a good time watching the game. I have a new color television set."

Too much undirected and inexpensive "fun" is threatening to a capitalistic system since such time is unproductive and unprofitable; so the system must absorb the threat by making fun and recreation expensive—by absorbing and co-opting fun into "leisure time". Think of the ways in which this has happened in this country in the last 50 years. Spectator sports, as I've already indicated, is one way. Sports and leisure time requiring a great deal of expensive equipment is another. Theme parks is another. People who could spent a day on a hike in the mountains or on a river or a stream will travel thousands of miles and spend thousands of dollars to go to a theme park to stand in line to be provided with sterilized, plastic adventure. Theme parks provide controlled, safe, sanitized "fun". The neo-Freudians of the 1960s would say that our natural need for fun and relaxation has been sublimated into leisure activity which is productive and profitable for society. Fun has now become big business.

As we have seen earlier, throughout the 1950s and into the 1960s, individual happiness and satisfaction became thoroughly identified with societal goals. The country, General Motors, and *we* were all in the same boat with the same values, interests, and priorities. Not only work, but recreation and play were big business. If we consider sex and the personal happiness found in the intimacy of close, personal relationships, we find that sex had become a big business also—in both obvious and not-so-obvious ways.

The Business of Sex

Perhaps one of the most obvious ways in which sex had become big business in the 1950s and early 1960s was the "commercial" use of sex in advertising. Vance Packard's book, *The Hidden Persuaders*,[5] provided us with one of the first revealing looks at the advertising industry in America and the way in which sex was used to sell everything from toothpaste to automobiles. Natural human needs and desires for sexual intimacy and satisfaction were very subtly but very effectively replaced with societal needs and desires.[6] Basic human needs are thus transformed into valuable commodities for society. The human need for sex gets sublimated into the need to buy—either expensive clothes, or expensive jewelry, or an expensive automobile. And, of course, in order to buy such things, and thus, in order to satisfy one's need for sex, a person must have money, which means that a person must have a job, which means that a person must be a productive member of society.

The 1950s and Non-Sex

Not so obvious was the way in which the very conservative societal attitudes towards sex in the 1950s turned sex into a big business. Perhaps the most accurate summary of teenage and premarital and (known) extramarital sex of the 1950s is to say that there wasn't any, or, in any case, very, very little. The social and legal restrictions were both thoroughgoing and enormously effective. The basic need for sex, driven by teenage hormones, was sublimated into activities which were valuable to society— team sports or consumerism. Everything from parental control to local zoning regulations to state statutes prevented anything like the freedom of sexual expression which was to come in The Sixties.

Sexual activity was permissible only within the rather strict boundaries set by society. Kissing, petting and "making out" were tolerated but still discouraged. Sexual intercourse, however, required commitment. Commitment meant commitment to marriage because of the possible (and probable) consequences of sexual intercourse—children. The lack of generally and easily available means of birth control and the woeful ignorance of teens and young adults in the 1950s about sex made it impossible for most of them to separate sex from pregnancy. Much has been made about the consequences of the "fear of the bomb" upon young people during the 1950s, but, on a day-to-day basis "the fear of pregnancy" was probably much greater. Getting married and having children means having a place to live, which means paying rent or mortgage, which means having money, which means getting a job, which means being a productive member of society. Consequently, once again, immediate human needs and spontaneity and hedonistic pleasure are absorbed by society and sublimated into long-term, delayed gratification.

The Promise Land
One the best songs which capture the way in which sex and pleasure were so thoroughly sublimated into the long-term, productive needs of a capitalistic society which is consumer-based and which requires an ever-expanding gross national product is "Paradise by the Dashboard Light", a song from Meatloaf's *Bat Out of Hell* album (1977). The structure of the song has a man and a woman, who are presumably now husband and wife, remembering the occasion when they were "barely seventeen" and first "went all the way" in a parked car.

In the lyrics, the boy and girl sing to each other. The boy is trying to talk the girl into "going all the way" and having sexual intercourse. He remembers the heat and passion of youth by singing that they were "glowing like the metal on the edge of a knife" and tells the girl "you're never gonna regret it." Since they are "barely dressed", the boy can see "paradise by the dashboard light". But, as the familiar saying from The Fifties goes, "you can look, but you can't touch." The metaphor of a baseball game is introduced to capture the progress of the boy's advances. He gets to first base. He gets to second base. He makes it to third base! Is he "going to score"? The voice of Phil Rizzuto, former shortstop for the New York Yankees and former broadcaster, is used in a mock play-by-play of the "game" which is going on the front seat of the parked car:

OK, here we go, we got a real pressure cooker
Going on here, two down, nobody on, no score,
Bottom of the ninth, there's the wind-up, and
There it is, a line shot up the middle, look
At him go. This boy can really fly!
He's rounding first and really turning it on
Now, He's not letting up at all, he's gonna
Try for second; the ball is bobbled out in center,
And here comes the throw, and what a throw!
He's gonna slide in head first, here he comes, he's out!
No wait, safe—safe at second base, this kid really
Makes things happen out there.
Batter steps up to the plate, here's the pitch—
He's going, and what a jump he's got, he's trying
For third, here's the throw, it's in the dirt—
Safe at third! Holy cow, stolen base!
He's taking a pretty big lead out there, almost
Daring him to try and pick him off. The pitcher
Glances over, winds up, and it's bunted, bunted
Down the third base line, the suicide squeeze is on!
Here he comes, squeeze play, it's gonna be close
Here's the throw, here's the play at the plate,
Holy cow, I think he's gonna make it!

The boy is trying to score, and the girl is trying to keep him from scoring. Well, is he going to or not? The tempo and the driving guitar pushes the boy and the audience relentlessly on toward an expected climax. But the girl sings, "Stop right there!" and "the play" is stopped. The immediacy of the present moment and the hot-blooded passion of youth must be balanced by the cool-headed reason of maturity and responsibility with concerns about the future and security. She wants to know

Do you love me?
Will you love me forever?

Do you need me?
Will you never leave me?
Will you make me so happy for the rest of my life?
Will you take me away and will you make me your wife?

And, she insists, "I gotta know right now/Before we go any further." The name of the game has suddenly changed. The boy tries to avoid having to answer and pleads with the girl, "Let me sleep on it." But she is adamant: "I gotta know right now." Although the boy resists, he finally is overcome by passion, and, as he now remembers,

I started swearing to my god and on my mother's grave
That I would love you to the end of time.
I swore that I would love you to the end of time.

Now, years after the remembered "first time", the boy is "praying for the end of time" so that he doesn't have to spend another minute with the girl to whom he made the promise. And, at the end of the song, both the boy and the girl lament the loss of that passion and intensity of their youth.

Boy: *It was long ago and it was far away*
       And it was so much better than it is today.

Girl: *It never felt so good.*
       It never felt so right.

Many people might interpret this song as depicting a struggle between men and women, and certainly, in the 1950s this is the way in which "the battle" was often waged. However, in the 1960s, with the protection that the pill offered for women and with the new-found sexual freedom for both men and women, the game changed. More importantly and more basically, "Paradise by the Dashboard Light" can be seen as a song about the struggle between two different aspects of human nature. The struggle is between the immediate needs of passion, spontaneity, sexual desire, and pleasure (which are identified with life in The Sixties) and the long-term goals of security, personal comfort, and social respectability (identified with life in The Fifties). As the conflict was to become regarded in the 1960s, it was the difference between Elvis Presley's "One Night" and Janis Joplin's "Ball and Chain".

Playboys, Playmates, and Sex

But what of the attempts to break out of the strict and conservative confines of the 1950s? Certainly one of the most prominent and successful attempts to break out of the mold of the repressed sexuality of The Fifties was *Playboy* magazine. In "The Playboy Philosophy", which was a regular monthly feature of the magazine for many years, we got a view of human sexuality which was widely divergent from the mainstream doctrine of the 1950s. The iconoclastic "philosophy" of human sexuality which we got from *Playboy* was promiscuous and casual. Sex and romance and love were separated, and "playboys" were encouraged to pursue their wildest fantasies of sexual pleasure with the "playmates" of their choice. We thus got a view of human sexuality far removed from the view of "Paradise by the Dashboard Light" and which seems to give vent to hedonistic desires and the priority of the pleasure of the immediate present moment over the delayed gratification represented by marriage, commitment, children, success, and consumerism.

Upon closer examination, however, the Playboy Philosophy regarding human sexuality is not as revolutionary and as threatening to the status quo as it first appears to be. The sexual freedom depicted in the Playboy view of human sexuality is anything but "free". The image of the Playboy and everything that goes with that image is very expensive. To attract all of those beautiful, voluptuous, willing playmates, after all, requires expensive clothes, jewelry, cologne, and exotic, fast automobiles and yachts. Seduction requires the very best food and wine at the most expensive restaurants. Even to be a member and get into one of the original Playboy Clubs required a man to be wealthy and successful. So, the Playboy Philosophy which seems to focus on hedonism and spontaneity and the present moment really requires having a lot of money, and that means, for most people, having a job and being a productive, contributing member of society. Consequently, "the wildest sexual fantasies" of the Playboy Philosophy and "the American Dream" are fundamentally very close to one another. The playboy must still have the commitment to career and consumerism. He simply doesn't have the commitment to personal relationships.

This attempt by the Playboy Philosophy to liberate human sexuality from societal restraints is successful only on a superficial level. On a more fundamental level, it is simply another example of what Herbert Marcuse called the "repressive tolerance" of a modern, technological society. Such a society can be tolerant of dissent because of its limitless "absorbent power" to take such dissent and use it for its own purposes. By turning playboys and playmates into big business, whatever threat they might have posed is absorbed. "True" and "natural" needs for pleasures are re-interpreted into "false" and "social" needs by society.

Many pleasures require people to be productive members of society in order to be able to afford them, and it is possible to cultivate an enjoyment of the present moment without denying the fact that such moments might be expensive. Here the question is whether the effort results in a person's ability to achieve the desired pleasure or not. Just exactly how much actual sex with exactly how many of those beautiful, perfect playmates was there? Well, actually, very little. But if you could not have the actual sex with the actual playmates, then instead, you could buy the magazine and all of the necessary playboy paraphernalia—expensive clothes and fast cars and boats. Playboy sex makes sex big business also. The money just goes into different pockets. It is all just business as usual, and basic human sexuality has still been sublimated into commodities and products which serves the interests of society.

The Pill
The invention and public availability of the birth control "pill" is arguably one of the most significant events in all of human

history, both because of its medical and social consequences. The sexual freedom which came about largely as a result of the general availability of an affordable and effective means of birth control was qualitatively different from the apparent sexual freedom of the casual sex of the Playboy Philosophy.[7] Along with the changing social and political climate of The Sixties, and the increased knowledge about human sexuality which was becoming available, the pill was to produce a genuine sexual revolution. One of the most important elements about the pill, aside from its affordability and availability, was that it gave women control over their bodies and allowed a woman to decide if and when to be sexually active and to prepare for that eventuality.

Free Sex

Separating desired sexual intercourse from the fear of undesired pregnancy removed what had been one of the strongest parental and societal inhibiting controls on pre-marital sex. Thus, sex between consenting men and women became possible with a degree of freedom which was unparalleled at any previous time in American history. As a consequence, the spontaneous and "free" sex which has become so identified with The Sixties became possible for both men and women.

Why was it that the "free sex" among the members of the younger generation in the 1960s posed such a threat to society and provoked such a vehement response from the "older generation"? Well, "free sex" did not simply mean sex free from the fear of pregnancy. And it did not simply mean that people did not pay money for it. Playboy sex was "free" in this sense. "Free sex" meant sex "free" of parental and societal constraints, in a particularly liberating sense. "Free sex" meant freedom from all of the associated societal values and needs, including marriage, children, clothes, cosmetics, automobiles, yachts, and fine food and wine at expensive restaurants. Free sex did not make money for anybody! In this sense, "free sex" was a threat to American society because it could not be sublimated or absorbed by being turned into big business. "Free sex" was sex which was pleasurable and valuable and rewarding *intrinsically*, that's to say, in and of itself, and without the accompanying guilt (or "hangup") of being unproductive by indulging in the pleasure of the present moment. In other words, by focusing upon the *intrinsic* importance of sexual pleasure *here and now*, without the attached necessity of the delayed gratification of worrying about the future, "free sex" became an ideal hedonistic pleasure.

Sex and Music
Much has been written about the relationship of sex and music. Surprisingly, much of the identification of sex with rock music comes from the early period of rock 'n' roll in the 1950s. Think of the controversy concerning Elvis's gyrating hips, and the fact that when he appeared on the Ed Sullivan Show, he was only shown from the waist up. Early critics complained about the pounding, sexual rhythm of rock 'n' roll. All of this took place during the time of sexual repressiveness of the 1950s. As conscious preoccupation, actually formulated in the lyrics of the songs, the *carpe diem* theme of sex was introduced in The Sixties with classic rock.

Why Don't We Do It in the Road?
Seizing the day, living for the moment, and emphasizing the present over the future produced a new kind of "love song". There are many candidates from which to chose to illustrate this theme of *carpe diem* sex, and they seem to fall into two distinct categories. One kind of song is blunt, crass, and mildly offensive with none of the lingering romantic sentiments of "traditional" romantic ballads. All of these songs contain the very simple and direct message of "Sex Now". Included in this group is "Why Don't We Do It In the Road?" (written by Lennon and McCartney) from "The White Album" by the Beatles (the double album, *The Beatles*, 1968):

Why don't we do it in the road?
No one will be watching us
Why don't we do it in the road?

"Let's Spend the Night Together?" (written by Mick Jagger and Keith Richards) by the Rolling Stones also falls into this category. In the song, Jagger is trying to line up a date for the evening, but it is a date which obviously involves sex since the invitation is to spend the night. We can assume that it is a woman to whom he is talking, but, given the rumors about Jagger's bisexuality, it might be a man. In any case, he needs the person to whom he's talking only for the night. There is very little romance involved here and no flowers or nice dinner plans. Jagger simply wants to satisfy the basic sexual needs of his date and himself. And if the date won't agree to spend the night, Jagger suggests that they could just fool around and make out for a while. (Permission to quote from this song was denied, presumably because of my reference above to Jagger's alleged bisexuality.) Perhaps the most obvious and blunt song in this category is, "Why Don't We Get Drunk [and Screw]?" by Jimmy Buffet. These songs have little to recommend them except being good, clean fun and for the embarrassment and anger which they provoked in the "adults" of the older generation. The message is simple and direct in these songs and no analysis or explanation is provided or needed. These songs are all action and little or no theory, and the sex is complete *carpe diem* sex.[8]

Love the One You're With

A second category of love song contains songs which still express the *carpe diem* theme regarding sex, but the messages are more subtle and less obvious. Some explanation or justification is offered in these songs to explain or "justify", to some degree, the kind of sexual relationship or encounter which is being advocated in the song. A good example of this kind of *carpe diem* sex song is "Love the One You're With" (written by Stephen Stills) by Crosby, Stills, and Nash. This song, which enjoyed some Top 40 success in 1971, appeared both on Stephen Stills's solo album *Stephen Stills* (1970) and the live Crosby, Stills, Nash, and Young double-album *Four Way Street* (1971). In what is probably the best known anthem to casual sex, Stills encourages us to take advantage of the opportunities of the present moment when we are separated from the person that we "really" love. When things are really rough, when you've got some sort of problem, and you're confused and don't know what to do, a little tender loving care from whomever you happen to be with at the moment will make everything look much better. We at least get some sort of reason for indulging in the pleasure of the moment since if you "Love the One You're With" you will presumably be in better shape then to deal with your problem—whatever it is. Casual sex is thus seen as therapeutic as well as pleasurable. You should not ask too many questions or delve too deeply into the mysteries of all of this. Being sexually attracted to the other person is all that is necessary. The present moment is to be *experienced*—not analyzed. You become aware of your existence by *acting*—not by contemplation. So, "just do it."

"You Ain't Seen Nothing Yet," written by Randy Bachman and performed by Bachman-Turner Overdrive, from the *Not Fragile* album (1974), is in the same vein as "Love the One You're With":

> *Any love is good love*
> *So I took what I could get*
> *Yes, I took what I could get*
> *And she* [a "fancy" woman whom he's just met] *looked at me*
> *With those big, brown eyes and said,*
> *"You Ain't Seen Nothing Yet."*

Help Me Make It Through the Night
Some of the songs in this category still retain much of the tender, romantic quality associated with traditional "love

songs." Kris Kristofferson's "Help Me Make It Through the Night," is a beautiful, melodic, romantic love song which is full of poetic images of the beloved to whom he is singing. Sammi Smith's version of this song made it to Number Eight in 1971.[9] As Kristofferson, who has never received his just due as a superb lyricist for his early songs, spins his soft, velvet web, we have to stop ourselves and think about what the lyrics are really saying to realize that this song is about a one-night stand. Kristofferson's lyrics lovingly describe a beautiful, tender encounter where two people manage to provide solace and comfort to each other, but remember, this is only a one-night stand.

> *Take the ribbon from your hair*
> *Shake it loose and let it fall*
> *Laying soft upon my skin*
> *Like the shadows on the wall.*
>
> *Come and lay down by my side*
> *Till the early morning light*
> *All I'm taking is your time*
> *Help me make it through the night.*
>
> *I don't care who's right or wrong*
> *I don't try to understand*
> *Let the devil take tomorrow*
> *Lord, tonight I need a friend.*
> *Yesterday is dead and gone*
> *And tomorrow's out of sight*
> *And it's sad to be alone*
> *Help me make it through the night.*

Kristofferson explicitly incorporates the main focus of hedonism and *carpe diem* commitment by disavowing any interest in yesterday or tomorrow or moral questions about right or wrong. It's only tonight that's important.

Another song by Kristofferson, "Me and Bobby McGee," which was a Number One hit in 1971 for Janis Joplin,[10] has a similar theme about the very special nature of a short-term relationship. In addition to being a showcase for Janis Joplin's voice at its best, "Me and Bobby McGee" again focuses our attention upon the hedonistic enjoyment of the present moment. "Feeling good" is what this song is about, and "feeling good was good enough for me, good enough for me and Bobby McGee." The relationship depicted in the song is a very simple one shared between two people who are "busted" and hitchhiking around the country, playing the harmonica and "singing the blues". And, years later, the singer remembers Bobby and still has such a strong attachment that she'd "trade all my tomorrows for one single yesterday" with Bobby McGee. Of course, Joplin did not simply sing about "living for today", she did live for "today", and the excesses of such a "philosophy" explain why she is not alive today.

In the same category are several other songs which repay listening, including "Ruby Tuesday" by the Rolling Stones which reached Number One in 1967, "Chevy Van" by Sammy Johns which got to Number Five in 1975,[11] "It Ain't Me, Babe" by Bob Dylan, and "Cactus Tree" by Joni Mitchell.

Drugs

The theme of *carpe diem* was also prominent in The Sixties drug phenomenon. We naturally therefore, find songs about drug experiences. It was not without good reason that Ian Dury entitled his song "Sex and Drugs and Rock and Roll".

"Psychedelic rock" is identified with the rock groups which originated in and around the San Francisco Bay Area and whose music and life-style were supposedly influenced by drugs. These groups included Jefferson Airplane, Big Brother and the Holding Company, Quicksilver Messenger Service, and, especially perhaps, The Grateful Dead. Quite a few other groups, however, also did songs which are, in one form or another, about drug use. There are ongoing controversies about whether certain songs were intended to be interpreted as "really" being about drugs through some secret, "decoding" mechanism known only to privileged cognoscenti. Such controversies have surrounded "Lucy in the Sky with Diamonds" and "Get Off of

My Cloud" despite denials from McCartney and Jagger. But there are numerous other songs explicitly concerning the use or effects of drugs.

One way to try to understand the whole "drug culture" of The Sixties is to see the ingestion of drugs as another form of rebellion by youth and another form of "rejection of the parental society".[12] There is nothing wrong with understanding the use of drugs in this way, but it certainly does not tell the whole story. There was a certain amount of "escape" from the present involved in drug use—escape from perceived oppression by parents and society; however, there was also a strong theme of escaping *into* the freedom of the present. We can see in at least some of the features of the drug culture of the 1960s the same hedonistic and *carpe diem* theme which we have seen was expressed in sexual behavior. Yet many Sixties drug consumers were fascinated by the experience of the present moment in a more profound and more literal sense.

One of the most dramatic subjective effects of taking some drugs is the increased importance of the present instant. With some drug experiences, time appears to be slowed to the point that the present moment seems to be extended indefinitely. With other drugs, the details of various senses, especially sight, but also smell and hearing, become magnified to the point that immediate sense perception completely occupies a person's attention. "Sensory overload" and "blowing my mind" are expressions which mean being overwhelmed and "blown away" by the sensory experience of the here and now. During such altered states, the entire person is involved in the experience of the present moment.

During our normal experiences, as William James and numerous other philosophers and psychologists have pointed out, we feel a "flow" to our experiences. In other words, we experience a succession of events where one event "flows" smoothly into another. In this sense, experience is like a movie where the individual frames of the film produce a smooth, fluid, flow of events. When a person is really "into" certain kinds of drug experiences, it is impossible for the person to be "removed" or "distanced" from what is happening *right now*. The normal "flow" is interrupted, and the individual experiences begin to flicker by more slowly. In extreme cases, if a person gets "locked into" the present moment, something like a "freeze frame" results. During such experiences, the person experiencing the effects of the drug cannot be calculating or planning for the future. In fact, there may not seem to be any future. As much as anything else, this "freeze-frame effect" of some drugs may explain why some people are not able to understand the consequences of their actions and why there have been such tragic consequences for some people who harmed themselves or others while under the influence of drugs.

Part of the normal "flow" of experience is the distinction, which we all acquire at an early age, between ourselves and everything else. Normally, we have no difficulty in telling the difference between our bodies and our clothes or our bodies and their immediate environment. However, during some drug experiences this distinction is reportedly lost. Space becomes malleable—including our place in it. Such effects of drugs tend to undermine what Immanuel Kant regarded as the very *a priori* preconditions of all human experience—Space and Time.

According to Kant, to perceive the world is to organize our experiences of the world in certain ways. Hence our minds and senses have to be so constructed, in advance, that they are able to organize our experiences. But then, there must be certain very fundamental ways of experiencing the world which do not come from the world but from our own human equipment. It follows that when we report on our observations of the world, these reports of ours can never be pure, uncontaminated copies of the world. They are always constructions of ours, partly determined by our own mental constitutions. For example, Kant thought that we could not make sense of the world at all except by taking for granted some very general notions of Space and Time. But then, our observations can never prove to us that Space and Time are really "out there" in the world. We can never achieve direct access to what Kant called "things in themselves".

Kant called the very fundamental assumptions which we cannot avoid bringing to our experience "a priori", meaning that they are logically prior to experience rather than conclusions from experience. Philosophers have chewed over Kant's "a priori" for the past 200 years, and there is still no general agreement as to whether such "a priori" categories really have to govern our conception of the nature of reality. By utterly transforming our experience, certain altered states of consciousness challenge the Kantian view. Drug states may make a person wholeheartedly doubt that Space and Time exist at all. Powerful hallucinogens may also induce their users to doubt who they are, or to suppose that the "real" world is an illusion, less real than some of the entities they "perceive" with the aid of drugs.[13]

It's easy to see how such experiences might threaten our understanding of rational human experience if the fundamental categories through which we organize experience are altered. This explanation provides a serious content for the common expressions from The Sixties such as "different state of mind", "messing with your mind", "mind games", and "mind fuck".

The effects of some drugs differ from the effects of others, and some drugs are more dangerous than others. The drugs of choice differ from generation to generation and from time to time and from locale to locale. The most common and preferred "illicit" drugs of the 1960s were marijuana, mescaline (peyote), mushrooms, and LSD. The most common and preferred "illicit" drugs today are cocaine and heroine. The licit drugs remain fairly constant. They are alcohol, nicotine, and caffeine. The casualties in the United States in the last 30 years from the use of the drugs alcohol and nicotine have been enormous.

Some people believe that the government should prohibit or regulate the use of drugs which may be damaging to a person's health. According to this view, the state has the right both to protect its citizens and to take measures designed to lessen expensive health care costs for the medical treatment of those individuals. However, there are some rather serious philosophical issues surrounding the right of society or government to control the actions of individuals, and we are a long way from any agreement.

The main philosophical issue here is one regarding the

freedom of the individual. John Stuart Mill, a nineteenth-century British philosopher, insisted that "society" and government have no right to interfere with any person engaging in what he called a "self-regarding" act, an action with consequences only for the individual performing the action. An "other-regarding" act is an action with consequences which involve other people. A defender of individual liberty would say that if a person wants to smoke dope or ride a motorcycle without a helmet, then since these are self-regarding actions no one else has the right to tell them that they can't. If, though, my smoking dope affects other people in some way (say by endangering them), or if my not wearing a helmet while riding my motorcycle affects other people in some way (say by raising their insurance rates), then these are other-regarding acts and may then become fair game for governmental control.

With this distinction between self- and other-regarding actions in place, *factual* questions about how actions affect people become very important. It is clear that as a society we have not been consistent in applying this distinction in the face of the facts. Consider, for example, the following description of the effects of a particular drug from a popular introductory psychology textbook:

> In large doses it causes stomach pain, vomiting and diarrhea, cold sweats, dizziness, confusion, and tremors. In very large doses . . . [it] may cause convulsions, respiratory failure, and death.[14]

Such a drug sounds really dangerous and obviously has potentially deadly consequences for individuals and society. No, it is not LSD or heroine or cocaine or marijuana, or airplane glue. It is nicotine. Nicotine is the cause of one-third of all of the cancer deaths in the United States.[15] According to the American Lung Association, in 1990, 390,000 Americans died from the effects of cigarette smoking, and 16 percent of *all deaths* in the United States are the result of smoking![16] The health costs of nicotine-related diseases are staggering—$65 *billion* a year![17] There are grounds for viewing cigarette smoking as an other-regarding action. With the most recent suggestions from some studies that "secondary" smoke may harm innocent by-standers, public smoking of tobacco products is even more of an other-regarding act. Nicotine, however, remains, a legal drug. Why? Well, society has simply absorbed nicotine and turned it into big business.

Two things seem rather clear: First, for all of the talk about the drug culture of The Sixties, the casualties of illicit drug use today are much greater than they were then. Second, the combined casualties from the use of licit drugs, then and now, far exceed the combined casualties of illicit drugs.

Goddamn the Pusher!

It may be surprising for many people who have not actually examined the music carefully, but there are more songs from the 1960s *against the use of drugs* than there are encouraging the use of drugs. For example, in "The Pusher", written by Hoyt Axton,[18] from *Early Steppenwolf* (1967), Steppenwolf sings, "Goddamn the pusher!"[19] There were the tragic, early deaths of friends, associates, or rock stars from drug overdoses which inspired several songs lamenting the heavy loss and pain caused by drug use—witness the deaths of Janis Joplin, Jim Morrison, and Jimi Hendrix as well as scores of lesser-known people associated with rock music. Such a sentiment is found in "Snowblind Friend", also written by Axton, from *Steppenwolf 7* (1970). In this song two friends are talking about a third friend who has just suffered an overdose of cocaine (or heroin).[20] The friend was last seen "lying on the pavement with the misery on his brain." The friend's "connection" was made from a telephone number which "he found upon the wall of some unholy bathroom in some ungodly hall." He spent his last dollar on some "comfort for his mind", and now, of course, he's blind.

The friend, who is now blind, figuratively and perhaps, literally, had "said he wanted heaven but praying was too slow." So "he bought a ticket on an airline made of snow." Whatever religious and spiritual hopes and beliefs there might have been in heaven and some future life in paradise have been traded in on a belief in the power of the material world to provide paradise now. The attempt is to find *now* what religion can only promise at some remote time in the distant future.

The sadness of losing a friend to drugs is also the theme of Neil Young's "Tonight's the Night" (1975), dedicated to Danny Whitten who died in 1972 of a heroin overdose and who was a member of Young's band, Crazy Horse. "Every junkie is like a setting sun," Young sings. There's the last beautiful spark of light, and then it dies.

White Rabbit

One of the best known and still widely played "drug songs" is "White Rabbit" by Grace Slick from Jefferson Airplane's album, *Surrealistic Pillow* (1967). "White Rabbit" is drawn from Lewis Carroll's extremely popular children's story, *Alice in Wonderland:*

> *One pill makes you larger*
> *And one pill makes you small*
> *And the ones that mother gives you*
> *Don't do anything at all*
> *Go ask Alice when she's ten feet tall.*

In Carroll's story, Wonderland is a land that Alice reaches by eating "magic" ("drugged") cakes and drinking "magic" potions which come with the instructions, "Eat me" and "Drink Me". In Wonderland, things are terrifyingly different for Alice from the way they are in "real" life, and she has a very difficult time coping and adapting. For example, punishment is given to a person *before* a crime is committed so that the punishment can prevent the crime. Logic is abandoned and contradictions are common. Things just don't make sense to Alice. When things don't make sense, when "the White Knight is talking backwards" and things are upside down, when "the Red Queen is on her head", then we must remember what the dormouse said:

Feed your head.
Feed your head.

The increasing tempo and the rising crescendo at the end of the song bring us along with Alice to the place where we become disoriented from feeding our heads.

There are several other songs performed by various groups which seemed to contain explicit messages about drugs, including "Sky Pilot" by the Animals, "Journey to the Center of the Mind" by the Amboy Dukes, "Crossroads" by Cream, and "Eight Miles High" by the Byrds. One of the best known songs related to drug use is Bob Dylan's "Everybody Must Get Stoned", a memorable song which makes a very clear use of the pun on 'stoned'. *"They* stone you," Dylan says at nearly every turn and opportunity, and "everybody must get stoned." We get the shift in meaning for 'stone' between the active and passive voices of the verb. *They* hurt you and attack you and accuse you all of the time, so just get high!

The known risk of drug use served as little deterrent to many people seeking the experience, the escape, or the vague promise of enlightenment which was thought to lie in the use of drugs. The effect of drugs upon human consciousness and perception was also receiving some consideration by serious writers, as evidenced by Aldous Huxley's *Doors of Perception,* enormously popular in the 1960s.[21] In this work, Huxley pursues the scientific basis for understanding the effects of mescaline upon human experience—even to the extent of reporting upon his own experimentation with the drug. Huxley holds that, in our ordinary experience, we human beings are too controlled and limited by our reason, which determines the categories that "filter" and "bracket" experience. The use of certain drugs can loosen the bonds of reason and expand the boundaries of experience by opening the doors of experience wider for us.

> To be shaken out of the ruts of ordinary perception, to be shown for a few timeless hours the outer and the inner world, not as they appear to an animal obsessed with survival or to a human being obsessed with words and notions, but as they are appre-

hended, directly and unconditionally, by Mind at Large—this is
an experience of inestimable value to everyone and especially to
the intellectual.[22]

With the use of drugs we are thus able to have "direct
experience" in contrast with "filtered" or "systematic experience," and ideally, Huxley suggests, in a fashion which would
give great comfort to Timothy Leary, we should all have a
chemical trip through the Door in the Wall of perception into
the new expanded consciousness of "transcendental experience."[23] We would all benefit from such a trip, Huxley claims.

> the man who comes back through the Door in the Wall will never
> be quite the same as the man who went out. He will be wiser but
> less cocksure, happier but less self-satisfied, humbler in ac-
> knowledging his ignorance yet better equipped to understand
> the relationship of words to things, of systematic reasoning to the
> unfathomable Mystery which it tries, forever vainly, to compre-
> hend.[24]

In terms of drugs which produced psychedelic, hallucinogenic effects, although the promise was vague enough, the
"payoff" in terms of the "heightened", qualitatively different,
or even mystical *experience* was thought by many people to be
worth the risk. The *experience* was the only important thing.
When Jimi Hendrix entitled his first album, *Are You Experienced?* (1967), he was simply confirming the fundamental
importance of experience for his listeners.

The Experience Machine
There are many serious philosophical questions to be raised
about the potential dangers of any situation which is capable of
providing an individual with all of life's experiences—all
packaged, sealed and delivered. Robert Nozick, for example,
asks us to consider the hypothetical situation where each of us is
offered the opportunity to "plug into" a super-incredible,
super-powerful "experience machine" where our brains could
be stimulated through electrodes with all of life's exciting and

satisfying experiences which we might choose while "we" (our brains and our bodies) are somehow supported in some kind of life-sustaining support tank.[25]

You could have all of the experiences associated with climbing a mountain, writing a book, being a super-star athlete, or a super-star rock musician. Or perhaps the experience is the experience of seeing god?! You would *really believe* that these things were happening since *the experiences* would be indistinguishable from "real" experiences. Besides, if they are your experiences, then they are real after all, aren't they? Well, would you plug in? If the variety and quality of experiences are the only things which matter to you, or if they are *so* important that they obscure other possible things which matter, then, it seems, you would choose to plug in. It's the actualization of Paul Simon's "Big, Bright Green Pleasure Machine," and it certainly seems to be able to satisfy Freud's "pleasure principle."

Why might a person choose *not* to plug into the Experience Machine? Well, think about the other things besides experiences which are important to being *a person?* What about *actions?* A crucial part of what makes us what we are as individuals are the ways in which we *act*, but, of course, if we simply passively *receive* experiences—either from the experience machine, or drugs—we are not acting, even if we have the entire experience of acting. By acting we receive the sense of *accomplishment,* and there is an aspect to accomplishing something which is distinct from having the experience of accomplishing it. We certainly would not regard both with the same sense of moral approval.

Wouldn't it also matter what kind of persons we are? What kind of character traits would a person who spends all of his or her time plugged into the machine develop? For example, could a person plugged into the Experience Machine be loving, or funny, or interesting, or courageous?[26] The people who are plugged into the machine will think that they are funny or interesting or courageous, but what would we say about them?

There is much more to what constitutes an individual identity for each of us than the unique experiences which we each might have had. If all of the other ingredients for personhood are present, then a person who has had a greater variety of unique experiences might, in some sense, be a more complex and complete person (and definitely a more interesting person). However, while having certain experiences might be "neat" or "cool" or "mind-blowing", experiences alone cannot make us fully persons.

Some experiences are such so they hinder or prohibit the development of the complete person. For example, the limiting experience which prohibits the development of the person is death. Other experiences which interfere with a person's ability to act and develop and maintain certain character traits or *virtues* are obviously harmful and should be avoided, and this is certainly true of many experiences which may be pleasurable, including some drug experiences. Hedonism, however, emphasizes *the bare experience* of pleasure, and even with the known risks, many people in The Sixties sought the benefit of the immediate, direct payoff of the pleasure of the present moment from drugs. As Bruce Springsteen says in "Blinded by the Light" from the album *Greetings from Asbury Park* (1973) and made into a Number One hit by Manfred Mann's Earth Band in 1977):

> *Mama always told me not to look into the . . . sun.*
> *But Mama, that's where the fun is.*

Rock 'n' Roll

The number of rock songs written about the very special nature of rock music is surprising. In one sense, I suppose, it's a form of self-promotion—something like, "buy these records because they will do wonderful things for you." In this sense, there is something of the tent evangelist, faith healer, shaman, pusher, and medicine man packaged into a lot of rock music.

"Do You Believe in Magic?" the Lovin' Spoonful asked in 1965. "The magic's in the music, and the music's in me." What sort of magic are we talking about here? Well, we have seen how sex and drugs provided two avenues of escape and two different ways of immersing oneself in the present moment. Another way of doing the same thing is "in" rock music itself. We simply *experience* the music, in something of the same way that we "experience" sex or drugs, in order for the magical effect to take place.

One example of the ability of music to take us into and keep us in the present moment is provided by what was a rather common manner of listening to rock music in the 1960s. Relaxed in a "beanbag" chair (or maybe in a "butterfly" chair or on velour pillows on the floor) late at night with the lights out (or maybe with the "light box" blinking) and the volume turned up listening to a familiar piece of music, one could almost imagine (with or without the assistance of drugs) that everything, including the music, was in one's head. A person could easily imagine that he or she was *imagining* the music—an existentialist, *solipsistic* experience. Solipsism is the philosophical position which declares that I and my experiences are all that exists. Other things, including other people, exist only as a part of my experience, according to solipsism. The existence of everything is reduced to *my* immediate sense experience.[27] After all, how do I, the author, know that you, the reader, really exist if I have never experienced you? And even if I have experienced you in the past, how do I know that you still exist if you are not a part of my experience *now*?

The pleasure of experiencing the music is immediate and direct, and the volume makes it impossible to "tune it out". By "getting into" the music, we lose ourselves, our worries about the past, and our plans for the future. Everything is *now*. Anyone who doubts this effect of rock music has very limited experience. The dancing and clapping and swaying and singing and shouting which were such a familiar part of so many concerts during the 1960s and 1970s were completely spontaneous and unscripted immersions in the present moment. "Get with it, man. You've got to let yourself *go!*"

There is no moment other than the present one. This is not music that promises some better state at some future time. Religion promises that. The "promise" of rock 'n' roll which we find in these particular songs is that right *now*, for a few moments, you can leave the rest of the universe behind and immerse yourself totally in the present moment. "Get it while you can." It's happening *now*, man. If you wait, plan or calculate, then you'll miss the moment. Kick off your shoes and get with it.

American Pie

Several songs explicitly recommend rock 'n' roll over other kinds of music. For example, "Roll Over, Beethoven" by Chuck Berry and "Old Time Rock 'n' Roll" by Bob Seger. One of the songs which immediately comes to mind as belonging in the category of rock music which is *about* rock music is Don McLean's "American Pie" which climbed to Number One in 1972.[28] This song, inspired by the tragic deaths of Buddy Holly, Richie Valens, and the Big Bopper, has attracted a cult following over the years with people trying to figure out what each little reference means by trying to identify the performers that McLean is describing in the song. Some of these are obvious, and some are more obscure. This is an interesting enterprise, but the importance of the song lies not in its particularities but in its generalities. The overall, impressive impact of the song is to capture the tremendous importance of *music* for those who were "into" music. The music is raised to the status of a religion. "Do you believe in rock 'n' roll?" is asked with the same seriousness and fervor that is associated with the question "Do you believe in god?" And McLean follows this question with another theological question: "Can music save your mortal soul?" The message in these songs is that the tremendously important thing about this kind of music is not to be found in analyzing it but in experiencing it. The magic is *in* the music— not in what we think about it, say about it, or write about it. Don't *think* about it, just do it! Forget your mind, and do what your body tells you to do. This is music to be experienced with your hands and feet and heart and not with your brain. With this music, we return to the happy-go-lucky music of the 1950s where the medium is the message, except that now the lyrics of the songs are telling us exactly that (the message is that the medium is the message). Notice that McLean asks, "Can music save your *mortal* soul?" We're not talking about immortality here or heaven or paradise or some future life. We're talking about what music can do for you *now*, in *this* world, and at the present moment.

Celebrate

The music in this category is happy music—hand-clapping and feet-moving music. If you can stand still during this music and not dance, or at least clap your hands or pat your foot, then there is no hope for you. This is music which touches something fundamental and universal in human nature. The Doobie Brothers tell us that all we have to do is "Listen to the Music" (Number Eleven in 1972).[29] The Doobies tell us that "what the people need is a way to make them smile" because "some are heavy" and "some are sad". Well, the Doobies have just the thing that the doctor ordered. We've "gotta let the music play":

> We'll be happy and we'll dance
> We'll dance the blues away.

And the use of the tambourine in the arrangement makes it almost impossible not to dance.

Sly and the Family Stone also use a tambourine in their arrangement of "Dance to the Music" (which made it to the Number Eight spot in 1968).[30] "Dance to the music, dance to the music, dance to the music" is repeated over and over again like a mantra or chant. And people did dance to this music! With the rhythm and beat, it is almost impossible not to. In fact, on the same *Dance to the Music* album (1968), there is a medley called "Dance to the Medley" which goes on for twelve minutes and thirteen seconds, and when you danced to this, you were able to lose *all* your cares. With "celebrate", "celebrate, dance to the music" repeated over and over again, it eventually sinks into the subconscious where everything is celebration and music and happiness, all mixed together. And people celebrated until they were exhausted. As Rare Earth sings in "Celebrate", we all "just want to celebrate another day of living."

Shake That Tambourine

The uses of the tambourine in "Listen to the Music" and "Dance to the Music" ought to alert us to something special about this instrument. This is a *happy* instrument, made to accompany *dance* music. There are precious few dirges which use a tambourine. Now there are many songs which are about people who play various instruments. For example, there's Carole King's "Jazzman", written by Carole King and Dave Palmer from Carole King's album *Wrap Around Joy* (1974), who can "sing you into paradise or bring you to your knees." David Gates emphasizes the special powers of the guitar player in "The Guitar Man":

> *He can make you love*
> *He can make you cry*
> *He can bring you down*
> *He can get you high.*

And Billy Joel tells us of the spell which can be woven by "The Piano Man", from the album of the same title (1973). Like a bunch of junkies needing another fix, the patrons in the bar plead with the piano man to "play a song for me" so they can "forget about life for a while." And the magic of his music has them "feeling alright". The witch doctor has conjured up another magical cure.

However, there's something special about the tambourine. And in "After Midnight", written by John J. Cale, and recorded by Eric Clapton 1970, it is no accident that "after midnight" when we're gonna "let it all hang down" that we're "gonna shake that tambourine." And can you imagine a song about a green guitar or a green drum hitting Number One? Yet "Green Tambourine" by the Lemon Pipers hit Number One in 1968.

Mr. Tambourine Man

When Roger McGuinn changed the $\frac{2}{4}$ timing of Bob Dylan's "Mr. Tambourine Man" to $\frac{4}{4}$, he turned a folk classic into a rock classic and a Number One hit for The Byrds in 1965.[31] The Byrds' version of "Mr. Tambourine Man", perhaps more than any other single song, is responsible for creating the genre of music now known as folk-rock. The Byrds condensed the five minutes and 21 seconds of Dylan's original version into only two minutes and 18 seconds—the price to be paid for a Top 40 hit. They use only one verse of Dylan's original, and eliminating lyrics from rock music's greatest lyricist is always a serious loss. Unfortunately, many people have only heard the Byrds' version of this song.

"Mr. Tambourine Man" is a song of escape. Many Dylan fans in the 1960s and even today understand this song only as a drug song, drugs as the means of escape, and Mr. Tambourine Man as the Candyman, the Pusher. The one verse used by the Byrds tends to confirm this interpretation:

> *Take me for a trip*
> *On your magic, swirling ship*
> *All my senses have been stripped*
> *And my hands can't feel to grip. . . .*

Drugs did offer a very popular means of escape for many people in The Sixties, and Dylan has always refused to answer questions directly about the use of drugs or the importance of drugs for his songs. Yet there is much more to "Mr. Tambourine Man" than the metaphorical references to drugs. If this is a song *just* about drugs, why do you think that Dylan would choose a *tambourine* to carry that message? Tambourines are simple, rhythm instruments unable to carry a melody. Wouldn't a guitar or maybe a saxophone be better as a symbol of a drug dealer—someone able to "weave a spell" and put people "in a trance"?

This song is also, and perhaps primarily, an acknowledgment of the magical attraction of music: "Mr. Tambourine Man, play a song for me," Dylan writes, and "in the jingle-jangle morning, I'll come following you", and so will the rest of us—like children following the Pied Piper. The music is also an escape—"escaping on the run" to where "but for the sky there are no fences." The music, as well as drugs, can make us "forget about today until tomorrow." Perhaps we are all stoned when we follow the Tambourine Man and perhaps it is just the music that gets us high. In either case, get aboard. The magic, swirling ship is leaving. And the whole trip is a "Magical Mystery Tour".[32]

Let the Music Play

Your tour director and captain of the ship is the "Rock 'n' Roll Band". In this song by Tom Scholz, from Boston's first album, *Boston* (1976), we get a good description of what it is like to be "living on rock 'n' roll music." "Everybody's waiting, getting crazy, anticipating," they sing, waiting, not for Godot or the second coming of Jesus, but simply for "the music". So, we're "dancing in the streets" and not worrying "about the things we're missing" just to "let the music play, play, play!"

Think of the ways in which celebration and music are used in religious ceremonies to unite and cement the relationships among the faithful. The comparisons with rock music go much deeper than just the superficial similarities such as the burning of candles and lighters at rituals and concerts. There is a power in music, and it is a power which has been recognized since ancient times. "Make a joyful noise." Hosanna! Hallelujah! In a more contemporary fashion, think of the admonition to "take your burdens to the Mardi Gras," as Paul Simon says, in "Take Me to the Mardi Gras" from *There Goes Rhyming Simon* (1973). "Let the music wash your soul." There is definitely something magically cleansing about the power of music. It can be both a catharsis and an inspiration.

There is also good reason and a definite line of philosophical argument to support the claim that the effects of music go far beyond simply the immediate psychological effects upon the people who happen to be listening to it at a particular moment. In some situations and under some circumstances, when people believe in something, simply believing in whatever it is plays an important role in *actually making something true*. Now, on one level, this must sound like a lot of "hocus pocus", and, on one level, it is. However, on a deeper level, there is something very serious to the claim that if you believe *certain things* strongly enough you can make those things come true.

The Will to Believe

In a philosophical essay called "The Will to Believe"[33] William James outlines the circumstances under which a person's strength of belief can actually make certain things true. In other words, under certain conditions, we actually "create" truth. On the surface, this may sound very far-fetched, but it is really just a matter of common sense. Imagine, for example, a pole vaulter, at the end of a runway about to attempt a vault. This person might be thinking many different things. She might be thinking something such as, "Oh my god, what am I doing here? Look at all those people up there in the stands watching me. I've never tried to jump this high before, and I know that I can't make it. I'm going to fall and make a fool of myself." Well, if she's thinking something along these lines, then the chances are high that she will not make it. But she might be thinking something such as, "Oh boy, now's my chance to show them what I can do! I'm ready! I *know* that I can do it!" And, if she's thinking something similar to this, then she very well might make it over, and *one of the important reasons which made it true that she could make the jump is that she believed it strongly enough.*

In the field of human endeavors, within certain limitations, a person's belief makes a very significant difference to whether a particular endeavor is successful or not. We now know especially in the areas of sports and the performing arts, how important "positive thinking" and "the right attitude" are. Much of the importance of our attitudes and beliefs for our performance is now common sense. There are also though more controversial areas in which the same sort of issue is now debated. Psychologists have done many experiments with the effects of "placebos". A placebo is simply a "sugar pill" with no active ingredients, but, *under certain conditions,* when certain people take a placebo while believing that they are taking a strong, effective medication, the effects of the medication are actually experienced. Yes, this suggests that some people are actually cured of some diseases by simply believing strongly enough that they will be cured when, in fact, the "medicine" they take has only completely inactive, benign ingredients.[34] Some such explanation might lie at the heart of some reports of the consequences of hypnosis, alternative medicines, and faith healing.

What about music? Can music be a placebo? Can music somehow enter causally into the physical world to make things happen? Is it really magic? We have already seen what the music and musicians have to say about music, but some philosophers have also attributed a unique status to music. For example, the German philosopher Arthur Schopenhauer (1788–1860) believed that music occupies a very special place as the highest of all of the arts. All of the other arts, Schopenhauer thought, are representative or imitative and, as Plato said, copies of Ideas. Music, however, is different in that it provides us with what Schopenhauer called a *direct* and *immediate* "objectification of the Will".[35] By this Schopenhauer meant that while the other arts copy *things* in order to represent something to the observer, music doesn't "copy" anything. The powerful and penetrating effect of music allows us momentarily to escape from the constraints of the physical world and the slavery of the Will during the aesthetic experience. In other words, in music we can momentarily escape from physical needs and desires and from the "shackles" of reason. We simply *are.* In music, we thus find the closest thing to Reality itself.

What does all of this mean for rock music? If people believe something strongly enough, then, in some circumstances, that belief will be an important part of making things happen. If you want to end war and poverty and bring about peace and brotherhood, then if you sing about doing those things long enough and loud enough and sincerely enough, maybe you can actually make those things come true simply by singing about them! Maybe, just maybe, if enough people believe—say,

10,000 or 25,000 or 50,000—really believe and sing loud enough, "with four part harmony and feeling", then we can change the world and "make it happen". Can you just imagine, Arlo Guthrie asks toward the end of "Alice's Restaurant", what would happen if one person, two, three, or 50 people a day were to walk into an army induction center and sing a bar of "Alice's Restaurant?" Well, we'd have a *movement*, "the Alice's Restaurant Anti-Massacre Movement."

Do *you* believe in magic? Do you believe in rock 'n' roll? Can music save *your* mortal soul? Dance to the music. Listen to the music, and remember to sing loud.

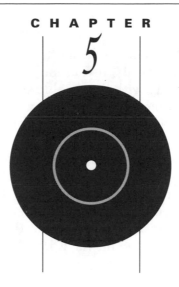

Keep on Trucking:
A Majority of One

When we think of the sundry "movements" and "revolutions" which have flickered across the landscape of human history and the various mottos which have come to identify those movements for us today, we are impressed by the power of words to capture abstract political and philosophical ideals. Those words, frequently in short, simple, aphoristic form, can bring to mind, for the student of history, entire epochs of complex social, political, and philosophical issues. Such "sayings" become proud epithets for significant periods and struggles in the development of civilization. "Liberté, Egalité, Fraternité" will forever be the cry of the French Revolution. "No taxation without representation", attributed to James Otis (1763), is now identified with the American democratic struggle against the British monarchy. And "Don't Tread on Me" was the motto on the first "official" American flag (1775).

What about the memorable mottos and sayings from the major social and political "revolution" of The Sixties which historians will identify with this "noble struggle"? Many of the candidates which come to mind may be a bit surprising to some people since they come from the songs of classic rock music. "We Shall Overcome" and "This Land is Your Land" were both supplied by Pete Seeger, and were, of course, titles of songs, as was "I Ain't Marching Anymore" by Phil Ochs. "I Am Woman" came from Helen Reddy, and "Trucking" from The Grateful Dead. One of the more common and poignant sayings and the title of this chapter was taken from the song, "Keep on Trucking", a Number One hit for Eddie Kendricks in 1973.[1]

The Rugged Individual

There is a common theme to many of these familiar songs: the indomitable human spirit and the independence and freedom of the rugged individual. It is a theme of the struggle of *the individual* against others—a theme frequently embellished as the battle of a lone individual, perhaps weak, scared, lonely, bloody-but-unbowed, against an overwhelmingly superior hostile force. It is a theme of individual dignity and worth. It is the sentiment which gave us such sayings as "I'd rather do it myself" and "keep on trucking" and "keep on keeping on" and "hang in there".

The theme of the struggle of the individual was played out in much of the popular culture of The Sixties. In the movies, the struggle for dignity by the lone individual was the main theme of enormously popular movies in the 60s and early 70s such as "The Graduate", "Harold and Maude", "Easy Rider", "Cool Hand Luke", "The Great Escape", "The Magnificent Seven", "The Hustler", and "Billy Jack".

In these movies, the hero or heroine becomes heroic in stature and nature simply by trying to be themselves—often in a very human, somewhat fumbling and bumbling manner. They're just trying to sort things out in such a way that they can manage to maintain their autonomy, independence and dignity, and "fate" (an uncontrollable circumstance) puts them in a situation where they are pitted against the authority and legitimacy of established society. The heros then become misfits, renegades or outlaws, and they are driven to desperate measures in order to assert or defend their autonomy. It is illustrative how many of these hit movies end with the hero in a standoff or shootout with the "duly recognized" representatives of society—parents, police, sheriffs, or armies.

The Fugitive
In The Sixties, we saw on television each week, week after week, "The Fugitive" starring David Janssen as Dr. Richard Kimble, an accused murderer "on the run" from justice and "law and order". As the Fugitive tried to avoid capture, he also strove to find the real murderer of his wife, a one-armed man. Of course, the dramatic impact came partly from seeing whether the greatest danger would come from the police lieutenant chasing him or the murderer. He could trust no one and was constantly on the run. And the road "goes on forever" as Gregg Allman sang in "Midnight Rider" in 1970.

> I'm not gonna let them catch me, no
> Not gonna let them catch the Midnight Rider.

Frequently, people he trusted and believed in turned against him, and he would manage to escape only to be "on the run" again and, as the title of the Number One hit in 1972 by Gilbert O'Sullivan has it, "Alone Again (Naturally)".

An even more pungent Sixties distillation of the plight of the embattled misfit is the cult TV series "The Prisoner", conceived by and starring Patrick McGoohan, in which each episode opens with a dialogue concluding with the exchange: "I am Number Two. You are Number Six." "I am not a number. I am a free man." (Followed by guffaws from the omnipotent Number Two.) Each episode depicts the authorities' ingenious yet unsuccessful attempts to break the will of The Prisoner, and The Prisoner's ingenious yet unsuccessful attempts to escape.

On the Run

The theme of the lone individual as a fugitive "on the run" is very common in songs from The Sixties. These were very popular songs which rose to high positions on the Top 40 charts and which still receive a lot of play time on FM radio stations. The theme of these songs obviously struck a very responsive note with many people. The story line is usually never as well-defined as it is in the case of "The Fugitive". It's generally not clear why a person is on the run, or from whom, or to what; nonetheless, the theme of the alienated individual who is unaccepted by and outcast from society and "running" is very explicit. Whatever the threat and wherever the protagonist is headed, "keeping on moving" is the important thing. Bruce Springsteen's first single ever to make it to the Top 40, "Born to Run", from the album of the same title (1975), is a fine example of this kind of song. The entire album is a concept album with songs such as "Thunder Road", "Backstreets", and "Tenth Avenue Freezeout" all about being "out in the streets" and "on the road". "Born to Run" is a combination of "trying to get away" and "trying to find love" at the same time. "We gotta get out while we're young," Springsteen sings to Wendy, whom he is trying to convince to run away with him. We've got to get out of this "death trap" of a town, he says, "cause tramps like us, baby we were born to run." Even though he's "a scared and lonely rider", he's going to run till he drops and "never look back" trying to find some place where he and Wendy can "walk in the sun". But, until then, he's just "born to run".

In "Running on Empty", Jackson Browne takes up the story of the lone and lonely individual, "born to run" and just "running on—running on empty, running on—running blind, running on—running into the sun" and "running behind". He looks into the eyes of his friends and sees that they are also running with the same frantic and hopeless compulsion to "keep on moving". He doesn't even know what he's "hoping to find". Even though he's running on empty and into the sun, he must keep on "running on".

Frequently, musicians see themselves and other musicians in the role of "fugitive". For example, Paul McCartney and

Wings' "Band on the Run" from the album of the same title (1973) is a good illustration. This song became a Number One hit for Wings in 1974.[2] The lyrics indicate that the members of the band have been locked up for some reason, and now they have escaped. They're a rogue, runaway, fugitive band. Now "the jailer man" and "they" are searching for the members of the band, searching for "The Band on the Run".

Like a Rolling Stone

Many other excellent songs deserve time and attention here, including "Midnight Rambler" by the Rolling Stones, "Rambling Man" by the Allman Brothers Band, "Free Bird" by Lynyrd Skynyrd, and, of course, Dylan's great song, "Like a Rolling Stone" from *Highway 61 Revisited* (1965), Dylan's best album and one of the best rock albums ever produced. In addition to "Like a Rolling Stone", this album contains "Ballad of a Thin Man", "Just Like Tom Thumb's Blues", and "Desolation Row", as well as the title track. "Like a Rolling Stone", which rose to Number Two on the Top 40 chart[3] despite being six minutes long, is a truly classic "classic rock" song which captures all at once the alienation, aloneness, and fugitive status of the individual:

> *How does it feel*
> *To be on your own*
> *With no direction home*
> *Like a complete unknown*
> *Like a Rolling Stone?*

The novels most popular during this period are also replete with the same theme of the struggle of the individual against society. *Catch-22* by Joseph Heller, *One Flew Over the Cuckoo's Nest* by Ken Kesey, *Slaughterhouse Five* by Kurt Vonnegut, *Nineteen Eighty-Four,* by George Orwell, and *Atlas Shrugged* and *The Fountainhead* by Ayn Rand were just a few of the most widely-read novels which continued the same theme—individuals trying to find or make their way in a hostile and frequently absurd world, with powerful, demonic forces seeking to destroy them for being themselves and "speaking the truth" as they see and know it. The contest is played out against "Big Brother", "Big Nurse", "The Establishment", "Authority", "the government", "the System", and "Them".

The freedom and variety of the individual were also evident in changes which took place in the social practices and dress of the youth culture of The Sixties. We went from the group bunny-hop in the 1950s to dancing without partners in the 1960s. The spontaneous, non-competitive, free play with frisbees was preferred to organized, competitive sports. And we changed from three-piece suits and Gucci loafers with tassels to bell-bottomed jeans, tie-dyed tee-shirts, and sandals.

Do Your Own Thing, Man

Thus, as Charles Reich emphasizes, the value of the individual was paramount in the consciousness of the youth culture of The Sixties.[4] This is not the "Be True to Your School" generation of the 1950s and early 1960s which the Beach Boys sang to and about. That song hit Number Six in June, 1963,[5] five months before John Kennedy was killed. Literally overnight, the song and its theme became childish, absurd, inappropriate, and ineffective for an entire generation. The commitment in the 1960s was to oneself, and a direct adoption of Polonius's advice to Laertes in Shakespeare's *Hamlet*, "To thine own self be true." This did not mean "Me First" as it did for the money-hungry yuppies during the Reagan years of the 1980s. There is no profit motive involved here. On the contrary, being true to oneself simply means being true to one's beliefs and principles, and not "selling out".

"Be yourself" and "do your own thing" became the mottos, and there are many songs which encouraged variations upon this central theme. "Go Where You Want to Go," the Fifth Dimension sang in 1967, "be what you want to be." The Beatles encouraged us all to think for ourselves and not to look to them or anyone else for answers in "Think For Yourself", written by George Harrison, from *Rubber Soul* (1965):

> *Do What you want to do,*
> *And go where you're going to,*
> *Think for yourself*
> *'Cos I won't be there with you.*

Respect

Many songs express the same theme by emphasizing the dignity and worth of the individual and many songs capture the struggle of the individual for autonomy and dignity. Many of the songs mentioned earlier, with their themes of social and political alienation, would serve equally well to illustrate this theme of rugged individualism. However, the songs we consider here go beyond describing the conflict between the individual and society or state. These songs specifically assert, emphasize, and glorify the dignity and worth of the individual. For example, Aretha Franklin's recording of Otis Redding's song "Respect" hit Number One in 1967.[6] Even though the lyrics are confined to the context of a romantic relationship, the metaphorical meaning is clear, and implicitly, these lyrics are easily interpreted as being about respect for individuals generally. "All I'm asking . . . is just a little bit . . . just a little bit . . . just a little bit of R-E-S-P-E-C-T." Respect for oneself from other people is something which is fundamental to human dignity. Self-respect is fundamental to self-esteem as the Staple Singers remind us in "Respect Yourself", a song which rose to Number Twelve in 1971,[7] and which coincided with the beginnings of the Black is Beautiful and Black Pride movements. Cultural, ethnic, racial and individual pride and dignity—self-respect—is the last bastion for the individual in the struggle against an over-powering, hostile society bent upon the destruction of individual freedom.

A Majority of One

This theme of "rugged individualism" draws upon a very mixed, but rich, philosophical tradition. Earlier we saw that the main reason utopian community experiments failed in The Sixties was because the participants had a commitment neither to a powerful, unifying ideology nor to a strong, effective authority. The reason for the lack of such cohesive elements was the formidable individualist sentiment which was so prevalent in The Sixties.

The well-known phrase "a majority of one" comes from Henry David Thoreau's essay, "Civil Disobedience", written in 1849. He says: "Any man more right than his neighbors constitutes a majority of one." Now just think for a moment about what this remark actually says. First of all, the kind of issue at stake here involves the question of "right" (and therefore, presumably, also "wrong"). So, the issue at stake is a moral issue, or perhaps a political or legal one where significant moral principles are at stake. A person might recognize the authority of a legislative body to decide *some things* (on which side of the road to drive) without recognizing the authority of that legislative body to decide *all things* (matters of religious practice or free speech). And, in the process of deciding such issues or resolving conflicts between the state and the individual about such issues, Thoreau claims that a lone individual constitutes a majority if that one person is more "right" than everyone else. This gives to the phrase "a majority of one" a meaning very different from that now commonly imputed to it: "50 percent plus one". In Thoreau's sense, the phrase means that a single, lone individual *against* the majority, or against everyone else, can be a majority of one.

There are two presuppositions for such a view of the individual and the individual's relationship to the state: First, there must be some criterion, or set of criteria, for determining what is right and wrong, which is theoretically prior to and functionally independent of the state. In other words, "right" cannot simply mean whatever the state says that it means. Secondly, there must be some decision procedure—some practical mechanism—for applying those criteria in particular cases for actually determining, in different circumstances, what is *actually* right and what is *actually* wrong. This procedure or mechanism must also be theoretically prior to and functionally independent of the state. The net effect of all of this is the acknowledgement of the authority of the individual to decide both the criteria for determining right and wrong and how those criteria are applied. These "rights" of the individual are "inalienable" in the sense that they can never be legitimately taken away from the individual by the state even though the individual might voluntarily agree to relinquish certain of these rights, in certain areas, to the state.

Rights

As we have seen earlier, Rousseau championed a theory of human nature according to which individual human beings are, by their inherent nature, innocent and good. The legitimacy of state authority over the individual is derived from a "social contract", according to Rousseau, which is a kind of hypothetical, negotiated agreement whereby the individual tolerates and supports and obeys the state in return for certain services provided by the state. This is simply a hypothetical way of understanding a situation where the individual and the state both have needs and interests which each expects the other to fill. (Social contractarians don't necessarily accept that there ever was, as a matter of historical fact, any actual social contract.)

In Rousseau's version of the social contract, his view of human nature means that since human beings, in their "State of Nature" with no government, are basically good, their need for the state is very limited. Hence, the corresponding authority of the state will also be very limited. The notion of individual "rights" plays an important function in limiting the state's authority. Individual rights or "human rights" are rights which are universal and natural; they are rights which we human beings possess simply by virtue of being alive and a member of the species *Homo sapiens*. Human rights are not bestowed upon people by governments as legal rights are. Since human or natural rights are pre-governmental, they are thought to serve as a guide for and a limitation upon how a government is structured, specifying the nature and limits of its authority. This thread of social and political philosophy, which runs from Rousseau through Thomas Jefferson and Thoreau has been enormously important in the development of liberal political democracy.

The Question of Relevance

Many people recall the demonstrations and political unrest of the 1960s. Various different political and philosophical themes and traditions coalesced into widespread opposition to the political institutions, policies, and practices of the United States. Abstract philosophical theory became translated into political action. The main two areas in which the confrontation developed on the national level were civil rights and the war in Vietnam. However, there were numerous related issues, more local in nature, which raised similar questions of political ideology and philosophical theory, for example, the Free Speech Movement at Berkeley and the student strike at Columbia.

The political activism of The Sixties was rooted both in the political philosophy of Henry David Thoreau and in the philosophical theory of human nature of Jean-Jacques Rousseau. These are philosophical traditions to which teachers and scholars in the United States had continually acknowledged our indebtedness. Generations of students in high schools and colleges across the country had regularly read Thoreau's *Walden* and "Civil Disobedience" and Rousseau's *Émile* and *Social Contract.*

Much of people's focus of attention in the 1960s was on the present moment—what's happening *now.* This was true, as we have seen, in terms of hedonism and the *enjoyment* of the present moment, but it was also true in terms of political activism. Activists wanted answers to political and social problems *forthwith*. The academic and detached study of completely abstract theories of economics, politics, and philosophy is not getting us anywhere or accomplishing anything, they thought. What we really need is *relevance* to the problems we are facing *now*. What we need to do is to *apply* these remote, abstract theories to the social and political problems of today to get some immediate political *action*. So the rallying cry of activists and the litmus test of intellectual theories became one of *relevance* and *action*. After all, the phrases "student activists" and "political activists" were descriptive of what identified these groups. They were not called "student theorists".

I Think, Therefore I Am

The history of Western philosophy is filled with aphorisms which encapsulate the main points of different arguments and theories and which are now used to identify those different theories. René Descartes's well-known claim, "I think, therefore I am" has some claim to be one of the best known one-liners in the history of Western thought. Descartes was a dualist, which means that he thought that the basic reality of things could be reduced to two fundamental kinds of substance —mental and physical. He also believed that a person is a unique combination of these physical and mental substances. For Descartes mental substance, by its very nature, is essentially private: each of us has direct access to and knowledge of only our own mental self and its experiences. In the whole world, I am the only person who is directly and immediately aware of my intentions, volitions, and sensations. Only I can *decide* that I will read a book, *will* to raise my arm, or *feel* the pain of my cut finger.

Much of Descartes's theory about the nature of persons has become very widespread as "common sense" in contemporary American society. However, this theory has generated much controversy and has, in the minds of many philosophers, been discredited. One important aspect of Descartes's theory of persons is the part which is supposedly captured by the saying

"I think, therefore I am." This claim by Descartes comes at the end of a process of skeptical doubt during which he searches for the most indubitable claim he can find, and this is it. By doubting, by thinking, by introspecting, by reasoning, I am absolutely positive that I exist, he claims. Even if he is dreaming or even if an omnipotent and malevolent god might be trying to play a trick on him, he cannot be deceived about his own existence since *he*, as a thinking thing, would have to exist in order to be deceived.

This claim and the kind of reasoning behind it has great appeal for many people. However, a sometimes unrecognized and unappreciated consequent of Descartes's philosophy, commonly called Cartesianism, is that it places the identity of the self in the realm of the private and mental. For Descartes, we are sure of our own existence because of mental activity, and, to use Descartes's own example, we do this individually and privately. This means that our relationships with the physical world, including our relationships with other people, are secondary and derivative to the definition of what it means to be a person. The best and most certain evidence we have, according to Descartes, of who we are and what we are is our own private, mental sensations.

This leads to a very limited view of the self which the Moody Blues recognize in the song "In the Beginning", written by Graeme Edge, from the album *On the Threshold of a Dream* (1969). The title of the album is similarly a reference to Descartes, because of his use of his inability to be absolutely sure of the difference between dreams and reality. The Moody Blues aren't too sure that Descartes's theory of persons works. The opening chord is eerie and ethereal, and the slowly building crescendo is reminiscent of Richard Strauss's *Thus Spake Zarathustra*, used at the beginning of the movie "2001: A Space Odyssey". The First Man is having a conversation with The Establishment, who sounds a great deal like Hal, the computer, from "2001". Expressing the uncertainty and doubt which has beset many a student of Descartes, the First Man says, "I think, I think I am, therefore I am—I think." The last "I think" has a decidedly puzzled and questioning tone to it.

The next track on the album is the song, "Lovely to See You" by Justin Hayward. This is an upbeat, joyous celebration of friendship, and whether the juxtaposition is deliberate or accidental, it provides a sharp contrast between the Cartesian and the non-Cartesian view of the self since in this song it is the relationship with other people which is fundamental to the self rather than private introspection by the individual.

I Act, Therefore I Am

Descartes has been attacked by many philosophers on several different points. For example, in the title of the first chapter of *The Concept of Mind*, Gilbert Ryle sarcastically refers to Descartes's theory as "The Ghost in the Machine". Ryle argues that the idea of a non-physical, mental, or spiritual substance being "contained in" or somehow in interaction with a physical body is nonsense. The Police adopted the title of Ryle's chapter for the title of their 1981 album, *Ghost in the Machine,* and one of the popular tracks from that album, which continues the Cartesian theme, is entitled "Spirits in The Material World".

Other philosophers opposing Descartes and his theory of persons argue that we are who we are and we come to know who we are by our *actions*, including, and perhaps including *especially*, our actions involving other people. The issue is not whether we simply develop a certain self-image through our actions involving other people; rather, the issue is whether it is through the actual occasions of doing something, of performing some action, and of experiencing the reaction of other people to our actions, we become aware of ourselves *as persons*. In this sense, our interactions with other people are crucial for our own awareness of ourselves as persons.

The Other

Jean-Paul Sartre, a twentieth-century French existentialist philosopher, is a good example of a thinker who advocates this understanding of self-identity. Sartre gives serious philosophical meaning to Robert Burns's wish, "To see oursels as others see us!" (from "To a Louse"). In fact, Sartre maintains that it is only through our actions involving another person, "the Other", that we can be aware of our own identity. "I must obtain from the Other the recognition of my being,"[8] Sartre says, because it is only through the way in which I see myself regarded by other people that I become aware of my own self. "As I appear to the Other, so I am," he says.[9] A simple example of what Sartre means here occurs in the sexual interaction between two people. It is one thing to feel sexual desire for another person, but it is quite a different thing to realize that the other person feels sexual desire *for you*. In such a situation, you are able to experience yourself *as desired by the other person*.

In songs from the 1960s, the idea that self-identity is based upon a person's actions is very prevalent. While we might not find an explanation or an argument as detailed as Sartre's theory about "the Other", a very similar notion is expressed in several songs. This theme is sometimes expressed in terms of the way in which a person's identity is inseparable from a romantic love relationship with another person. In other words, we find and identity ourselves through our relationship with someone else. In "Sentimental Lady", written by R. Welch, from Fleetwood Mac's album *Bare Trees* (1972), the lyrics say "I come so together where you are."

Expressions such as "getting it all together" and "getting your shit together" came to express the notion of a person developing something of an organized set of beliefs and patterns of behavior which were supposed to provide emotional and intellectual stability—something of a self-identity. People described "getting it all together" by describing what a person was "into" or not "into". "John is so together," someone might say, "he is completely into Yoko." We have already seen how John Lennon described the fundamental nature of such a relationship with another person in "God". Paul Tillich, a twentieth-century American theologian, described god as "the ground of being"—that which is responsible for all being. But, in "God", from *John Lennon Plastic Ono Band* (1970), where he describes what is most fundamental to his own being, Lennon says, "Yoko and me and *that's* [my emphasis] reality." Yoko is his *Other*.

Individuals can also come to identify themselves by interacting with groups—especially by resisting a group and acting against the rules of some authority—parental or societal. The desperate and anonymous attempt at assertion and recognition by an individual in a hostile and alien world is the theme of one of Paul Simon's more interesting songs, "A Poem on the Underground Wall" from Simon and Garfunkel's *Parsley, Sage, Rosemary, and Thyme* (1966). Although this song never made it to the Top 40 charts as a single, it is, I think, a much better song than "I Am a Rock", a song with a somewhat similar theme, which made it all the way to Number Three in 1966.[10] In "A Poem on the Underground Wall", Simon cleverly describes a man hiding in the shadows of the subway, the underground; so, he is able to play upon the double meaning of 'underground'. The man is obviously afraid and lonely while he watches everything. "His restless eye is leaping, scratching all that they can touch or catch." Then the subway train arrives with other people and symbolically opens its doors of welcome wide, but the man doesn't come out of hiding to accept the invitation to join the other people. The train leaves, and then the man comes out clutching his "crayon rosary", and he slashes "a single word, a poem comprised of four letters" upon the advertising on the walls of the underground. This is his desperate act of assertion, and he dashes up the steps of the subway with his heart "laughing, screaming, pounding". The song ends when the man runs away to seek "the breast of darkness" to be nourished and "suckled by the night".

It is humbling to see how a great artist and master lyricist such as Paul Simon can take such a simple act of an anonymous single man and turn it into a momentous action for all mankind. But isn't this a strange and bizarre incident to be the basis for a song? It is amazing to me that people can listen to this song, and even be moved by it, and never confront what I think is the crucial message. Isn't it interesting that Simon doesn't tell us what the word was that the man wrote on the wall? There was a time when I first listened to this song when I thought that it would make a great difference to my understanding of this anonymous man if I knew what his "poem comprised of four letters" was. Was it 'LOVE'? Or 'HELP'? Or was it some vulgarity like 'FUCK' or 'SHIT'? Was it a threat like 'KILL' or 'HATE'?

Well, in some sense and on one level, it would make a difference in how we understand this person, but on a very fundamental, existential level, it really doesn't matter what the word was. The important thing was *the action*. It is simply the act of scrawling a graffito which brings him to life and allows him to assert himself. He is alive, and his heart is "laughing, screaming, pounding" from the simple *act of assertion*. He has done something daring, he has broken the rules, and he is alive, and he is *somebody*. He becomes an individual through his action.

Civil Disobedience

If the criteria for moral good and evil are prior to and independent of society, as Thoreau's claim about "the majority of one" requires, and if individual human beings have a nature which allows them to form independent and direct judgments about applying these criteria in particular situations, then we have the theoretical framework within which the judgment of the individual can be pitted against the collective judgment of society and the state. The practice of civil disobedience in the 1960s represents the application and implementation of this long-standing theoretical framework. Civil disobedience is philosophy at its most relevant point. It is theory become action.

The practice of civil disobedience in the 1960s within both the Civil Rights Movement and the Anti-Vietnam War Movement was based upon a very carefully and thoroughly articulated political philosophy. People *studied* theories of civil disobedience. During this period, Thoreau's "Civil Disobedience" and Martin Luther King's "Letter from a Birmingham

Jail" became two of the mostly widely read and interminably pored over political tracts ever written.

Much of the controversy at the time surrounded the question of actually breaking the law in order to protest or in order to pursue a particular political interest. "Law and order" advocates insisted that it was all right for individuals to form their own judgments so long as they did not disobey the laws of the state, and civil disobedience advocates insisted that if a law conflicts with the privately held moral beliefs of the individual, then the individual is justified in breaking the law. Law and order advocates insisted that law-breaking is law-breaking, no matter what the reasons; so all law-breakers are the same. Civil disobedience advocates insisted that not all law-breaking is the same and that not all law-breakers are the same.

This discussion and debate can get very complicated, and there was much sophisticated discussion and debate about these issues at the time. For example, if civil disobedience is to be identified and distinguished from other forms of law-breaking, then what are the conditions for doing this? Some advocates held that civil disobedience must involve a person's actions which are public, directed at some immoral law, and not for direct financial gain. Furthermore, the person practicing civil disobedience must not resist arrest or punishment. Now each of these conditions is debatable, and, believe me, they were debated.

The crucial aspect of civil disobedience, however, is the recognition of the role of the individual as the final arbiter in matters of conscience. Perhaps the individual appeals to religious beliefs, as Muhammad Ali and scores of other conscientious objectors to the war in Vietnam did, or perhaps the individual appeals only to moral values and his or her own conscience. In either case, the individual is recognized as "a majority of one", standing against the will of the majority, society at large, and its chosen representatives.

In songs which are directed to the individual, Sly and the Family Stone urged us to "Stand", and Burton Cummings to "Stand Tall". "Think For Yourself," the Beatles said. And in their only song ever to break into the Top 40, "Hold Your Head Up" (1972), Argent admonishes us in a line which is repeated over and over again, "hold your head up, hold your head up, hold your head up, hold your head high." Whatever comes your way, "Take It Like a Man," Bachman-Turner Overdrive sings, and Gloria Gaynor sang in 1965: "I Will Survive".

There are examples of songs in this genre which can be found both earlier and later than the period from the mid-1960s to the mid-1970s, but the sheer number of songs of this type indicate how salient the theme of the rugged individual was during this period. The theme of the same lone, defiant individual continues in later songs. "I don't care what you say any more," Billy Joel says, this is "My Life" (from *52nd Street*, 1978). The lyrics of this song are very similar to the lyrics of "It's My Life", a Top 40 song by The Animals (1965). The challenge to everyone else is explicit and direct:

> *It's my life, and I'll do what I want.*
> *It's my mind, and I'll think what I want.*
> . . . .
> *Show me I'm wrong.*

John Cougar Mellencamp's "Authority Song" (1984) and Tom Petty's "I Won't Back Down" (1989) are also both very similar songs. All of these songs insist, as the song that became Frank Sinatra's theme song puts it, I'm going to do things "My Way."[11] The notion was echoed in Loverboy's 1981 "Turn Me Loose".

Beelzebub

Comedian Flip Wilson's famous line, "the devil made me do it", is a humorous way of raising a serious question about human nature. Is there a devil in us all, a savage, corrupt nature which must constantly be kept in check? Are people basically good or evil? We have seen earlier how the different answers to these questions separate those who follow Rousseau and those who follow Hobbes. In terms of the current debate over who deserves to be the final arbiter—individual conscience or state authority—in matters of significant moral concern, this differ-ence is manifested in the relationship between the individual and the state. Do good individuals make good governments or do good governments make good individuals?

Theories of human nature need not contain any specifically theological connotations. In a completely secular fashion, the appeal to "human nature" can be used to capture the notion of a deep, primordial, selfish force in human nature which is potentially evil and destructive. For example, Freud's Id is such a force. According to Freud, the Id is a fundamental drive in all of us, whose only purpose is the immediate gratification of our appetites. It is a force which is amoral and alegal because it is pre-moral and pre-legal. Civilization and its moral and legal rules provide a thin veneer which covers this underlying, primordial part of human nature to keep it under control. Given such a view of human nature, the state with its social restraints become necessary in order for human intelligence, the Ego, to flourish.

One English translation of the Greek word, 'Beelzebub', is 'Lord of the Flies', the title of a novel by William Golding which was both extraordinarily popular and bitterly controversial in the 1960s.[12] In *Lord of the Flies*, Golding tells the story of a group of English school boys shipwrecked on a deserted island. The boys, as products of a "proper" English boys' school, are taken, both metaphorically and literally, as representing the very best that society can produce—England's Best and Bright-est. The story which unfolds is one of savagery and barbarism as the boys "revert" to what Golding represents as their "natural state." That thin veneer of civilization is ripped away, and underneath is a pack of savage beasts. The message from Golding is clear and unmistakable: it is only within the confines of society and government that the savage beast within human beings can be controlled. (The novel is a rejoinder to R. M. Ballantyne's *Coral Island*, an old-fashioned, optimistic boy's adventure story in which the marooned lads remain decent all the way through, and revolting cruelty comes only from the dark-skinned natives.)

Golding joins Hobbes and Freud as providing the literary

and philosophical framework for the "law and order" advocates of The Sixties. According to this view, it is only society and the state which can provide the context for deciding right and wrong. Law and order are what control the devil within us, and it is only collectively that human beings can overcome their savage nature. Thus, the state must be the final arbiter of right and wrong.

On the other side are Rousseau, Thoreau, Jefferson, and King. To these writers we owe the literary and philosophical framework within which the basic value and worth of individuals and the notion of individual "rights" are generated. If individuals can be noble, good, and just *qua* individuals, without the authority and control of a government, then good government will be the product of the endeavors of such good people. Good laws will then be the laws which embody the underlying good qualities of human nature. Individuals will have natural rights to be protected from excesses and abuses by government, and the individual conscience will be the final arbiter of what is right and wrong in matters of "moral conscience".

This debate was carried on in many different variations and contexts in The Sixties. One favorite ploy of the civil libertarians who sided with Rousseau, Thoreau, Jefferson, and King and who supported the notion of civil disobedience, was to read the following quotation and then ask another person whether he or she agreed with it. This ploy was actually used in a scene from the 1971 cult movie, "Billy Jack". Here's the quote:

> The streets of our country are in turmoil. The universities are filled with students rebelling and rioting. Communists are seeking to destroy our country. Russia is threatening us with her might, and the republic is in danger—yes, danger from within and from without. We must have law and order. Without law and order, our nation cannot survive.

At the time, people would guess that the quotation had come from Richard Nixon, Spiro Agnew, or John Mitchell, but the surprising answer is that it comes from a speech made by Adolf Hitler in 1932, in Munich.

Now, to suggest that something is tainted *simply* because it was said by a particular person, no matter how odious, is a completely fallacious, *ad hominem* argument. On the emotional level though, the level where much of this dispute was conducted, this ploy never failed to produce a heated exchange. The main point at stake is a theoretical and philosophical one about human nature—about our "original", primordial nature *qua* human beings. No amount of actual data or examples will resolve that question since it is not an empirical question of fact.

Beyond Good and Evil

Another philosophical source for the theme of the importance of the individual is the existentialist thought of German philosopher Friedrich Nietzsche. There is a similar emphasis upon the individual and the authority of the individual in his writings. The truly noble individual, according to Nietzsche, must become a moral law unto himself, according to Nietzsche, avoiding "slave morality" and establishing a "master morality". There is no objective basis for morals or laws: laws and moral values are not to be *found* in the world. All values must be *created* by people, and the truly noble individual is the one who refuses to allow himself to be controlled by the mediocrity of the masses. The really exceptional person is able to rise above other people and make his own rules and laws. Indeed, one of Nietzsche's major works, written in 1886, is entitled, *Beyond Good and Evil*. This is one of those rare cases in philosophy and literature where the title of the work not only captures its main content but also serves as an effective summary. In this book, Nietzsche offers a number of different aphorisms to help the individual develop the "master morality", by rising above society's definitions of good and evil.

The theme of being a law unto oneself is expressed in "Miles From Nowhere", from *Tea For the Tillerman* (1971), when Cat Stevens sings about the awesomeness of being completely on one's own "miles from nowhere" with "not a soul in sight". Now, he says, "I can make my own rules, the ones that I choose." He is beyond the standards of "good and evil" of society. The clear implication is that you can make yourself be whatever you are going to be by your own decisions, actions, and rules, and ultimately, only you, yourself can do that.

Similarly, in "The Fuse", from *The Pretender* album (1976), Jackson Browne says,

> *Forget what life used to be*
> *You are what you choose to be*
> *It's whatever it is you see*
> *That life will become.*

Sisyphus

In "The Myth of Sisyphus", Albert Camus, another existentialist philosopher, tells the story of how Sisyphus has been condemned to a life of torment in Hades. That life consists in the endless task of repeatedly rolling a huge, round rock up a steep hill. Each time, after Sisyphus manages to get the rock to the top, after an enormous effort, the rock rolls to the bottom, and he must begin the job of getting it to the top again. Nothing ever changes. Nothing will ever change in the future—ever! This is to be Sisyphus's destiny for all eternity.

Now the point of the story is this: The plight of Sisyphus is representative of human life. Other people and events seem to have complete control over our lives, and whatever we do, it's all going to end in death anyway. How do you manage to survive such a meaningless and contemptible existence? You are kept in a situation over which you have absolutely no control. You are swept along by unseen forces which you can neither identify nor understand. Nothing you try to do matters in the slightest. You are the contemptible plaything of some far-distant, unseen, omnipotent god. What do you do? How do you live? How do you make your existence meaningful and count for something in such a completely meaningless situation?

Our lives are such that, if there is any value to be found in them, it must be value which is created and imparted by the individual. We each must make our lives meaningful and *give* meaning to life by the way in which we live our lives.

If we are Sisyphus, for example, we decide that we are going to be the best rock-roller that ever existed, and we commit ourselves each time to rolling the rock better than we did the time before. We must each stand with our heads high, bloody, but unbowed, and we *resist* by refusing to acknowledge the absurdity of our situation. By resisting and by *asserting* ourselves in creating a life of meaning, we distinguish ourselves from the riffraff who kick the dirt and snarl and curse their fate and hang their heads. We lift ourselves by our bootstraps above other people, not with the intention of helping or saving the world but with the intention of saving ourselves by standing our ground and spitting in the eye of Fate. And no matter how hopeless and absurd our situation is thought to be, maybe we can gain or maintain our dignity and worth as individuals by making some small difference and by making the overwhelming forces which grind us down at least take some notice of us.

I Am

There are several songs of classic rock music which have as their theme the simple act of asserting oneself. For example, "I Am . . . I Said" by Neil Diamond. This song made it all the way to Number Four on Billboard's Top 40 in 1971,[13] but when you listen to the lyrics, you realize that Diamond is singing about the simple fact that he exists. He's "lost between two shores" (New York and Los Angeles), and he has no home. So, what does he do. He simply *says:* "I am." And he doesn't even say it *to anybody!* "No one heard at all", so he's not trying to prove anything to anyone else. To try and cope with the "emptiness deep inside", he merely *asserts* his existence and thereby *asserts* himself.

> *"I am," I said.*
> *"I am," I cried.*
> *"I am."*

We must assert ourselves and our autonomy and our freedom in whatever circumstance we find ourselves. It's one thing to be a "Free Bird" and to have our freedom by being able to fly away, but if we are a "Bird on a Wire", from *Songs From a Room* (1969), as Leonard Cohen sings, or "a drunk in a midnight choir" we must still try in whatever way possible "to be free".

"I Stand Alone," Al Kooper said. "I Will Survive," Gloria Gaynor sang. And "Go Down Gambling" advises Creedence Clearwater Revival. Why? Well, in the description we get of Don Quixote's foolish and foolhardy quest from "Man of La Mancha", in "The Impossible Dream", we are told that "no matter how hopeless" we must "fight the unbeatable foe" and "run where the brave dare not go." Even if we think that there is not a chance of succeeding, we must never give up. We must continue to try because our salvation lies in the trying. The victory is in the struggle. It doesn't matter that, in the end, the individual is ground down. It matters that "one man, scorned and covered with scars" made his best effort and took his best shot. Take a stand. Take a chance. "Go down gambling" even if you are a "natural loser" or "Born to Lose", and "you may never have to go at all." Be somebody. Fight. Resist.

As if we needed a reminder, we had Paul Simon to tell us that Dylan is not Dylan Thomas. But both Dylan and Dylan Thomas urge us to find our identity and *make* ourselves human by asserting ourselves against others and our mortality, and we each must do this on our own. Although it is convenient and comforting to think that Dylan is singing about somebody else, we are all in the position of Mr. Jones in "Ballad of a Thin Man"—trying to make sense of an absurd situation. "Something's happening, but *you* don't know what it is, do *you* . . .?" And you don't have a lot of time to figure it all out. As Dylan warns in his apocalyptic song of warning, "All Along the Watchtower", "the hour is getting late", and since "life is but a joke", what are *you* going to do about it? Well, you are on your own. And you'd better "look out, kid" 'cause somebody "wants eleven dollar bills, and you've only got ten." You're a day late and a dollar short. Don't ask for help, and "don't follow leaders" 'cause "you don't need a weatherman to know which

way the wind blows" ("Subterranean Homesick Blues"). You're
"on your own, with no direction home, like a complete unknown, like a rolling stone" ("Like a Rolling Stone"). The
poetry of "the other Dylan", Dylan Thomas, bore a similar
theme, urging us to resist, make the most that we can out of life
while we can since death is always waiting for us.

> Do not go gentle into that good night,
> . . . .
> Rage, rage against the dying of the light.[14]

The Hero
The kind of hero from fable and folklore, from literature and
cinema, which has particularly appealed to the American
public also embodies the same existentialist theme of the lone
individual pitted against over-whelming forces and impossible
odds. This is also a rich theme of world literature. Cervantes's
Don Quixote, the Knight of the Sorrowful Countenance, who
spent his life tilting at windmills, daring to dream "The
Impossible Dream", fits this pattern. The entire story of Hom-
er's epic Greek poem, The Odyssey, is also the record of the
struggle of its hero, Odysseus (Ulysses to the Romans), against
other men and women, and the gods. Odysseus struggles to
make his way home after the Trojan War. He is cursed by the
gods, especially Poseidon, the God of the Sea, which is particularly inconvenient since Odysseus must cross the Aegean Sea to
get back to Greece. He makes mistakes which cost the lives of
friends, he endures times of self-doubt, he gives way to tempta-
tion and self-indulgence, but he continues his struggle and
never gives up. Similarly, the Tales of Robin Hood capture the
theme of the hero who is pitted against the powerful forces of
evil. This time it is the notorious Sheriff of Nottingham who has
usurped power in England while Richard the Lionheart is away
on the Crusade. And, again, it is the lone individual who is on
the side of right and justice.

The Good Guys and the Bad Guys

This same image of the lone and lonely hero is etched forever in American history by the influence of the American frontier upon our popular culture. The image of the cowboy, translated onto the big screen by the movie industry, gave us the archetype of the cowboy as hero. These roles nearly always embodied the same theme which quickly and easily became solidified into a formula: the lone cowboy, a misfit and wanderer, the embodiment of truth and justice, does battle against the forces of evil. The cowboy wins, the cowboy continues his quest, his "odyssey" to find more evil to vanquish.

Of course, there were variations on the basic theme, but the essentials remained the same. Partners were sometimes necessary for purposes of narration and humor; so we had The Cisco Kid and Pancho, Roy Rogers and Pat Brady, the Lone Ranger and Tonto, Gene Autry and Smiley Burnette, and perhaps, the favorite pair for most people, John Wayne and Gabby Hayes.[15] But in the end the Lone Ranger really was *lone*. When the time came for the showdown with the bad guys, it was always the hero, standing alone, who carried the fight against the bad guys.

On the frontier, where "law and order" was yet to be institutionalized in the form of a government, a man had to "Stand Tall" by going beyond society's Good and Evil and becoming a law unto himself. This meant, of course, that the difference between the good guys and the bad guys was not explained in terms of their social acceptability or legal status. There were "lawmen" and "outlaws", but the distinction between the two is frequently blurred, and the lone hero, the "good guy", is frequently pitted against the "official", legal authorities who are depicted as corrupt and in cahoots with the bad guys. The difference between good and bad is explained in terms of some individual, private moral code.

Desperado

There are many songs which illustrate this theme of the lone individual standing for "truth, justice, and the American way" against the forces of evil. All of these songs glorify the struggle of the individual against society's rules, laws, and authorities. One of the best concept albums which elaborates this theme is *Desperado* by The Eagles (1973). The entire album is about the life of an outlaw, a desperado. At the beginning of the album, "Twenty-One" tells the tale of a young man on his way to becoming a outlaw who is "fast as I can be" (with a gun) and thinks that he is going to live forever. The album takes us through being "Out of Control", a "Certain Kind of Fool", and an "Outlaw Man" who wades too deep in "Bitter Creek". In the end, we hear the lament sung to the aging desperado who has been on the run and "out riding fences" too long. This kind of life is a hard one, and the Eagles sing to the desperado (to themselves, to us?), "You'd better let somebody love you before it's too late."

In "What About Me?" from the album of the same title (1971), Quicksilver Messenger Service represents the younger generation in the role of "outlaw" in society, "on the run" and forced to "take a stand" because society's "rules and regulations . . . don't do anything for me."

> *And I feel like a stranger in the land where I was born*
> *And I live like an outlaw, and I'm always on the run;*
> *And I'm always getting busted, and I've got to take a stand.*
> *I believe the revolution must be mighty close at hand.*

Bad Is Good

The image of the bad guy as hero is the major thrust of several songs. The main theme is that "bad is good". In 1974 *Bad Company* by the group Bad Company with the song "Bad Company" in which the group prepares to "take our final stand" became the Number One album in the United States.[16] This theme of bad guy as good guy, which started with Jimmy Dean's Number One hit "Big Bad John" in 1961, is continued in "I Fought the Law and the Law Won", by the Bobby Fuller Four in 1966, and "I Shot the Sheriff", a Number One hit in

1974 by Eric Clapton. Other popular songs which contain the same theme are Jim Croce's "You Don't Mess Around with Jim," Number Eight in 1972 and "Bad, Bad Leroy Brown", Number One in 1973.[17] Both of these songs are about popular heros who are villains and ruffians.

This theme was very successfully revived by Michael Jackson in 1987 with his number one hit, "Bad", but it is very difficult to imagine anything of the outlaw and the lone individual standing against society in someone who has been so abjectly and slavishly commercial in his career as Jackson. We must see this success, I think, as simply another example of the process of sublimation mentioned earlier. If you want to sing about being bad and outside society, then someone or some company or some business in society will pay you a lot of money to do it, if you're willing to do it the way they want you to and in a way which will make a lot of money for them (and, of course, for yourself).

The theme of the bad guy as the good guy has been a dominant one in much of black music. In his fine book, *Mystery Train*, Greil Marcus devotes an entire chapter to how this theme finds expression in the Myth of Staggerlee.[18] The character from Lloyd Price's Number One hit "Staggerlee" in 1959 has its origin in numerous folk stories and legends of the black man who defies a white society. As Marcus says,

> It [the story of Staggerlee] is a story that black America has never tired of hearing and never stopped living out, like whites with their Westerns. Locked in the images of a thousand versions of the tale is an archetype that speaks to fantasies of casual violence and violent sex, lust and hatred, ease and mastery, a fantasy of style and steppin' high. At a deeper level it is a fantasy of no-limits for a people who live within a labyrinth of limits every day in their lives, and who transgress them only among themselves. It is both a portrait of that tough and vital character that everyone would like to be, and just another pointless, tawdry dance of death.[19]

In the story of Staggerlee, we find just how bad "bad" can be. Staggerlee, the song says, "shot poor Billy . . . just to watch him die." And Lloyd Price urges Staggerlee on, "Go, Staggerlee.

Go, Staggerlee." Staggerlee is the ultimate personification of bad as good and outlaw as hero. He is, as Marcus summarizes, "nobody's fool, nobody's man, tougher than the devil and out of God's reach."[20] He is a law unto himself, "beyond good and evil".

There are many other fine songs with this theme, notably one of my favorites, Paul Simon's "The Boxer", from Simon and Garfunkel's *Bridge Over Troubled Water.*

Easy Rider

In the 1950s, this same image of the heroic lone individual who is outside society underlay the mass appeal of comic books to American children. The names of the heroes change. There are Superman, Batman, Spiderman, Captain Marvel, and, my favorite, Plastic Man, along with many others, but the essential formula remains intact. During the late 1950s and into the 1960s, the decade of "the car", the cowboy riding his horse on the open range gives way to the trucker or the biker driving his rig or his bike on the open road. The lure of the open road replaces the lure of the open range, and "pulling a load" or just driving across the country replaces driving cattle or riding fences. The trucker and the biker carry the same image of the misfit and loner, outside society, who is "doing his own thing" and going his own way—the completely free and autonomous individual.

Steppenwolf's "Born to Be Wild", popularized in the 1969 cult movie "Easy Rider", is the epitome of this kind of song. "Head out on the highway", "looking for adventure", Steppenwolf sings as Peter Fonda and Dennis Hopper start their cross country trip to New Orleans. It is also no mere accident that practically the only people who befriend the long-haired, freaky bikers on their trip are cowboys. In a symbolic scene missed by many people, Peter Fonda repairs the tire on his chopper while the cowboy is putting a new shoe on his horse. One cultural image is superimposed upon another.

There are many other cowboy songs from the 1960s which

glorify riding and driving on the open highway, or use driving or riding as a metaphor for living. There is "Trucking" by the Grateful Dead and "Keep on Trucking" by Eddie Kendricks, which hit Number One in 1973.[21] In "Take It Easy" from their first album, entitled *Eagles* (1972), the Eagles use the metaphor of riding down the highway as living life. "Take it easy," they warn, and "don't let the sound of your own wheels drive you crazy."

"Willing" by George Lowell of Little Feat is another song about simply driving on the highway and doing whatever it takes (including drugs) to be able to continue. You've got to be "willing" to "be moving". Keep on moving. Keep on trucking. "Keep on Choogling," Creedence Clearwater Revival sang on their *Bayou* album in 1969. While 'choogling' is one of those countercultural neologisms which came out of the 1960s whose meaning is not crystal clear, it definitely carries the connotation of "keeping on", "keeping on moving," "keeping the faith", "moving on", and "moving on down the highway". So, choogle on, baby, and choogle on down the highway, man.

The Beat of a Different Drum
While there are many points of major differences between Nietzsche and Rousseau, Jefferson and Thoreau, there is a fundamental emphasis upon the importance of and the final, ultimate moral authority of the individual. Although the fundamental view of human nature which can be used to generate a theory of natural rights is not to be found in Nietzsche, he does provide the two presuppositions discussed above for making sense of the notion of "a majority of one". The truly noble and liberated individual must rise above the morality of "the crowd" or "the herd" and take the responsibility for providing the criteria for moral right and wrong. The individual must also take the responsibility for applying those criteria—for actually deciding right and wrong. Indeed, it is only by actually *acting* upon individually-held beliefs that the individual can rise above the crowd or the herd.

We have seen that there is an enormous difference in the attitudes and treatments of the individual according to different political and economic theories. There is also a wide range of attitudes toward the individual even within liberal democratic political theory. A good place to begin to understand this difference is to ask what can be expected or demanded of an individual in order to promote "the common good", the welfare of everyone. In recent philosophical dispute, the two extremes on this issue are represented by John Rawls[22] and Robert Nozick.[23] Rawls has argued that there is a "Principle of Fairness" which, under certain circumstances, requires and obligates individuals to support and co-operate with ventures in a society which are mutually advantageous, *whether or not the individuals wish to do so.* Such a principle serves as a basis for the legal doctrine of eminent domain, which allows the state to seize private property when it is needed for some public purpose determined by a state legislature or some other body. So "they" can "pave paradise" and "put up a parking lot", as Joni Mitchell sings in "Big Yellow Taxi", if some legally constituted body decides that this is what would serve the public good.

Nozick, on the other hand, champions the right of the individual against the notion of the public good, and says, "No way! You've got no right to take *my* paradise for a parking lot!"[24] An individual cannot, according to Nozick's argument, justifiably be made to participate or support a communal activity which is for the common good *even if that individual has benefitted from the activity.*[25] Neither the state nor groups of individuals can give you some benefit and then demand that you pay for it unless there was some prior agreement in which you agreed to do so.[26] Imagine, for example, walking down the street and stopping to listen to a band that is playing in a public park. The concert ends, and you are told that you must pay because you listened. Should you have to pay? Nozick insists that no one is obligated to pay for any service or benefit which he or she did not explicitly contract for in the beginning, and there's no way, according to this argument, that the state should be permitted to take *my* paradise for a parking lot.

Nozick opposes what are called "end-state" principles for distributing goods and services, that's to say: those principles which attempt to produce a certain state-of-affairs, such as helping the poor and needy. According to his theory of *entitlements*, an individual is entitled to complete control over any services or property which is acquired according to certain principles, and no representative of the state or society has the legitimate authority to tell the individual what to do with that property.[27] (The individual may then voluntarily opt to help the poor and needy.) Even taxes, according to Nozick, amount to the same thing as forced labor.[28] In the conflict between individual rights and state authority, Nozick's argument always supports the side of the individual.

During The Sixties, frequent attacks upon political activists and protestors from the political right and conservatives contained the accusations that various protests and demonstrations were "communist-inspired" or that the activists were "playing into the hands of the Communists" were repeated regularly. We have seen that many criticisms of modern capitalism can indeed be traced back to Karl Marx, and there were undoubtedly influential members of The New Left[29] (such as Herbert Marcuse) who unequivocally advocated socialist political theory. The same was true of some of the major groups of activists such as Students for a Democratic Society (SDS), and some major protest figures (such as Angela Davis) were members of the Communist Party. However, criticisms of capitalism do not necessarily lead to socialism, and a lot of people accepted the criticisms of capitalism without accepting or even understanding socialism or Marxist theory.

The themes of rugged individualism and "a majority of one" champion the authority of the individual against all forms of economic, political, or governmental dominance and control—including capitalism and, perhaps especially, *socialism*. Although some socialists have thoughtlessly denied it, socialism can provide much less tolerance of the individual and individual rights and "entitlements" than capitalism can. Without "end-state principles" socialism cannot get off the ground. In the pervasive themes of the rugged individual and "majority of one" and the common expression of these themes in the literature and music of The Sixties, we find abundant evidence that, for the most part, the political activism and protests of The Sixties had very little or nothing in common, at a fundamental philosophical level, with socialism or communism.

The themes of the rugged individual and "majority of one", voiced in Sixties popular culture and especially rock music, reinforce most of the other themes which we find there. For this reason, these are two of the most outstanding themes from The Sixties. The Organization Man of The Fifties, who identified with society at large and kept step with General Motors, was replaced by the flower child of The Sixties, who kept time with a very different music. In the words of Thoreau,

> If a man does not keep pace with his companions, perhaps it is because he hears a different drummer. Let him step to the music which he hears, however measured or far away.[30]

In The Sixties, that music with a different drummer was classic rock.

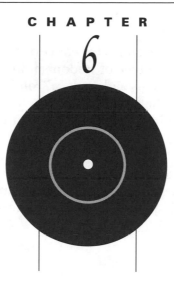

CHAPTER 6

Brother Love's Traveling Salvation Show: The Theology of Rock

In their early stages, both rock 'n' roll and rock music were, for the most part, considered complete anathemas by organized religion in America. The personal, social, and political alienation which stamped The Sixties resulted in a rejection of established social institutions, including the major forms of organized religion. The result, as we have seen, was a conspicuous theme of secularization among the members of the youth culture. This implied the introduction of new myths and symbols to replace the old religions myths and symbols in an attempt to capture the spiritual aspect of human existence. As we have seen, many people in The Sixties were pursuing answers to fundamental philosophical and theological questions about the meaning of life, but they did this within a very different framework and employing categories very different from those of traditional Christianity or Judaism.

There were some grounds for concern by religious believers. The very prominent theme of hedonism in rock music and the emphasis on "sex, drugs, and rock 'n' roll" presented a significant philosophical challenge to the teachings of the predominant forms of organized religion. The beat of rock 'n' roll, the lyrics of rock, and the lifestyles of the musicians and their audiences were all viewed by many religious believers as harmful and even downright evil. The irreverence of rock music for the dominant culture, including mainstream theology, was viewed as sheer blasphemy by many of the religious faithful.

Satanic Rock

More extreme reactions came from fundamentalists and the religious right. A major campaign, including record burnings, was organized by a baptist minister in Florida in 1976.[1] Another record burning in Minnesota, by two brothers who were both fundamentalist preachers, in 1981, reportedly included the destruction of a half-million dollars worth of records and tapes.[2]

Accusations by fundamentalists concerning "satanic" meanings of rock lyrics and "backward masking" of hidden satanic messages became commonplace and were taken seriously in many quarters. For example, the California State Legislature considered a bill in 1982 which would have required special labeling of rock music containing "subliminal" messages, and a committee of the legislature, the Committee on Consumer Protection and Toxic Materials, actually held public hearings on the proposed bill.[3] The offending recordings were supposed to have included "Revolution 1" by the Beatles, "Snowblind", by Styx, and "Stairway to Heaven", by Led Zeppelin. The bill never made it out of committee. Nonetheless, a Republican congressman from California was inspired to introduce a bill in the United States Congress which would have required a label for songs determined to contain satanic messages. The label would have read: "Warning: This record contains background masking that makes a verbal statement which is audible when the music is played backwards."[4] In its admittedly sometimes questionable wisdom, Congress allowed the bill to die with no action. Other satanic rumors persisted though. For example, the name of the group, KISS, was rumored to be an anagram for 'Kids in Service to Satan', and AC/DC was alleged to be a cryptic symbol for 'Anti-Christ/Devil's Child'.

Religion and Rock

I confess to having been fascinated by the possibilities of backward masking and tried, on numerous occasions on different kinds of equipment, to produce the secret satanic messages; however, the results were always indecipherable gibberish. The only conclusion which I can draw is that satanic verse must lie in the ear of the beholder.

Instead of being worried about backward masking and possible hidden 'satanic' messages, religious leaders should have addressed the explicit or evident meaningful content of the lyrics of rock songs. We have found in the lyrics of many songs serious indictments of many aspects of American culture and significant philosophical themes which, if they are to be responded to at all, ought to be responded to on the level of intelligent, reasoned discussion. For some religions believers, the issue of backward masking was a smokescreen to enable them to evade having to address directly the tough questions and problems raised in the lyrics of classic rock.

The rather obvious religious atmosphere which came to surround rock performers and performances in The Sixties and the near-divinity status with which they were endowed by their devoted fans touched a very sensitive chord with religious fundamentalists. John Lennon's too-often repeated remark that the Beatles were more famous than Jesus Christ is just one example. The tragedy of his death is ironically compounded by the fact that he was killed by a self-professed born-again Christian. Ironically, confirmation of Lennon's claim of his status is to be found in the repeated description of his death by the media as an "assassination"—a description usually reserved for the murder of a major religious or political figure. In his tribute to Lennon following his death, Dave Marsh explicitly compares the murder of Lennon to those of the Kennedys and Martin Luther King, Jr.[5]

Some comparisons were deliberate and explicit such as Neil Diamond's "Brother Love's Traveling Salvation Show" from the album of the same title (1969) in which the singer and the concert become a parody of an evangelistic preacher and a gospel tent meeting. The album comes complete with a "Do You Want to be Saved?" Salvation Game which is "played" by answering questions such as "Are you a groupie?" Other comparisons were less explicit but still obvious—such as thousands of fans "lighting candles" of supplication to their idols at concerts. The attacks upon organized religion and the sarcastic references to orthodox theology in many rock songs are bitter and vitriolic. To appreciate the stinging vehemence of the lyrics of these songs, we need only remember some of the songs we have discussed earlier including "With God on Our Side" by Bob Dylan, "Are You Bombing with Me Jesus?" by Shurli Grant, and "God" by John Lennon. The sarcastic criticisms of organized religion in the lyrics to these and similar songs give a whole new ironic meaning to the notion of "oral tradition" in religion.

Eventually, in an if-you-can't-beat-them-join-them, why-should-the-devil-have-all-the-best-tunes   maneuver,   mainstream religion was to develop the Christian Rock genre which included such songs as "Spirit in the Sky" by Norman Greenbaum, "Put Your Hand in the Hand" by Ocean, "Oh Happy Day" by Edwin Hawkins, the Broadway rock musicals "Jesus Christ Superstar" and "Godspell", and the songs of Amy Grant. Fundamentalist groups were also quick to adopt Dylan's born-again albums, *Slow Train Coming* (1979) and *Saved* (1980). "When He Returns" from *Slow Train Coming* is typical of the songs on these albums: With a solo piano accompaniment and a distinctive gospel sound, Dylan sings of how He (Jesus) who knows our needs before we even ask is coming again to bring peace on earth. And in "Slow Train" (also from *Slow Train Coming*) Dylan warns that we had all better straighten ourselves out and abandon our "earthly principles" (and presumably, "get right" with God) because we could die at any moment (the slow train's coming).

Rock and Mysticism

The way in which questions and problems concerning spiritual and religious beliefs are posed in rock music constitutes an interesting counterpoint to the theme of secularization. Although, as we have seen, the "death of god" and the secularization of society had an enormous impact on the popular culture of The Sixties, the secularization was never absolute or universal. Alongside the rejection of organized religion and traditional, mainstream Christian and Jewish theology, there was also the quest for some new source of new symbols and myths which might provide some spiritual meaning to life and some spiritual guidance.

This search led many people to Eastern religions, various forms of meditation, astrology, or other sources of non-traditional forms of spiritual teachings. George Harrison's interest in both Indian music and religion is well-known. After a trip to India in 1966, Harrison studied both the music and religion of India very seriously. He studied the sitar with Ravi Shankar, certainly the first (and probably the only) sitar player to become a household name in counterculture communes in The Sixties, and he introduced Indian music (and the sitar) into rock music in "Within You Without You" from *Sgt. Pepper's Lonely Hearts Club Band* (1967). This one song on one of the best and biggest-selling rock albums ever produced, the meeting of the Beatles with the Maharishi during his visit to England in 1967, and the trip to India by the Beatles in 1968 to study meditation with the Maharishi all provoked an enormous interest in the mysticism of Eastern religions and meditation—an early foray into multiculturalism whose effects are still felt today.

Don Juan

There was tremendous interest during this period in literature with mystical or spiritual themes—whether in fiction or non-fiction. The mystical writings of Carlos Castañeda and *The Teachings of Don Juan*[6] became enormously popular. Don Juan was a Yaqui Indian shaman from Mexico who used peyote and other hallucinogenic drugs to raise his consciousness and to receive a higher level of mystical enlightenment than anything thought possible according to Western philosophy.

Akin to this genre of literature was J. R. R. Tolkien's trilogy of books called *The Lord of the Rings*. Tolkien, an Oxford don who also wrote *The Hobbit*, fills *The Fellowship of the Rings*, *The Two Towers*, and *The Return of the King* with convincingly-drawn characters in a fabulous, magical world of elves, wizards, hobbits, and humans. The main story line which runs through the three volumes is based upon a continuing battle of ultimate good against ultimate evil. These spellbinding stories held tremendous appeal to many young people of The Sixties, unknowingly seeking some sort of spiritual component in their lives.

The *I Ching*

The search for new forms of spirituality went in many different directions in The Sixties. The *I Ching*, an ancient text of Chinese philosophy which some scholars attribute to Confucius, has been around for thousands of years, but, in The Sixties, the *I Ching* became for many people a do-it-yourself kit for predicting or making decisions about the future. Those who consulted the *I Ching* for spiritual guidance believed that the writings provided a way of understanding and predicting the future. A person is supposed to compose "hexagrams" by rolling dice or using some other arbitrary means to select individual lines from the text. The different lines of text represent the interplay and the respective strengths of "yin" and "yang", respectively the female and male cosmic principles in the universe. As an individual composes his or her individual hexagrams from the *I Ching*, the ancient text is thought to provide spiritual guidance for that person's life, and many people in The Sixties refused to make important decisions until they had consulted the *I Ching*. Recognition of the importance of such hexagrams is provided by Russ Giguere who, when he left The Association in 1970, named his first solo album *Hexagram 16*. A curious tribute to the influence of the *I Ching* is to be found in Philip K. Dick's extraordinary novel, *The Man in the High Castle*.

Many people in The Sixties tried to replace the lost spiritual component of their lives in other ways as well—frequently preferring obscure (and what many people would call "lunatic fringe") sources of that spirituality to the dominant, established religions. The prophecies of Nostradamus, a sixteenth-century French doctor, seer, and astrologer, were taken very seriously by many people. Those who do take Nostradamus seriously believe that he provided predictions and messages in his cryptic "quatrains" which have been proven true by subsequent historical events. However, these quatrains, much like the hexagrams of the *I Ching*, are also notoriously vague and subject to many different interpretations so there has always been a great deal of discussion and controversy over trying to interpret the cryptic prophesies of Nostradamus.

The spiritual quest of The Sixties was a private, individual quest. The moral, religious, and spiritual teachings and practices which received their legitimacy from the dominant culture meant little or nothing to those people for whom spiritual quests represented a way of escaping and avoiding the influence of that dominant culture. Since the search for some spirituality in their lives was prompted by the general rejection of dominant society, it was important that spirituality be found outside the mainstream of dominant society and outside the mainstream of organized religion and Judeo-Christian theology.

Siddhartha

The true spiritual quest was understood to be like that of Siddhartha in the novel *Siddhartha* by the popular existentialist novelist and Nobel Prize winner, Hermann Hesse. This book probably did as much to popularize Buddhism in the United States in the 60s as any other single source.[7] Hesse's fictional account of Siddhartha's quest for spiritual enlightenment takes him through different stages—both conventional and non-conventional. It is a truly human quest, with struggles and misdirections and trials and errors. Other people dismiss him as a "strange" fellow with "crazy" ideas. In the end, he reveals the spiritual truth which he has discovered: the Buddha is all, all is One, we are all the same—the stone, the river, trees, animals, human beings are all One. And the most important thing in the world is love.

The message of *Siddhartha* is straightforward. After all of his travels and travails, at the end of his search for the meaning of life and enlightenment, the ultimate answer is very simple— love. This does not mean romantic love or even friendship since these are affections directed toward specific individuals. This is the love of fellow human beings—love for all of humankind— brotherly and sisterly love for everyone. In various ways this same theme has been embodied in much of world literature, poetry, and philosophy, and since the times of Buddha and Jesus, such a simple message has been both powerful and threatening.

All You Need Is Love
The theme of such a universal, spiritual love was also, of course, a major theme of many classic rock songs from The Sixties. For example, consider again the cult movie, "Billy Jack", whose story revolves around an experimental pacifist commune which is racially and ethnically mixed. The pacifist members of the commune are assaulted, raped, and murdered by the townspeople. The theme song for "Billy Jack" is "One Tin Soldier" by Coven which made it to the Top 40 in 1971.[8] The lyrics describe the conflict between "the Mountain People" and "the Valley People", but the message is a general one about conflicts between different peoples everywhere. The Mountain People have a "treasure" which the Valley People want. "Go ahead and hate your neighbor," the lyrics say, you can "justify it in the name of Heaven." Finally, the Valley People attack and kill the Mountain People to discover and capture their "treasure". When they turn over the stone which protects the sacred treasure, the words 'Peace on Earth' are all they find, and "one tin soldier rides away."

A very similar theme occurs in "The Boy With the Moon

and Star on His Head" by Cat Stevens, from the album *Catch Bull at Four* (1972). We find here, in both symbol and content, the kind of interest which later led Cat Stevens to abandon music altogether to convert to Islam. In "The Boy With the Moon and Star on His Head", Stevens tells what is, on the surface, a bizarre story of fathering a child by "the gardener's daughter" while he is on the way to his wedding. But the union with the gardener's daughter is a symbolic union which takes place under "the holy magnolia" with the "naked earth" beneath them and "the universe above". When the child of this mystical and magical union, The Boy With the Moon and Star on His Head, arrives and grows into a man, everyone is in awe of this special messenger from the gods, and people come from far and wide to hear his words of wisdom. The song ends with, ". . . and 'Love' is all . . . he said."

Perhaps one of the most explicit and poignant examples of this kind of expression of the importance and power of love is the song, "All You Need Is Love," by Lennon and McCartney. "All You Need Is Love" was released as a single in 1967 and appears on the album, *Magical Mystery Tour*, also released in 1967. The first line, after a few brassy bars of the *Marseilleise*, the archetypal herald of Revolution, is simply, "Love, love, love, love, love, love, love, love, love." The refrain, repeated over and over again, is "All you need is love." Earlier, in 1965, Jackie DeShannon had sung the same theme: "What the World Needs Now is Love (Sweet Love)". The lyrics of this song confidently proclaim the superabundance of resources, a conviction which was not to survive The Sixties but which helps to explain the feeling of the time that many appalling problems could be easily dissolved given goodwill and enthusiasm. The power of love is also the theme of "Revival", written by Dicky Betts, from the Allman Brothers' second album, *Idlewild South* (1969) and also *Beginnings* (1973). In "Revival", we get the real gospel flavor of a revival meeting complete with organ, gospel choir and hand-clapping. The refrain, repeated over and over again, is,

> *People can you feel it? Love is in the air.*
> *People can you feel it? Love is everywhere.*

Monism and Dualism

Siddhartha's declaration that All is One is an example of what philosophers call metaphysical *monism*—the belief that the basic building blocks of everything in the universe are ultimately reducible to and explainable in terms of *one* kind of substance. Body and mind, material and immaterial things, and living and non-living things are all, ultimately and fundamentally, made of the same *single* metaphysical "stuff".

In Western philosophy, metaphysical monists have been in the distinct minority, and metaphysical dualists have been much more persuasive. We have already seen how Descartes's dualism with its division of the world into mental and physical substances has influenced Western intellectual thought. The theologies of both Judaism and Christianity are also dualistic, with their teachings of an immaterial and immortal soul which is supposed to survive death.

Whatever the other desirable appeals of metaphysical dualism might be, it does have the affect of dividing the universe up into different kinds of things—of separating things from one another. Indeed, the very doctrine of dualism is defined as making a fundamental distinction between two different kinds of things—the mental and the physical—a distinction which cannot be resolved or explained away. Now many people still regard this as a desirable feature of dualism, but if your main purpose is to try and explain how everything in the universe is similar and if you want to emphasize fundamental, universal harmony in the universe, then metaphysical dualism greatly complicates your task.

The Sixties was a period during which the sameness of people, the universal qualities of humanity, and cosmic harmony were of ultimate importance for many people. We should therefore expect to find such intellectual themes expressed in the popular culture, including the rock music, of this period, and we do.

In 1969, Seals and Crofts became converts to the Baha'i faith.[9] Baha'i is a product of Islamic belief which grew out of a Shiite Muslim tradition in Persia (now Iran), and was founded in the nineteenth century by Baha'u'llah, a follower of the heretical Shiite, Bab-ud-Din (Gate of the Faith).[10] Baha'i is now outlawed in Iran, but has a very active following in the United States.[11] This religion is characterized by an extreme egalitarianism and a metaphysical monism: We are all equal and everything is One. In particular, all religious beliefs, traditions, and practices are equal, and the main religious purpose of a devout follower is to work for a general ecumenism of all people (under Baha'i, of course). Baha'is thus seek spiritual union with all of human kind and god.

Seals and Crofts's very familiar tune, "Hummingbird", from their *Summer Breeze* album (1972) is a simple, straightforward expression of Baha'i beliefs. The Hummingbird is a divine harbinger from heaven of a "New Day" which is dawning for all humankind. The "spirit-voices" are whispering to us, preparing us for the divine union which is to come. We will fly up to heaven with the Hummingbird. Seals and Crofts quote from the Baha'i scriptures: "Lift us up to the Heaven of Holiness. Oh Source of our being." Don't leave us behind, Hummingbird! "Hummingbird don't fly away, fly away." Finally, "the draught [draft, potion] of understanding, wisdom, peace and love is ours."

This same hope for a divine union with other people and with god is the main theme of Seals and Crofts's "When I Meet Them", a song about that glorious day when we are all finally united in God's love—that's the day "when I meet them . . . my brothers and sisters." By "brothers and sisters" lyricist Jim Seals does not mean simply his fellow believers. He means all of humankind! On that happy day, he says, he wants to see "everybody singing, everybody, dancing, everybody clapping, everybody happy. . . ." This same theme of ecumenism and spiritual unity dominated the 1976 Seals and Crofts album, *Get Closer*.

Astrology

The Sixties saw the development of an enormous interest in astrology as a possible source of the new spiritualism. The belief that the relative positions of the distant stars and their constellations as well as the planets can influence human affairs and other events on earth is an ancient one. The origins of astrology are found in ancient Greece, India, China, Egypt, and Persia, and as you might well expect there are many varieties of astrology. In at least one popular school of astrology, observing and interpreting the celestial bodies and their groupings, as represented in the Zodiac, as a means to understanding and predicting human behavior is antithetical to modern science and most major religions. The distant causal influence of celestial bodies upon us amounts to the troublesome notion of "causal influence at a distance", and the completely mechanistic view of the positions of the stars precludes any sort of divine influence. Many people still believe, of course, that individual horoscopes, based upon the positions of celestial bodies at the moment of a person's birth, can be used to foretell events in that person's life.

Another element of astrological theory involves not individual horoscopes but what is known as The Great Year. According to astrological interpretations of the Cosmic Clock, as the earth progresses on its journey through the heavens, it passes through a cosmic cycle every twenty-six thousand years. During this cycle of the Great Year, the earth comes under the influence of each of the twelve constellations which make up the Zodiac for a period of approximately two thousand, two hundred years (26,000 divided by 12). During each of these twelve "ages" the earth is supposed to be influenced by the characteristics of the particular sign of the Zodiac which dominates that age. The Age of Leo is the first age in the cosmic cycle of The Great Year, followed by The Age of Cancer and The Age of Gemini.

The Age of Aquarius

Aquarius, the water bearer, is the seventh age in the Great Year following upon the heels of The Age of Pisces. Although the reasons for claiming a particular date for the beginning of the Age of Aquarius are obscure, there is common agreement among astrologers that we are now "on the cusp" of entering

The Age of Aquarius. Some fix the actual date for the beginning of The Age of Aquarius at 2010 A.D.[12] We are thus in the "dawning" of The Age of Aquarius.

The particular characteristics which are supposed to dominate human affairs during the two thousand, two hundred years of The Age of Aquarius are peace and love, harmony and brotherhood (and sisterhood).[13] During this age, spiritual perfection is the most important goal of human existence which means spiritual harmony with oneself, one's fellow human beings, and one's world. Passing from The Age of Pisces to the Age of Aquarius means passing from an age dominated by preparation, acquisition, competition, and work to an age dominated by harmony, satisfaction, and happiness.

In one sense, it is easy to understand why so many people wanted to believe in The Age of Aquarius. We might say that The Age of Aquarius was coming at just the right time because people needed to believe in something which emphasized the positive aspects of human nature. Wouldn't it be nice, one might think, if something like The Age of Aquarius were really possible? After all, aren't the politicians always talking about World Peace? And don't most of the world religions preach brotherly love and peace? Some versions of astrological interpretation of The Great Year see The Age of Aquarius as part of a divine plan for us human beings.

The Age of Aquarius is not believed to be the end of things in any apocalyptic sense. The dawning of "The Age of Aquarius" is not "The Eve of Destruction". The Great Year is a continuous cycle, and The Age of Aquarius is to be followed by the Age of Capricorn, and once the entire cycle is completed, it is repeated endlessly. But for over two thousand years, we will enjoy the peace and harmony of The Age of Aquarius. Peace, brothers and sisters.

"Age of Aquarius" by The Fifth Dimension from the album, *Aquarius/Let the Sunshine In,* soared to Number One in the spring of 1969. Originally from the Broadway rock musical "Hair", this song embodies all of the major themes of the changes which are supposed to occur during the Age of Aquarius according to the astrological interpretation of the Great Year. The Fifth Dimension sings

When the moon is in the seventh house
And Jupiter aligns with Mars
Then Peace shall guide the planets
And Love will steer the stars.

What does it mean for the moon to be "in the seventh house"? Remember that the Age of Aquarius is the seventh age in the astrological Great Year, following the Age of Pisces, and it is the position of the planets which heralds the changing from one age to another. As the influence of Aquarius replaces the influence of Pisces, Peace and Love and Harmony will become the forces which dominate human affairs.

In contrast to the messages of doom and gloom, "The Age of Aquarius" contains a message of hope and revival for a time when the stars themselves conspire to "Let the Sunshine In". This hope for a time when peace and happiness will abound is a recurring theme throughout the period of classic rock. These songs do not contain a message of a cataclysmic apocalypse when everything will be destroyed; instead, they contain a message which involves the passing of an age when "things as we know them" will be destroyed. In this sense then, such songs are apocalyptic since they involve messages about the end of an age and the beginning of "the New Heaven and Earth" when Love is the only thing which matters. For example, Gale Garnell's Number Four hit from 1964, "We'll Sing in the Sunshine", is an expression of a very similar hope for a bright and happy future time when peace and love will characterize all human relationships. The use of the sun and sunshine as a metaphor for love is too common in literature, poetry, and musical lyrics to need any lengthy explanation here. Since the time of the ancients, the light and warmth of the sun has been identified in fable, legend, and mythology as a source of good for human beings. Songs about love and sunshine abound: for example, "Here Comes the Sun" and "Good Day Sunshine" by the Beatles, "Sunshine", by Jonathan Edwards (a Top 40 hit in 1972), and "Sunshine of Your Love", by Cream, another Top 40 hit in 1968.[14] The image of a sungod is reintroduced in "Sunfighter" by Paul Kantner and Grace Slick from the album with the same title. On the album cover, a newborn baby (presumably their son, whom they named 'God') is being held aloft by a pair of hands, and the bright red and golden sun of a new dawn creates a halo around the baby's head. We thus get the graphic juxtaposition of God and the sun. The innocent, infant Sunfighter is the defender and savior of the earth—a new messiah. It is he who must tame the "night-time hurricane" of the destruction of the earth.

> *The sword of the Lord don't mean nothing to me if He won't get down*
> *On the people making such a mess of the land and the sea all around me.*

The Sunfighter, in the saving act of divine love, must "Mount the earth and learn to ride her—feel the land moving under you."

Apocalyptic Rock

A dominant part of the search for spirituality in The Sixties involved a great deal of interest in traditional and non-traditional (Western and Non-Western) spiritual teachings about the end of the world. The end of things—not just the end of human civilization but the end of *everything*—has held a particular fascination for theologians and philosophers through the ages. Interest in and predictions about the Apocalypse have influenced the popular culture of almost every age, and, in the late 1960s and early 1970s, this fascination with the end of the world erupted into a plethora of different spiritual and "philosophical" views about "the End". It is not surprising that views about the Apocalypse found their way into the popular culture of The Sixties. There are many rock songs from this period which contain depictions of various scenarios not only of the cataclysmic end of human existence, but of the possibility of judgment and punishment for the wicked and redemption and reward for the righteous.

This genre of classical rock music with its theme of the apocalyptic end of the world was something completely new to popular music. Some spiritual music—church hymns and gospel music—had included such a theme, but such dire prophesies had never found their way into popular music. Songs with such a somber and "negative" theme represented a dramatic departure from the rock 'n' roll of the 1950s, the rock music of the early 1960s, and all the rest of American popular music.

The songs of Apocalyptic Rock were powerful songs which both reflected and reinforced a general feeling of dread and impending doom. These are serious, somber, ominous songs. For example, from the funeral dirge beat on the drums at the very beginning of the "Eve of Destruction" we are aware that this is a different kind of song. The dreadful news is announced in Barry McGuire's harsh, irritable voice (which bears more than a little resemblance to Dylan's). "You don't believe we're on the eve of destruction," Barry McGuire repeats sarcastically in the song written by P.F. Sloan which reached Number One in 1965.[15]

Many of these songs of Apocalyptic Rock made it to the Top 40, and many didn't; many are still well-known and receive air time on FM radio while others are buried in albums which are becoming more and more obscure by the moment. These songs both resulted from and helped to reinforce the general hopeless feeling of anger, frustration, victimization, and alienation which characterized so much of The Sixties. Understanding the feelings of fear and apprehension along with the anger and frustration which accompanied the firm conviction of many people in The Sixties that the human race was rushing headlong into its own destruction would go a long way toward understanding what was unique about this period.

Among songs which will repay careful scrutiny are "Bad Moon Rising" and "Who'll Stop the Rain?" by Creedence Clearwater Revival, "Spirit in the Sky" by Norman Greenbaum, "A Hard Rain's Gonna Fall" by Bob Dylan, "Share the End" by Carly Simon, "The House at Pooneil Corner" by Jefferson Airplane, "Before the Deluge" by Jackson Browne, "After the Gold Rush" by Neil Young, and "Wooden Ships" by Crosby, Stills, and Nash.

The Book of the Dead

Perhaps there have been people in every age of human history who have believed that human beings are in some way able to survive death. There is an amazing amount of similarity in these different beliefs from different parts of the world. The earliest records we have of such beliefs and religious practices tied to those beliefs are those of ancient Egypt around 2000 B.C. In the earliest accounts which have been deciphered from "The Book of the Dead", composed from fragments chiseled on the walls of tombs, we discover that in The Kingdom of Osiris, the souls of the dead are judged, and Osiris, the god of the dead, is responsible for reward and punishment. The heart of the dead person is then weighed in the "scales of judgment" against an ostrich feather. A heart which is made heavy by the weight of evil deeds will result in punishment, and a heart which is light with goodness will result in the reward of eternal paradise.[16]

Zoroaster

In the history of what was called Persia in ancient times, which encompassed the present-day territories of Turkey, Iraq, Iran, and Pakistan, we find the records of the earliest form of ethical monotheism—the belief in a single, all-powerful god responsible for deciding the standards and judgments of human moral behavior. According to the teachings of Zoroaster (or Zarathustra), in approximately 1000–800 B.C., earth is a place where the struggle between good and evil is waged, and each of us is involved in that struggle. This struggle will ultimately bring the world to a cataclysmic end with the final battle between good and evil. At that time, there will be a general resurrection of the dead, and the "test of fire" to separate the good from the evil. In a metaphor which we now find reminiscent of the belief of the ancient Greeks that a soul had to be ferried to Hades across the River Styx, souls must, according to Zoroastrianism, cross a bridge over the bottomless pit of Hell. The evil souls are cast over the side, and the good souls cross safely into paradise.

The Celts

The Celts were a pre-historic people who are thought to have migrated to the British Isles from what is now Northwest Germany. At the time when the Romans came to the British Isles, the Celts represented the dominant culture which had been in place from many centuries. The Druids, the priests of the Celts, shrouded in mystery and folklore, were thought to have divine, mystical powers, and are believed to have been responsible for Stonehenge, the circle of gigantic stones near Salisbury in England. The Druids led the Celts in various rites and rituals, including the practice of animal and human sacrifice. The same interest in and knowledge of astronomy which led to the building of Stonehenge also led to the belief in a cataclysmic doomsday when the earth would be destroyed by fire and when all human beings would perish. The sky would fall, and a great fire would consume all human souls to prepare the way for a new race of people on a new earth.

Revelation

It is generally agreed by scholars that members of the early Christian church in the first century believed that "the Kingdom of God" about which Jesus had preached was close at hand.[17] They were wrong, of course, but the Christian view of the end of the world and the coming of "the Kingdom of God" has come to dominate much of Western culture. Its influence is evident in much of Renaissance art, and even the word 'apocalypse' originally simply meant a revelation concerning the future; however, since the book of *Revelation* in the New Testament contains such cataclysmic prognostications about the end of the world, the word 'apocalypse' has taken on an entirely different meaning to include these dire portents.

According to *Revelation*, the End is not going to be a pretty sight. In a series of visions, the details about the cataclysmic end of the world and the coming of the Kingdom of God is supposedly revealed to the writer of the book of *Revelation*.[18] The prophesies are revealed when the seven seals on the holy scroll are broken. The seven seals are generally understood as containing the portents, the advanced warning signs of the destruction of the world. Much has been made of the mystical importance of the number seven,[19] and various different people through the ages—serious scholars and complete nut cases alike—have tried to unravel and translate the mysteries of the seven seals. Numerous "prophets", ranging from rather obscure television evangelists to such infamous public figures as Charles Manson, Jim Jones, and, most recently, David Koresh, have claimed to speak with divine authority to foretell the coming of the end of the world, usually drawing upon *Revelation.* In 1972 the minor rock group Aphrodite's Child released an album, *666*, devoted to the Apocalypse.

Daniel and *Ezekiel*

The apocalyptic images of the book of *Revelation* are similar to images from other religious sources such as the books of *Daniel* and *Ezekiel* in the Old Testament whose depictions of the cataclysmic end of the world are closely paralleled in *Revelation.* According to *Daniel* and *Ezekiel,* the battle between good and evil will end and the Messiah will appear, to destroy evil and to save the righteous from the carnage which will devour the wicked. The devastation portrayed in *Daniel* and *Ezekiel* which will be brought upon the unrighteous is as terrible as anything described in *Revelation.* Fathers will eat their sons, and pestilence, famine, wild beasts, and the Sword of the Lord will bring down the wrath of God (Ezekiel 5:10; 17), and the land will become desolate and waste (Ezekiel 6:14). God will sit in judgment of good and evil, and the forces of evil shall finally be overcome. The evil will perish, and those who have been faithful will be rewarded in heaven with eternal bliss (Daniel 7:26–27).

Many of the apocalyptic teachings of Islam and Hinduism are very similar to those of Christianity and Judaism. Islam teaches that a great fire will come to destroy the world and at that time, there will be a divine judgment of the good and the wicked. The good will enter into an eternal paradise, and the wicked shall perish. At the sound of "the last trumpet" by the angel Gabriel, the dead shall rise to be judged with the living.

The *Koran* (the Qur'an) describes the final scene in the same terrifying detail as the books of *Daniel* and *Ezekiel* and *Revelation* do in The Bible:

> *When the sun shall be darkened,*
> *When the stars shall be thrown down,*
> *When the mountains shall be set moving,*
> *When the pregnant camels shall be neglected,*
> *When the savage beasts shall be mustered,*
> *When the seas shall be set boiling,*
> *When the souls shall be coupled,*
> *When the buried infant shall be asked for what sins*
>   *he was slain,*
> *When the scrolls shall be unrolled,*
> *When heaven shall be stripped off,*
> *When Hell shall be set blazing,*
> *When Paradise shall be brought nigh,*
> *Then shall a soul know what it has produced.*[20]

And there shall be signs and portents which will come before the end to give us time to prepare.

Three major deities have been recognized within Hinduism since the beginning of recorded history of religions: Brahma, the Creator; Shiva, the Destroyer; and Vishnu, the Preserver. Brahma creates the world but is not involved with or in the world in any way. Shiva is the god responsible for disease, war, and death—all of which are thought to be necessary for regeneration and new life on earth, and Vishnu is the god responsible for preserving life by keeping evil in check through both judgment and love.

Vishnu is said to have already had nine *avatars* ("descents", meaning animal or human embodiments of gods) which include Krishna and Gautama, the founder of Buddhism.[21] The arrival of the tenth avatar of Vishnu, Kalki, will signal the apocalypse. Kalki will arive on a white horse and carrying a flaming sword of justice and righteous. The wicked will perish, and the faithful will be carried off to Nirvana and rewarded with eternal life in a pastoral paradise.

Several songs from George Harrison's first album after the break-up of the Beatles, *All Things Must Pass*, are inspired by

Hindu beliefs. This three-album set, which hit Number One in the United States album charts in 1970,[22] includes, in addition to the title song, "Hear Me Lord", and "My Sweet Lord", over which Harrison fought and lost a plagiarism suit in 1976.[23] *Living in the Material World* (1973) contains "Give Me Love," "The Light That Has Lighted the World," and "Living in the Material World" which chronicle Harrison's spiritual development. Harrison expresses his hope of escaping this material world through his religious faith. He says,

> *I'm living in the material world*
> *Living in the material world*
> *I hope to get out of this place*
> > *by the LORD SRI KRISHNA'S GRACE*
> *My salvation from the material world.*

The folder inside with the lyrics contains a striking depiction of Krishna, an avatar of Vishnu, glowing divinely and riding a chariot pulled by four white horses.

A Hard Rain's A-Gonna Fall

There are several classic rock songs which do not actually *describe* the destruction and mayhem which is to occur; they simply *warn* us of it in the abstract—without all of the gory details. Bob Dylan's songs, "A Hard Rain's A-Gonna Fall" and "All Along the Watchtower" fall into this category. The similarities in both of these songs to the apocalyptic component of Judeo-Christian theology are too close to be coincidental. "Watching" and "keeping watch" are recurrent Biblical expressions used in both the Old and New Testaments to capture diligence and steadfastness and preparedness of religious faith.[24] *Ezekiel* specifically uses the metaphor of a watchman in a watchtower for the way in which a prophet is supposed to warn the people of Israel as a spokesman of god. Just as the watchman warns people of dangers which threaten, the prophet serves as the watchman to warn people of the judgment and wrath of god.[25]

In "All Along the Watchtower", it is clear from the first line,

"There must be some way out of here", that the song is a warning from the watchman of the doom which is about to befall us. Is there a way out? Well, "life is but a joke" and "the hour is getting late." The wild animals are circling, the wind begins to howl, and "two riders" are approaching. What or who is meant by the "two riders?" One possible and very probable answer, given the whole context of the song, is that the "two riders" are Death and Hades, which, according to Revelation 6:7–8, are unleashed upon earth when the fourth seal is broken. Death and Hades come riding upon their horses "to kill with sword and with famine and with pestilence and by wild beasts of the earth."[26]

"A Hard Rain's A-Gonna Fall", written in response to the Cuban Missile Crisis of October 1962, is also clearly a warning of impending doom, and aside from the obvious allusion to the Deluge it also contains definite references to the book of *Revelation.* The use of the metaphor of rain for the comforting presence of God is a common one in the Bible.[27] True, God is reported to have employed rain to destroy the world in the time of Noah, but didn't God then give the rainbow as a promise that this would never happen again? Yet maybe the promise applies only to water, and are we so sure that Dylan's "rain" refers to water? This rain is a *hard* rain. Dylan's raspy voice and the driving intensity of the staccato beat punctuate the *hardness* of the rain as the phrase is repeated: "It's a hard, it's a hard, it's a hard, it's a hard", and, in case we missed the point, "it's a *hard* rain's a-gonna fall." As the warning is given by "my blue-eyed son, my darling, young one," he is asked, "What did you see?" and "What did you hear?" The answers are ominous images:

I saw a new born baby with wild wolves all around it.

. . . .

I saw guns and sharp swords in the hands of young children.

and

I heard the sound of a thunder that roared out a warning.

. . . .

I heard the roar of a wave that could drown the whole world.

The similarity of the images in the lyrics of "A Hard Rain's Gonna Fall" to those found in *Revelation* is striking. When the seven seals are broken in *Revelation*, the writer reports seeing and hearing different things which are supposed to portend the cataclysmic end of the world. When Dylan's "blue-eyed son" is asked to report on the things which he has seen and heard, the things which are to serve as portents of the end of the world, he describes *exactly seven* different things which he has seen and *exactly seven* different things which he has heard. Given the recurrence of the mystical number seven in *Revelation*, can the meticulous lyricist Dylan's use of the number seven here be accidental?

Several other songs serve as portents of a cataclysmic end to the world. Some of these are more explicit than others, and, of course, some are simply better songs than others. Barry McGuire's "Eve of Destruction" lacks the complexity and sophistication of the two Dylan songs; the straightforward lyrics and the caustic tone captured perfectly the cynical and pessimistic attitude which pervaded so much of The Sixties and it rose to Number One in 1965.[28]

Bad Moon Rising

Another song foretelling the destruction awaiting us all is Creedence Clearwater Revival's "Bad Moon Rising", written by John Fogerty. This is a good dance tune with a strong back beat, and it is sobering to watch people dancing to this song and even singing along without paying any attention to the fact that "the bad moon on the rise" portends the imminent end of the world. Is this metaphoric, in some way, of how we all live our lives—singing and dancing and having a good time and ignoring impending doom? Fogerty does not provide as much graphic detail as Dylan, but the message is unmistakably the same:

> *I see a bad moon a rising.*
> *I see trouble on the way.*
> *I see earthquakes and lightning.*
> *I see bad times today.*

And things don't get any better as the song continues:

> *I feel hurricanes a-blowing.*
> *I know the end is coming soon.*
> *I feel rivers overflowing.*
> *I hear the voice of raze [rage?] and ruin.*

I hope that you are ready, Fogerty laments. "Hope you have got your things [meaning, in the vernacular of the day, "your shit"] together. . . . There's a bad moon on the rise."

The End

Despite all of the warnings and portents, however, when The End comes, we will not be prepared for it. This is a familiar theme of much religious teaching. Jesus warned repeatedly that no one knows when the Kingdom of God will come.[29] Of the day of judgment, "no one knows, not even the angels of heaven," Jesus said.[30] Therefore, we must be ready because the End will come at a time when we least expect it.[31] As Jackson Browne observes in "The Road and the Sky",

> *Don't think that it won't happen*
> *Just because it hasn't happened yet.*

Warnings, however, as Carly Simon sings, have little or no effect. In "Share the End", which Simon co-wrote with Jacob Brackman, from the album *Anticipation* (1971), the major theme is the one of unpreparedness. And it is *we* who are unprepared. When the "baying of the hounds" is heard and the time is at hand for "universal dying"—when The End comes— none of us is ready for it. The priests, kings, madmen, and we are all in the same boat.

> *Please, Lord we're not ready*
> *Give us some time to work things out. . . .*
> *Please, Lord we're not ready*
> *Give us a day*
> *Give us an hour. . . .*

In the end, we will all "Share the End". The inevitable destruction which we face in the end is also the theme of "Death and Destruction" by the New Riders of the Purple Sage.

When the final hour finally arrives, the Four Horsemen of the Apocalypse are to be loosed upon the earth, including the rider of the pale horse, Death. Here's part of the picture described by the writer of Revelation when the sixth seal on the scroll is broken:

> there was a great earthquake; and the sun became black as sackcloth, the full moon became like blood, and the stars of the sky fell to the earth as the fig tree sheds its winter fruit when shaken by a gale; the sky vanished like a scroll that is rolled up, and every mountain and island was removed from its place. (Revelation 6: 12–14)

Not a very appealing picture, is it? But this is just the beginning of the death and destruction which are to occur as a part of the end according to *Revelation.* When the angels blow their trumpets, hail and fire and blood will fall from the sky, the sun and moon and stars will be smitten, and the seas will turn to blood (Revelation 8: 7–12). Locusts and angels on horses with heads like lions and breathing fire and brimstone will torture and kill millions of people (Revelation 9: 3–18). Finally, seven angels will pour out the "wrath of God" upon the earth. Painful sores will torture people, every living thing in the seas will die, the sun will scorch the earth with intense heat, and there will be lightning and thunder and the great earthquake (Revelation: 16: 2–18).

The House at Pooneil Corners

This scene of destruction is repeated in several rock songs, for example "The House at Pooneil Corners" written by Marty Balin and Paul Kantner and included by Jefferson Airplane on their album *Crown of Creation* (1968). The mushroom cloud on the album cover reminds us that The End might come in the form of a nuclear holocaust. The scene described in "The

House at Pooneil Corners" is as frightening and terrifying as anything you might find in *Ezekiel* or *Revelation,* and the stabbing guitar riffs and painful organ chords drive home the point. When the end comes,

> *Suddenly everyone will look surprised*
> *Stars spinning wheels in the skies*
> *Sun is scrambled in their eyes*
> *While the moon circles like a vulture.*

Everything and everyone turns into "Jelly & juice & bubbles— bubbles on the floor." Finally, the destruction is complete, and then

> *Everything someday will be gone except silence*
> *Earth will be quiet again*
> *Seas from clouds will wash off the ashes of violence*
> *Left as the memory of man*
> *There will be no survivor my friend.*

Everything is silence because the world has been cleansed: as the penultimate, anguished cry says at the end of the song, "All the idiots have left."

A similar end to everything is depicted by Neil Young in "L.A." from *Time Fades Away* (1973) which describes the catastrophic effect of "the big one," the long-awaited earthquake which is expected to hit southern California.

> *And the mountains erupt*
> *And the valley is sucked*
> *Into cracks in the earth.*

Young continues the theme of an apocalypse in the album *On the Beach* in 1974, a title taken from the novel of the same title by Nevil Shute which depicts the aftermath of a nuclear holocaust. (The movie, starring Gregory Peck and Ava Gardner, was released in 1959.)

The end of the world is a time when the last great battle between the forces of good and the forces of evil will take place, and, of course, in the end, the forces of good will win. The good will be rewarded, and the wicked shall perish. Satan will be cast into "the bottomless pit" and his followers into the lake of fire and brimstone and the dead will rise (Revelation 19:20; 20:2; and 20:5). "All the idiots have left."

The Ghost Dance

In 1890, following what history books usually call "the Indian Wars", several tribes of Native Americans developed their own special adaptation of Christian eschatology. The belief in the coming of the Messiah and the practices surrounding this belief evidently began with the Paiutes,[32] but most of the different tribes from the Dakotas to Arizona quickly embraced these beliefs. Here is how Wovoka, the Paiute Messiah, described his version of the coming apocalypse:

> All Indians must dance, everywhere, keep on dancing. Pretty soon in next spring Great Spirit come. He bring back all game of every kind. The game be thick everywhere. All dead Indians come back and live again. They be strong just like young men, be young again. Old blind Indian see again. . . . When Great Spirit comes this way, then all Indians go to the mountains, high up away from whites. . . . Then while Indians way up high, big flood comes like water and all white people die, get drowned. After that, water go way and then nobody but Indians everywhere and game all kinds thick. Then medicine man tell Indians to send word to all Indians to keep up dancing and the good time will come.[33]

Thousands of Native Americans came to believe that Jesus had returned to earth as an Indian to save the Indians, To facilitate their salvation, they built great bonfires, donned sacred Ghost Shirts with magic symbols,[34] and sang and danced the Ghost Dance from dusk to dawn. These widespread practices continued for several months in the Fall of 1890 until the murder of Sitting Bull on December 15, 1890.[35]

The point here is a general one: peoples of various cultures and at various times have recognized the power of music and dance—even the power to save one's soul. Thinking of the Ghost Dance might make us listen to such songs as "Let's

Dance" by Chris Montez (1962) and David Bowie (1983) or Van Halen's "Dance the Night Away" (1979) or King Harvest's "Dancing In the Moonlight" (1973) with a more serious and critical ear, but any direct connections with the Ghost Dance are very doubtful. Buffy Sainte-Marie, however, did write a song called "He's a Keeper of the Fire" which does have a much more straightforward connection to the Ghost Dance. The haunting, eerie howling and moaning at the beginning of this song conjures up images of unfamiliar people in unfamiliar places doing unfamiliar things. The lyrics make very clear that this song is about a medicine man, a holy man, performing sacred rites. "He's a prophet of a new day, baby," Buffy Sainte-Marie sings about "the Keeper of the Flame." "He's been tested by the blood. He's a walker on the hot coals, baby." He talks to demons and to the heavens. Can the Keeper of the Flame save us and take us to that Great Spirit in the sky? By dancing?

That Great Spirit in the sky is also the theme of Norman Greenbaum's Number Three hit in 1970, "Spirit in the Sky". It is amazing to me the number and kinds of different people who like this song. There are many people who are attracted to this song though they publicly acknowledge having no particular religious belief. It must be saying something to them. What the song expresses, of course, is the age-old hope of the human race for some continued existence after death, and that belief is expressed here in very simple, even childish terms: "I've got a friend in Jesus," Greenbaum sings. And when I die, he continues, "I'm gonna go to the place that's the best. . . . I'm gonna go up to the Spirit in the Sky." I'm gonna go to the place "that's the best"? This is hardly superlative poetry, but the simple belief in redemption and eternal life still has a strong appeal for many people.

The Remnant
Although Christianity has dominated much of American culture, it certainly is not unique among world religions in having

an *eschatology*—a theory about the end of things—death, judgment, heaven, and hell. Christianity was initially seen by many Jews as a fulfillment of prophecies which had been a part of Judaism for centuries before the time of Jesus. The Pharisees had believed in and taught that God would intervene to bring about the end of the world and would send a Messiah to save the faithful remnant and to judge the unfaithful. The Pharisees believed that there would be a resurrection of the dead and a last judgment after which the faithful and righteous few would enjoy a pastoral paradise with green pastures, clear, fresh streams of water, and plenty to eat.[36] It is this belief which first gave rise to the doctrine of "the Remnant." According to this doctrine, a remaining chosen few of the faithful and righteous will be spared the suffering and death which await the rest of us. The Remnant will be taken by God directly to paradise or to start a new Zion.

So, according to the doctrine of the Remnant, not everything and everyone will be destroyed at the time of the apocalypse. The chosen few will survive to begin again. This doctrine is not unique to Judaism, but it is particularly explicit and pronounced in Judaism. It is also explicit and pronounced in several classic rock compositions. The interesting thing about these songs is that interwoven with the descriptions of the death, destruction, and general mayhem which is to accompany the apocalypse, are the descriptions of the remnant escaping this world and setting off to a new one.

Wooden Ships

A fine example of a song whose main theme is the surviving remnant is "Wooden Ships." This was written by David Crosby, Paul Kantner, and Steven Stills and was included on the *Volunteers* album by Jefferson Airplane (1969) and on the premier album of Crosby, Stills, and Nash, *Crosby, Stills, and Nash* (1969), as well as on the album *So Far* by Crosby, Stills, Nash, and Young (1974). This song is Apocalyptic Rock at its best. The scene is one supposedly following the madness of a thermonuclear war, and the passengers on the wooden ships watch in horror as people die from radioactive contamination and as they search for food and shelter on the land.

We can only be saved on simple, wholesome, "natural" wooden ships. Nothing plastic, artificial or synthetic can save us. The select remnant will be spared, and they will sail away on their wooden ships—"free, happy, crazy people, naked in the universe." And it is the music which purifies. In a line which is reminiscent of the magical, redemptive quality of music, which we examined earlier, we are instructed to

> *GO RIDE THE MUSIC*
> *C'MON AND RIDE IT CHILD*

to save ourselves from destruction.[37] Maybe music *can* save our mortal souls!

There was little doubt in the minds of those who knew and listened to this song about who were the chosen few who would survive. It's "us" versus "them" again; "they" are the ones who ultimately destroy the world, and "we" are the ones who survive to start a free, natural life. The wooden ships, sailing "free and easy" on the water, will take us away from "this barren land" and to the promise of a new land where we can laugh and be happy once again. We find in this song two of the most memorable lines from the whole period—lines which capture aphoristically the anger, frustration, courage, determination, and, at the same time, the hope and optimism of a generation:

> *We are leaving.*
> *You don't need us.*

And, in the song, they do leave on their wooden ships. They are "free and gone".

The image of escaping a decaying and dying world by sailing away in ships was also used by James Taylor in "Highway Song":

> *Father, let us build a boat and sail away*
> *There's nothing for you here*
> *And brother, let us throw our lot out upon the sea*
> *It's been done before.*

After the Gold Rush

Another well-known song which also contains an explicit and dominant theme of a chosen remnant is "After the Gold Rush" by Neil Young for the album of the same title (1970). Maybe Young's "After the Gold Rush" was somehow the result of the bizarre interpersonal conflicts which always seemed to exist between Young and Crosby, Stills, and Nash. We'll probably never know if Young intended to show the world that, since David Crosby and Steven Stills had collaborated with Jefferson Airplane for the version of "Wooden Ships" on *Volunteers*, he could go one better with "After the Gold Rush". After all, Young does say in the middle of "After the Gold Rush", "I was thinking about what a friend has said. I was hoping it was a lie." Both of these very similar songs are great songs.

The use of the metaphor of a "gold rush" to capture the frantic, greedy, consumerism, planned obsolescence, and disposable, use-it-up-and-get-another-one attitude which characterized so much of the 1950s and early 1960s is particularly striking. So much is packed into this one phrase. What so many regarded as the pinnacle of the development of human civilization is compared to the cheap, fragile, shoddy storefronts of a gold rush town.

The vision comes to Young in a dream. *After* the gold rush, everything is supposedly destroyed or in chaos, and as Young watches from the "burnt out basement" in which he is lying, he sees "the chosen ones" as they board "the silver space ships".

> *They were flying Mother Nature's silver seed*
> *To a new home in the sun.*

Again, as in the case of "Wooden Ships", we have an apocalyptic song, but it is one with a dominant message of hope and salvation for the chosen few who are innocent—the Remnant.

Before the Deluge

It is characteristic of all devout religious zealots that they believe that *they* are the ones which are the chosen ones which are to constitute the remnant, but, of course, not everyone is going to be saved. An interesting feature of Jackson Browne's song "Before the Deluge" from the album *Late for the Sky* (1974) is that Browne cleverly plays upon this common belief that *we* are the ones to be saved. Many of *us* are going to be swept away along with *them* when the final deluge comes. We might expect god's wrath to rain upon those who have abused the earth and those "bad" developers who simply turn the beauty of the earth into power, Browne says. But his message is also pointed at those who think that they hold the high moral ground.

In the Old Testament, prophets such as Amos turned their prophecies of judgment and destruction upon Israel herself. It was acceptable for the people of Israel to hear pronouncements of doom and gloom from Amos for *other people*, but then Amos announces that God will similarly punish the people of Israel.[38] We can imagine the reaction of those listening to Amos. What, us? Aren't we the good guys? Browne does the same thing to his listeners. It's all right for him to tell us how those who "reach for the golden ring" will perish since we well know that Jesus said that it's easier for a camel to pass through the eye of a needle than for a rich man to pass into heaven.[39] But what about *us*? Well, when the Deluge comes, the surviving remnant will be much smaller than we had imagined:

> *When the sand was gone and the time arrived*
> *In the naked dawn, only a few survived.*

The message is not a pleasant one. Those of us who are "innocent" and those who are "dreamers" and those who are trying "to make their way back to nature" and those for whom "only the [present] moment matters" are all swept away in a moment "before the deluge" along with the "bad guys".

I hope that you all make it and aren't swept before the Deluge. If you're not sure about where you stand and what your chances are, then maybe you should "pack up the babies" and "grab the old ladies" and head out for "Brother Love's Traveling Salvation Show".

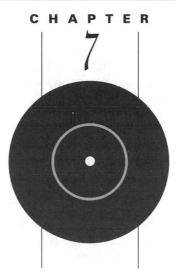

Too Old to Rock 'n' Roll, Too Young to Die

Fortunately or unfortunately, the world did not end with The Sixties. The wrath of God did not descend upon a corrupt, racist, and sexist corporate America in the form of a fiery apocalypse, and so, life goes on. The young, nubile flower children of the summer of love and the love-in and be-in in Haight-Ashbury in 1967 are now already middle-aged and rapidly sinking into senescence even as you read these lines. These former flower children and members of the Woodstock generation now have adult children of their own, and even grandchildren, and instead of expanding their consciousness, most of them worry more about receding hairlines, sagging bustlines, and expanding waistlines.

My Generation

Members of The Sixties Generation have already become the older generation against which future younger generations will rebel. Whatever happened to not trusting anyone over 30? Well, be serious. If you happen to know someone under 30 right now, what degree of understanding and judgment do you think that they possess concerning the complexities and vagaries of the modern social, political, and economic world in which we live?

Describing and evaluating the importance of the times and the music of "My Generation" is difficult because much, perhaps even most, of what was important about those times defies translation to members of other generations. Perhaps this is because so much of being a member of The Sixties generation was exactly that —*being*—being young, being free, being yourself, being whatever you wanted to be. It was an identity, as we have seen, which was defined in terms of actions and deeds, and as such, that identity resists description and analysis— especially as recorded *history.*

Courses on The Sixties are now common in most history and American studies departments at colleges and universities around the country! *WE* and our times and our music are now, even in our lifetimes, objects of *historical* scrutiny. It is significant that an effort is usually made to find instructors (or visiting instructors) to teach such courses who not only lived at the same time as but also lived *through* and participated in the activism of The Sixties. In matters concerning college curricula, this is one of the few areas where experience is weighed equally with formal training.

In The Who's "My Generation", a 1966 single, reproduced on *The Who Sings My Generation* (1966) and *Meaty, Beaty, Big and Bouncy* (1971), Peter Townshend addresses the over-thirties:

> *Why don't you just f-f-fade away?*
> *Don't try to d-d-dig what we all say.*

A minor gimmick was the stutter on key words, and if someone ever recommended, in 1966, that you "f-f-fade away", you weren't really with it if you didn't instantly recognize a more earthy exhortation beginning with "f".

Of course, very little, if any thought was ever given to growing old by members of the Woodstock Generation. After all, the overwhelming influence of the dominant theme of hedonism in the popular culture of The Sixties glorified a life of immediate pleasure. The ultimate subconscious desire, though it also frequently rose to the level of consciousness, was to "live fast, die young, and leave a beautiful corpse."[1] It is not surprising that we find explicit expressions of this intention in many songs, including "My Generation": "I hope I die before I get old," The Who sings. This thought was defining both of The Who and of the times which produced The Who, so much so that Dave Marsh takes it as the title of his definitive book on The Who.[2] James Dean was the epitome of someone who lived his life in the fast lane never thinking about or intending to grow old gracefully. His life and death are eulogized by The Eagles in "James Dean" (written by Jackson Browne, Glenn Frey, Don Henley, and John David Souther)from *On the Border* (1974). He was "too fast to live, and too young to die." Bye bye.

The Death of Rock
It is interesting, and perhaps illustrative, that a number of possible titles for this last chapter sprang easily to mind—all prompted by well-known rock songs, for example: "The Greying of Rock Music", "Where Have All the Flowers Gone?", "What a Long, Strange Trip It's Been", "The Death of Rock", "Only the Good Die Young", "Dust in the Wind", "Teach Your Children Well", and "Touch of Grey".[3] There are many others.

Writers and performers have been lamenting or celebrating "the death of rock" for almost two decades now. Perhaps it is definitive of modern American culture that individuals and movements are remembered and known more for their failures than anything else. The public record holds all of us to a high standard—especially our public idols. The passing of the golden age of rock music has prompted a number of eulogies on its behalf. This attention is perfectly justified since an age has definitely passed and *something* has died, albeit exactly *what* is hard to say.

The Greying of the Greening of Rock Music

The promise and expectations of the youth culture of The Sixties and its music had been enormous: brotherly and sisterly love, freedom for everyone, racial and even global harmony, simple, wholesome lives, and peace on earth. It was exactly such expectations which caused Charles Reich to wax eloquent about the age upon which we were supposed to be entering in the mid-1970s:

> Today we are witnesses to a great moment in history: a turn from the pessimism that has closed in on modern industrial society; the rebirth of a future; the rebirth of people in a sterile land.[4]

This rebirth was to have been the result of challenging and ultimately replacing the eroding institutions and relationships of modern American society. Reich continues to describe the radical transformation which was expected to take place in modern American society:

> If we think of all that is now challenged—the nature of education, the very validity of institutionalism and the legal system, the nature and purposes of work, the course of man's dealing with environment, the relationship of self to technology and society—we can see that the present transformation goes beyond anything in modern history.[5]

In the end, Reich concludes: "What is coming is nothing less than a new way of life and a new man—a man with renewed energies and imagination—a man who is part of the living world."[6]

However, those who were to bring about a new age of man and a new life for us all are now aging baby-boomers with silver streaks in their once golden locks. Those who dreamed and schemed about the transformation of society and "the greening of America" are now old and grey or well on their way. As Neil Young ironically wrote and sang in "Old Man" from his *Harvest* album, 1971:

> *Old man, look at my life.*
> *I'm a lot like you were.*
> . . . .
> *Give me things that don't get lost.*

But the eternal youth which was such a part of The Sixties when "life was so wonderful" has been lost, and the flower children have grown up to be "sensible and logical" as Supertramp sang in "The Logical Song" (1979). Now, everyone is pleading, "Please, tell me who I am."

I Have a Dream

Martin Luther King Jr.'s speech during the March on Washington in 1963 is one of the defining moments of The Sixties and of the political life of this country. The lines of this speech, which has become known as the "I Have a Dream Speech" are as well known to many school children today as the lines of Abraham Lincoln's Gettysburg Address. Of course, King was not the only one to have such a dream in the 1960s. Many people shared his dream and many others had dreams of their own. The naive, idealistic, romantic themes, which influenced and found expression in so much of popular culture in The Sixties encouraged such dreaming—about peace and love and brotherhood and the end of war, poverty, and bigotry. The underlying philosophical themes are what gave meaning and substance to those dreams.

Songs about dreams and dreaming in the 1960s and 1970s are perhaps second in number only to songs about love. So, we have everything from "Dreaming" by Johnny Burnette (1960) to "California Dreaming" by the Mamas and Papas (1966) to "Dream On" by the Righteous Brothers (1974) to "Dreams" by Fleetwood Mac (1977).

The Sixties was a period when certain kinds of dreams and hopes and aspirations dominated a very substantial minority of the population. The fact that those dreams were shared in a very personal way by hundreds of thousands or even millions of people explains the dramatic and emotional impact of King's words. The content and nature of dreams and hopes and aspirations are perhaps a measure of the defining characteristics of a culture, a people, or an age.

It is impossible to pinpoint any single event which marked the death of rock music though many have tried. The death of rock 'n' roll occurred as early as 1959 with the death of Buddy Holly and the conviction of disc jockey Alan Freed in the payola scandal, according to some. The death of rock is traced by others to Altamont in 1969, just four months after the festival at Woodstock, where Hell's Angels beat a fan to death at a Rolling Stones concert. Still others will point to the drug-related deaths of the legendary figures of rock—Jimi Hendrix and Janis Joplin in 1970 or Jim Morrison in 1971—or to the break-up of the Beatles in 1970. With the advent of the British punk rock group, the Sex Pistols, in 1976, with *Anarchy in the UK*, we get the avowed intention to kill whatever remained of rock music.

The Dream is Over

It seems that it is nearly always more difficult to determine when a particular period of history *ends* than when it begins. For example, the title of the final section of Todd Gitlin's book on the radical left in the Sixties is entitled, "In Search of an Ending".[7] It is hard to find an appropriate description for the end of The Sixties because the lasting influence of The Sixties and the changes brought about by and because of The Sixties are particularly difficult to determine:

> A biography ends with a death; the history of a war with an armistice; a scientific article with a call for more research; a balance sheet with a bottom line; a cautionary tale with a moral.

> Any finality I can imagine for this book seems false, for I write
> not just about history but imprisoned within it, enclosed within
> the aftermaths of the Sixties, trying to peer over the walls.[8]

Getlin has hit upon something important here. We are still
within the confines of the period of history which is perceptibly
influenced, to some degree, by The Sixties. It is still impossible
to say, from the standpoint of history, just what the ultimate
impact of The Sixties will be. We must await the final judgment
of history upon The Sixties and upon those of us who lived
through that period. But by whatever measures, by the early
1980s, when the impact of Reagan economics began to be felt
and dreams of six-figure incomes and BMWs and Porsches
replaced dreams of brotherhood and love, something was
indeed dead. Things had definitely changed. It is illustrative
that by the mid-1980s Janis Joplin's imperative to "get it while
you can" had taken on an entirely new meaning. Instead of a
directive to enjoy life and to indulge in "free" sex during the
immediate present, it would have been understood as a crass
call to acquisition and consumerism—make all the money any
way you can and spend it all on really expensive toys.

Early signs of these developments led John Lennon to say,
very early on, both in interviews and in song lyrics, that the
dream was over. In an interview with *Rolling Stone* in 1971,
Lennon said:

> The dream is over. It's just the same, only I'm thirty, and a lot of
> people have long hair. That's what it is man, nothing happened
> except that we grew up, we did our thing—just like they were
> telling us—most of the so-called "now generation" are getting a
> job. We're a minority you know, people like us always were, but
> maybe we are a slightly larger minority because of something or
> other.[9]

Lennon makes the same sad and powerful pronouncement in
"God", from *John Lennon/Plastic Ono Band* (1970), as we have
already seen. "The dream is over," he says. Now he believes in
nothing—except Yoko and himself. Now, as Cheap Trick
warned in 1979, we have to watch out for the "Dream Police".

Requiem for Rock

The news and the realization of the death of rock traveled slowly, and many people—performers and audiences alike— still persist in "Living in the Past"—something about which Jethro Tull had tried to warn us as early as 1972. Aging and aged rockers are a pitiful sight. The image of an aging, grossly overweight Elvis during the last few years of his life, going through the motions (barely) and covered with sequins and tassels, is not only embarrassing but painful. It is indeed melancholy to feel pity for the King. And, Paul Simon's "Graceland" notwithstanding, it is overwhelmingly *sad* to visit Graceland and see how the life and death of the King have been turned into a slick and sick Elvis Theme Park. It's a little like paying to see the blood on the limousine in which John Kennedy was killed. An icon has become a novelty—and the subject of ridicule. As the rap group, the Geto Boys, describe in the satirical rap song, "Trophy": Elvis is the winner of the trophy for the most appearances made after death. And, since Elvis isn't here (has anybody seen him?), another major con- tender for the award (and perhaps next year's winner), The Grateful Dead, will accept the award for Elvis. Oh, how the mighty have fallen, and oh, how the greatest of talents have become such easy targets for their conspicuously less gifted successors.

The sight of a dancing, prancing, aging Mick Jagger in Danskins is similarly embarrassing and sad. Watching Old Grey Beard Himself, Jerry Garcia, with his love beads (and with much more than just a "Touch of Grey") and withered, wrin- kled Chuck Berry is equally painful. They are now sadly *anachronistic*—out of place and out of time. Watching aging rockers is somewhat like watching newsreels of the 1960s or movies made *in* the 1960s (not *about* the 1960s). It is poignant and painful, and it stirs something buried deep inside of us, but it is also sadly comical—something like trying on your old bellbottom jeans or peasant dress in the attic.

Something of the same phenomenon takes place with aging athletes. They can't seem to let go, and we, their adoring subjects, can't seem to let them go with dignity and style. The sight of a fumbling Willie Mays trying merely to hold on one more day in a game which he dominated or a mumbling Joe Louis, reduced to shaking hands in the lobby of a gambling casino in Las Vegas with a trembling right hand which had so terrorized opponents, are lasting images of how we manage to drag those who have dared to rise above the rest of us back down to our level. We can then reassure ourselves that after all, they're only human. And we still have great stories to tell: "Oh, I saw Muhammad Ali when he came out of more than three years of retirement to fight Jerry Quarry in Atlanta. Man, he was something." AH, YES. BUT YOU SHOULD HAVE SEEN HIM IN HIS PRIME. It is a badge of honor and distinction to have lived so long and to have been "with it" so long to have seen the greats in their prime. Yes, having Eric Clapton win a Grammy Award in 1993 for "Tears in Heaven" was great, but you should have heard him with Cream in 1967 or Derek and the Dominos in 1970. YOU SHOULD HAVE HEARD HIM IN HIS PRIME. MR. SLOWHAND! HE WAS THE BEST! Clapton and Duane Allman battling it out with guitars on Derek and the Dominos' album *Layla* is like Ali and Joe Frazier going at it! Man, they were the best!

Can you imagine taking the great Secretariat and dressing him in a bonnet and a clown's outfit and having him lead the parade at Disney World? No, oldtimers games are not for me, and "golden oldie" concerts are not for me. I want my idols— sports and rock alike—in their proper places. An essential part of what made classic rock music what it was and what it is was the age and the times which produced it, which is why so much of this book has been about the events of the 1960s and 1970s as well as the rest of the popular culture of the period.

Rock Music for Sale

Joe McGinniss's book, *The Selling of the President 1968*, was the first major exposé of the influence of television, communications and advertising upon the presidential electoral process.[10] To the surprise and alarm of most people, politics had seemingly become a matter of Madison Avenue advertising and marketing. Now, it should come as no surprise for people to realize that the same thing has happened to rock music, but the corruption and commercialization involved in the selling of rock music produce a sense of loss and betrayal for the children of The Sixties which, for better or worse, they have never felt about politics. From Watergate to Iran-Contra to Abscam to the banking scandal in the House of Representatives, the culprits are, except perhaps for their immediate families and close friends, at a safe emotional distance. "Get the bastards" and "Throw the bastards out," people say. The public takes a fiendish delight in seeing a politician get caught and punished for some shady dealing because our initial expectations are so low for politicians, we do not feel the sense of betrayal which comes with an anguished cry of, "How could they do this to *us?*"

Rock music and rock musicians have not only been sold; they have become *the sellers.* The packaging of the music itself continues to get slicker and glossier and the marketing strategies to sell "the product" rock music has become continue to get more and more excessive. More importantly though, the music has been reduced to a marketing strategy itself. In some cases, the musicians write or perform some little ditty or jingle for a product which provides instant "product recognition".

Since the bulge in the population which is now the middle-aged baby boomers represents the largest single market for goods and services in our country, advertisers wanting to reach that market will obviously use the best means available. These Madison Avenue guys are no dummies. They know that people remember that the Lovin' Spoonful told us that "the magic's in the music", and they know that people remember the admonition of the Doobie Brothers to "Listen to the Music". And if music, as Don McLean asked "can save your mortal soul", then it stands to reason that it can also make you want to buy or sell your mortal soul. The magic which is in rock music and which *is rock music* and rock musicians has proven to be very successful in selling things and services to you and me (believe me, if it were not successful, then Madison Avenue would not continue to do it).

We're talking about huge amounts of money here—not just millions but *billions* of dollars. According to one incredible set of figures, the sale of rock records and tapes in 1972 accounted for a larger gross income than movies, professional sports, and theater *combined!*[11] It's no wonder that everybody wants a piece of the action!

So, many rock music and rock musicians have been reduced to the equivalent of sideshow barkers hawking their wares. Rock music is now used to sell everything from automobiles to soft drinks and beer to fast food and clothing to politicians. In fact, it has become difficult to avoid advertising using rock music and it has become difficult to think of products which are *not* sold using rock music.

Status Symbol Land

We live, like Jackson Browne's "Pretender", "in the shade of the freeway" in a world where "the ads lay claim to the heart and soul of the spender." It is, as the Monkees sang in 1967, just another "Pleasant Valley Sunday"—out here "in status symbol land." Except now, classic rock music is one of the best marketing "tools" for selling those status symbols.

Is there anything wrong with this? Surely the same thing has happened even to classical music. There are many examples. The two most recent ones which come to mind are the use of the final bars of Tchaikovsky's "1812 Overture" to accompany the exploding firewords on television announcing "The Memorial Day Automobile Sellathon" and the use of the opening bars of Richard Strauss's "Thus Spake Zarathustra" to draw our attention on television to the availability of the financial and investment services of a major company. And the masterpieces of Wagner, Tchaikovsky, Rossini, and other composers of classical music are used regularly for accompaniment for Saturday morning cartoons on television—largely, I am sure, because there are no royalty charges involved since these works are now in the public domain. Is there anything wrong with this? After all, didn't Beethoven and Strauss as well as Bach, Mozart and others write music for money? Well, yes, *BUT* there *is* a difference. Don't you think that Beethoven would, to borrow a phrase ironically popularized by Chuck Berry in "Roll Over, Beethoven" (1956), "roll over" in his grave to know that his music has been reduced to an advertising jingle? I do. But, of course, he doesn't know, and he didn't sign a contract for big bucks to write an advertising jingle for Juicy Fruit chewing gum!

This Note's for You

Neil Young has never been a person too careful with his words, which makes many of Young's songs—both the music and the lyrics—"unpolished" and sometimes unfocused. The listener is left with a strong, sometimes even overpowering feeling of the impact of a Young song which is still somewhat general and vague. The effect, for all that, can still often be very powerful, as I have already noted with regard to such songs as "After the Gold Rush". "Powderfinger" from his *Rust Never Sleeps* (1979) contains an equally strong and compelling message of alienation and cynicism.

Young's "This Note's for You" from the album of the same title with The Bluenotes (1988) is a noticeable departure from his usual style of songwriting. This song has no nebulous imagery or foggy abstractions. The title line is an obtrusively obvious play on the well-known advertising slogan for Budweiser beer. The lyrics are tight and focused, and he uses them to cut with the precision of a surgeon's knife, a contrast to his usual wide swaths of a broadsword. There is little doubt about the meaning or intended targets of his venom:

> *Ain't singing for Pepsi*
> *Ain't singing for Coke*
> *I don't sing for nobody*
> *Makes me look like a joke*
> *This note's for you.*

And, just in case anyone happened to miss the point, Young reiterates it for us:

Ain't singing for Miller
Don't sing for Bud
I won't sing for politicians
Ain't singing for spuds
This note's for you.

Finally, with a fierce pun and a forceful message which is characteristic of so many of his songs, Young proudly and mockingly exclaims at the end,

I've got the real thing
I got the real thing baby
I got the real thing
Yeah alright.

Of course, if Young were writing this song now, five years later, he would have many more targets from which to choose. Michael Jackson and Ray Charles were merely among the first and most obvious cases of musicians who have turned to marketing. Now, Bob Seger's "Like a Rock" is used to sell trucks, Willie Nelson writes jingles for Taco Bell, and John Oates provides music for HBO's special on *Sports Illustrated*'s swimsuit issue. There are, of course many others who have given a whole new meaning to the notion of "the greening of rock music" by turning rock music into a major "marketing tool".

Young's video for "This Note's for You" which features a Michael Jackson double with burning hair was banned on American television when it first appeared.[12] Ironically, in more ways than one, the video was named Best Video of the Year in 1989 at the MTV Video Awards Ceremony. Young had proclaimed his own innocence by announcing,

Don't want no cash
Don't need no money
. . . .
This note's for you.

But, protestations to the contrary, though the notes may be for us, the audience, they are still expensive. If you want them, you must pay for them. The notes are not for free. This is the way in which we have seen the threat posed by rock music co-opted and absorbed by "the system" repeatedly. Sure, if you want to write and sing a song which is critical of the music industry about the way in which rock musicians have "sold out" to business and industry and have prostituted themselves for money, we'll be glad for you to do it. We'll even help you produce it. We'll pay you to do it and give you a prestigious award for doing it—if you do it in a way which will guarantee a large enough share of the market. Do you think that it will sell? Its part of what has become "the American way". As John Cougar Mellencamp says in "Pink Houses",

> *Now ain't that America?*
> *Home of the free*
> *With little pink houses for you and me.*

The most often-quoted conclusion of Marshall McLuhan's analysis of mass, electronic media is his claim in *Understanding Media* that "the medium is the message." We saw how this dictum is an accurate description of the rock 'n' roll of the 1950s and early 1960s, though in a sense somewhat different to that intended by McLuhan. Taking even more violent liberties with the author's intentions, we can read the title of a later book by McLuhan, *The Medium is the Massage*,[13] as an accurate description of the commercial role assumed by rock music and rock musicians in the 1980s and 1990s. In between, during The Sixties, for some brief time, the medium and message "had their act together", and, as we have seen, rock music during that period had some serious messages for those who would listen and even for those who wouldn't. From then until now—well, "What a long, strange trip it's been."

The Opium of the People
As we have seen, there was an enormous sense of moral, political, and spiritual urgency in The Sixties. The themes which characterized the rock music from that period did not just accidentally and coincidentally find their way into the

music. Things mattered! Life mattered! Ideas and principles mattered! Truly existential choices were *forced* upon people by the events of those times, and it was impossible to evade these choices by running away because running away was also a choice. People had to take stands and be counted. There were feelings of vitality and urgency to life which emphatically pervaded the period and the rock music which gave voice to the issues about which people felt so strongly. Never before in any period of human history have the people and places, beliefs and causes, events and emotions, and the fears and dreams of the times been so dramatically encapsulated in music. And never before, because of the coming together of the technology and the culture which produced rock music, has a medium been in such a mutually interactive role with its message with each shaping and influencing the other on such a grand scale.[14] This is why understanding classic rock is essential to any serious understanding of The Sixties.

Where are they now—those rock idols and icons of The Sixties? Where are the ideas and ideals? Where is the sense of urgency and the feeling of vitality? Where are the beliefs that things matter in some sense which is greater than ourselves and that what we do—you and I—is important? Where is the belief that standing on values and principles is what is really important about a person? Where are those dreams and hopes of love and peace in the world? And what has happened to the music which gave voice to those dreams and hopes?

It was Karl Marx who characterized religion as the opium of the people. For "the Woodstock generation", who rejected organized religion early on along with the other institutions of the dominant culture, rock music has now earned that appellation. Give the people what they want! You want to feel good? You want music? We'll give you music. Drop your quarter in the slot and listen right here! Now doesn't that feel good? It's the "Big, Bright Green Pleasure Machine" Paul Simon warned us about except now *the machine is the music* which he employed to warn us! Oh, no, say it isn't so! It can't be! Not our beloved and hallowed rock music! But it is, of course. And *we* have done it—you and I. As Pete Townshend agonizes in "We Won't Get

Fooled Again", "Meet the new boss. Same as the old boss."
How could this happen after we were warned and were so sure
that we wouldn't get fooled again?

Hotel California

You and I are hard on our heroes. We want them up there in the
spotlight, on the stage, and in the history books—leading us
onward and upward. Heroes and idols—from serious political
leaders to pop culture heroes such as movie stars, athletes, and
rock musicians—walk a fine line. They must carefully balance
their talents, their differences and even their outrageousness
against some unspoken and undefined limit to their own drive
for artistic perfection and their capacity for self-doubt. The
public's fickle demands for messianic deliverance from their
common, everyday existence is always tinged with an undercur-
rent of envy and jealousy that it is *they* and not *we* who have the
talent or who got the breaks. They are walkers, artists, on a high
wire, doing a dangerous balancing act for high stakes. We love
them for being up there. We love it when they are successful.
However, many of them fall. And when they do fall, then we
never get tired of accounts and the analyses of the details of
their suffering or the gory particulars of their fall. Witness the
public's appetite for the details of the deaths of its fallen
heroes—the assassinations of John Kennedy and Martin Luther
King, Jr. A visit to the Luray Motel in Memphis, the site of the
assassination of King, is disturbing because of the commercialization and the extraordinary bad taste of displaying the grue-
some details of his final moments on earth. People, it seems, are
somehow exalted by and glorify in the deaths of their heroes,
and thirst to be told every last detail.

Rock music has supplied us with many martyrs. I've only
talked about the better-known ones. The entertainment business is a cut-throat business, as the Eagles have observed in
several songs from their *Hotel California* album (1976). We get a
good look at what a star's life is like in "Life in the Fast Lane".
It will "surely make you lose your mind," and once you get in

the fast lane, nothing is ever the same again. And you just go on and on, faster and faster, "trying to get off". It's like being on the back of a wild tiger that you either ride, or have eat you if you get off. There's always someone pushing you from behind — some "New Kid in Town" — someone who is better or that the people love more — someone who is a threat. No, at "Hotel California", once you check in, "you can check out anytime you like, but you can never leave." There's the fame. There's the adulation. There's the lifestyle. There are the drugs and the groupies. There's the money. There's the music. No wonder it is so difficult to ever leave. And no wonder that so many have "checked out" in one way or another. Very, *very* few have managed to "make it big" and then walk away as John Lennon did, to write and sing about it. "People say I'm crazy . . . [and] they give me all kind of warnings," he sang in "Watching the Wheels" from *Double Fantasy* (1980). "No longer riding on the merry-go-round, I just had to let it go." But he couldn't and didn't let it go because we wouldn't let him. It was a fan who made sure that he didn't. He tried to get off the back of the tiger, and the tiger ate the Walrus.

We all want leaders, and we place an enormous burden upon them to provide us with a vision or a dream which speaks to our deepest needs. Then we expect them to take us along — drag us along, kicking and screaming all the way — to that vision. No wonder Bob Dylan said, "Don't follow leaders" in "Subterranean Homesick Blues". If you want a vision and a dream, and you want to make it reality, do it yourself. The same reaction by John Lennon is reported by Dave Marsh in the "Open Letter to John Lennon" which Marsh published in *Rolling Stone* in 1978, asking Lennon to end his retirement because the world needed his artistic genius to interpret events. "I don't fucking owe anybody anything," Lennon said. "I've done my part. It's somebody else's turn now."[15] These larger-than-life expectations of a messianic deliverance are explicitly addressed in John Lodge's song, "I'm Just a Singer in a Rock 'n' Roll Band", from the album *Seventh Sojourn* (1972) by the Moody Blues. "If you want the winds of change to blow around you . . . don't tell me. I'm just a singer in a rock 'n' roll band." Don't look to us for answers. If "you can see exactly what to do, please tell me. I'm just a singer in a rock 'n' roll band."

Crucifixion

Of all the many classic rock songs which acknowledge the delicate balance between deliverance and destruction, one of my favorites is "Crucifixion" by Phil Ochs from his 1967 album, *Pleasures of the Harbor*. A compelling version of "Crucifixion" was recorded by little-known duo Jim and Jean on their album entitled *Changes*. In "Crucifixion" Ochs tells the tale of the morbid delight which we all take in the sagas of our fallen heroes. Which heroes? Well, take your pick—from Jesus to John or Robert Kennedy to Martin Luther King, Jr. to Jim Morrison or Janis Joplin. When iconoclastic rebels become "an assault upon the order" and represent "the changing of the guard", we embrace them and follow them and urge them on in their fight against "the establishment" and "them" and "evil". It's the battle of a hero of truth, justice, and right against overwhelming odds, and we love them for it. But the terrible truth is that "beneath the greatest love is a hurricane of hate", and "success is an enemy of the losers of the day", and "in the privacy of the churches, who knows what they pray?" Until, finally, with "the cross trembling with desire", the rebel and savior is crucified and "the eyes of the rebel have been branded by the blind." We who are left and who, of course, are innocent of the rebel's death, must know every detail. "Do you have a picture of the pain?" we ask. And "as the cycle of sacrifice unwinds", the important thing is that it's "good to be alive when the eulogies are read." And "with the speed of insanity, then he dies."

You Just Had to Be There

There are moments in human life which defy being captured by recorded history. For many people who lived through The Sixties, there were many such moments—from the Cuban

Missile Crisis and the Death of John Kennedy in the early 1960s to the resignation of Richard Nixon in 1974. Now I am sure that there are other periods of American history which contain such moments, but perhaps not so many of them concentrated into such a brief period. The momentous events crowded into that brief, fateful episode which we call "The Sixties" produced a sense of dramatic vitality, urgency, shared experience, and shared destiny. "It was the best of times. It was the worst of times"—from Woodstock to Altamont—and these events were the defining moments of what the members of that generation were and what they hoped to become. For a brief shining moment, people did "Come Together" as Lennon and McCartney urged us to do. The music, as a synthesis of what had come earlier both came together itself and brought people together. But we are, as Kansas reminded us, simply "Dust in the Wind". We all have our moment, "and the moment's gone." The moment of time which was The Sixties is definitely gone.

Just how much of The Sixties was real and how much is the result of an exaggerated sense of nostalgia is difficult to say. Much of it seems surreal, like a hallucination. The song "The Music Never Stopped" written by Bob Weir and J. Barlow from *Blues for Allah* (1975) by the Grateful Dead captures one aspect of attempts to reflect upon The Sixties. As a condensed version of "The Rainmaker", this song is simply about a band which comes to town in the middle of a drought to play, and play it does—with "a rainbow full of sound". It's a sound which the people have never heard before, and everyone starts dancing and clapping their hands. People forget all about time as the music plays, and they join hands with one another. Then, suddenly, there's a big storm, and the band is gone. Later, the people aren't sure whether it was ever there or not. But the corn crop is saved, and the people are happy, and singing and dancing because "the music never stopped." Though The Sixties are gone, and though it is difficult sometimes to distinguish fantasy from reality in The Sixties, the music from The Sixties is still here.

For all of its excesses, failed promises, self-righteous smugness, and foolish, naive romanticism—and for all of the casualties on both sides of the microphones—The Sixties was a unique period in history when the continuing social, political, cultural, and philosophical progression of modern human beings moved a few notches along the scale that measures human development and human progress. Maybe, to really appreciate this claim, you just had to be there.

In the classic science fiction movie, "Close Encounters of the Third Kind" (directed by Steven Spielberg in 1977), *music* is the universal language used to make contact with the aliens from outer space when their space ship descends upon Devil's Tower. The scene where single notes are sent and received back and where single notes become chords and chords become a dazzling succession of bars of chords is a powerful affirmation of the fundamental nature of music. For some short period of time for those who were there, and now reaching toward us across time, the notes and chords—the riffs and words—the back beat and melodies of classic rock music touched and provoked something in the same manner in this basic part of our nature.

Come Together

We have seen that classic rock music and the unique times and events which were The Sixties were inseparably linked, and each helped make the other what it was. The characteristics of the Sixties and the beliefs and attitudes of that generation produced a *unity*—a oneness—a sense of shared victimization and shared destiny—shared dreams and aspirations. And, perhaps most importantly, there was a sense of shared culture and music. Those who had rejected the dominant culture in one way or another and those who were desperately searching for some sense of self-identity created their own culture—they talked the same language, they had their own politics, they developed their own myths and symbols, they had their own heroes, they read the same books, and they made and listened to the same music.

Not only did they come together to make and listen to the same music, the music *brought them together*. The music itself was a unifying force. Rock journalists and writers, including Ben Fong-Torres, Charles Gillett, Paul Goodman, Greil Marcus, and Dave Marsh have repeatedly demonstrated the way in which rock emerged from different kinds of music including rhythm and blues, early rock 'n' roll, country, and folk. It is diverting to analyze the importance of the contributions of the different kinds of music which went into the melange which produced classic rock music, but the really important thing is that rock became the musical melting pot of all these different ingredients. It was a synthesis of different styles and genres which somehow yielded a common sound and the possibility of a common voice.

The common voice with which classic rock music speaks became possible because of the underlying philosophical themes which provided a cohesive message for the voice. There was a little something from everybody and for everybody in rock music. Rock thus became *our* music, and it was the product of and the glue for a *community* of people who had to some degree or other left their own communities behind in their search for themselves. Rock music in The Sixties provided a cohesion to a fragmented youth culture. It was both the effect and the cause of coming together.

Bob Dylan is reported as once saying, in 1991, "The world don't need any more songs."[16] While many people might agree with Dylan now, far fewer would have agreed 30 years earlier. Just think of what we would have missed!

The Dream Is Over

Some people think that the notions of unity and community are exaggerated with respect to The Sixties. Paul Williams calls the togetherness of the 1960s an "illusion of community".[17] It is this illusion of a sense of community which is missing from society and from rock music today, according to Williams.

> For a few brief years in the sixties there was something like a collective illusion, a sense of working together in service to a real and imminent greater truth. We believed that we were building

something. That feeling was so satisfying that even today musicians and fans alike listen to the music that was made then and bemoan the loss of the intangible Something that made it all so special once.[18]

The music from this time was both a cause of and a product of the sense of community. Was it all just an illusion? A dream? In a sense, it really doesn't matter in terms of comparing what went on in The Sixties with where we are today. Today, there is not even an *illusion* of shared community much less a genuine sense of one. As Williams concludes, "the magical sense of community came to naught, and blew away, and it's hard to put an illusion back together again."[19]

As Paul Simon tells us in his dissertation about failed dreams in "American Tune", we can't expect to be forever blessed, and all dreams come to an end at some time or another:

I don't know a dream
That's not been shattered
Or driven to its knees

Interestingly enough, one way in which the dream of "the magical sense of community" was lost was because of a general flight to privacy of many of those who lived through the 1960s. From the deserts of southern California to the mountains of Vermont, former flower children and members of "the Woodstock generation" have sought their salvation on a very individual and private level trying to survive with something of their dignity and their dreams still intact. These are former activists who wanted to change or save the world and who are now neither interested in nor likely to participate in demonstrations, marches, sit-ins or vigils unless the issue is one on a very local, even personal, level.

Was the dream really worth it? Could the dream ever have become real? There has been a lot of self-doubt. In "For America", Jackson Browne finds that the dream of individual "freedom" which was so important wasn't so sweet once he knew the truth. And in "In Dreams", one of several songs by Roy Orbison in which the dream is better than the reality, the lament about a lost love is metaphoric for the lost opportunities of meaningful relationships with other people. Freedom and community are very hard to get together in the same dream.

There are several classic rock songs which speak specifically to the syndrome of cynical social and political activists who now seek some kind of refuge in privacy. Billy Joel's song, "Angry Young Man", from the album *Turnstiles* (1976) describes the sad and unattractive spectacle of an aging angry young man who continues his cynical battle against the world. He is always defending some noble cause or another, and "he's proud of his scars and the battles he's lost." He stands on principle and makes sure that everyone knows it:

> *He refuses to bend, he refuses to crawl,*
> *He's always at home with his back to the wall.*

With his "fist in the air and his head in the sand . . . he likes to be known as the angry young man." To all of this Joel responds that he "once believed in causes too", but now, he adds, in a line which I am sure strikes a responsive chord in many children of The Sixties, "I found that just surviving is a noble cause."

A very similar theme is echoed in a very similar song by Styx in "Fooling Yourself (Angry Young Man)" (written by Tommy Shaw) from the album *The Grand Illusion* (1977). This song is a little pep talk to an aging and still bitter and cynical angry young man. "You see the world through your cynical eyes. You're a troubled young man." Styx tells this guy to snap out of it and get a life. In reality, "you've got it all in the palm of your hand . . . , and your future looks really bright to me," they say. Enough of this cynicism!

> *Get up. Get back on your feet*
> *You're the one that they can't beat.*

Make a life for yourself, and "just take your best shot."

And All the King's Horses and All the King's Men . . .

In *The Sound of the City,* published in 1971, Charlie Gillett identified what he called five distinct styles of rock 'n' roll from which the rock 'n' roll music of the mid-1950s developed.[20] *Five!* Five distinctive styles of rock 'n' roll! They were northern band rock 'n' roll, New Orleans dance blues, Memphis country rock (rockabilly), Chicago rhythm and blues, and vocal group rock 'n' roll.[21] The combination of these different styles of rock 'n' roll from their different cultural and geographical origins produced a kind of "collective identity" for rock music according to Gillett.[22]

If Gillett were writing today, how many styles of popular music might he identify. Fifty? A hundred and fifty? It is difficult to ask even how many styles of *rock* music there are since rock music has become so varied and fragmented and the borders of rock music have been expanded so widely that it is difficult even to make sense of the title any more. This is especially difficult since much of the "new" popular music— beginning with punk music in the late 1970s—expressly distinguishes itself from and contrasts itself to rock music.

The sense of community and togetherness of The Sixties, illusory or not, has been smashed into dozens of different pieces which don't seem to fit together into any kind of whole. Today we have rock 'n' roll, classic rock, punk rock, cyberpunk, heavy metal, new wave, rave, rap, dance/rap, gangsta rap, native-tongues rap, bass, hip hop, psychedelic hip-hop, rockabilly, Southern rock, progressive, alternative, free style, techno, house, grunge, reggae, dance-hall reggae, ragamuffin reggae, and undoubtedly several other new genres of "rock" music which will have come and gone by the time that you read this. Even with some serious effort to keep up with what is going on in contemporary popular music, it is too complicated and fragmented. Every day it seems there is news not just of some new group but of some completely new genre of music which is sweeping some part of the younger generation.

In a way it doesn't matter whether there are two dozen or three dozen or even more different distinctive styles of rock music today. The important point is that there is no sense of shared community—no sharing of messages, dreams, and aspirations—in these fragmented and fractionalized genres of music. The rock which was the melting pot of different racial and cultural sources has become the Humpty Dumpty of the music of today. What we have is a lot of different pieces which cannot be put together under any kind of single description, and people are not interested in putting them back together anyway.

Not only have the kinds of music multiplied and fragmented, but the *performers* have as well. Just as there is no single dominant genre of rock music any more, there is also no dominant individual or group in rock music which can command the kind of general attention and following which individuals and groups in The Sixties were able to do. Elvis was the earliest perhaps, but then, in the late 1960s and early 1970s, The Beatles, The Rolling Stones, Dylan, The Who, Elton John, and perhaps a few others were able to attract and hold the attention and the adulation of *millions* of fans. And the interesting thing is that though each of these groups attracted their own legions of faithful followers, they were not regarded (except perhaps in the case of The Beatles and The Rolling Stones) as competitors. Today, the drop in the overall sales of new releases, and the cancellation of highly promoted concerts and tours have music producers scrambling for new marketing techniques, and everyone's hoping, of course, to find that new star or group which will be "the new Elvis" or "the new Beatles". As we have seen, though, Elvis and the Beatles and their music were all a product of their times, and the times have changed and the music has changed along with the times.

Where Have all the Flowers Gone?

We have seen how a cohesive and mutually reinforcing set of literary, theological, and philosophical themes found expression in the classic rock music of The Sixties. These themes provided a fundamental unity and cohesiveness to the message of classic rock. There was never anything like a carefully thought-out, systematic development of these themes. No doubt, some uses of these themes were intentional and deliberate, and also with no doubt, other uses were unintentional and accidental. In whichever case, these themes both provided and expressed the collective identity of a generation and its music.

Where are they now—these philosophical themes of alienation and friendship and utopias and hedonism and *carpe diem* and autonomy and freedom and basic human goodness and self-assertion and peace and brotherhood and cataclysmic apocalypse and deliverance and salvation? Where are these themes which provided a conceptual vehicle for a generation to travel through one of the most important and difficult periods of American history? It was these themes and their expression in classic rock music which got many of us from then to now and from there to here. Well, maybe they're still around in new wave or rap or grunge, buried somewhere beneath the various obfuscating layers of fragmented identities, but I see very little sign of them, and I hold very little hope or expectation of finding them. The particular set of themes which we have examined in this book and the music in which they found their expression were not only products of their times but inseparably a *part* of their times, and we are not likely to see those times or their music anytime again soon.

Much of this may sound like a simple and straightforward apology for rock music and an elaborate and convenient rationalization for the excesses, wastes, and failures of The Sixties and the current garish commercialization of classic rock music and musicians. Why not just admit that whatever ideology it was that The Sixties had to offer has failed miserably? It seems that those people who were not victims of excessive self-indulgence and the flight to privacy have dropped back into society in a big way by selling out—both themselves and their music. Was it all just a big waste? And hasn't rock music been taking itself far too seriously for far too long? Doesn't classic rock music merely provide the object of another genre of popular writing with a strong popular appeal, including this book itself? Well, it would have been much easier and undoubtedly more profitable to write a revealing biographical study of some rock idol. The whole point of this book is to get people to think seriously about classic rock music and to understand it as expressive of some serious philosophical themes.

Minimally, if classic rock music was nothing else but a *vehicle*, as I suggested earlier, a vehicle to get us from there to here and from then to now, it was an extraordinarily valuable part of our culture. It is true that every generation has to go through difficult times while growing up, but not every generation has had to face the overwhelming crumbling and eroding and destruction of identifying cultural beliefs, ideals, and figures which occurred in The Sixties. This is what has made it a long, strange trip!

Some Dreams Die Hard

So, we're now long removed from The Sixties, and the long shadow of the 1960s which extended over the 1970s and 1980s is beginning to fade. For many people who were not even born when the Beatles split up, it takes the deliberate use of nostalgia as a marketing ploy to produce any sort of identification with The Sixties at all. All of which raises one last question which has not been faced squarely yet: What about the challenging, revolutionary aspect of the themes of classic rock music and the other popular culture of The Sixties? Has the threat to society passed? And did the desire to change society come to nought?

For better or worse, we got to where we are by the particular route that we took to get here. It is very difficult even to speculate about how the world might be different today if The Sixties had not been what they were. There are those who believe that, as a society, we are no better off in terms of social, racial, and sexual equality and justice than we were 30 or 40 years ago. I am not one of those. We have come a long way from the systematic and legally sanctioned racial discrimination of the early 1950s. We have also come a long way from the systematic and legally sanctioned sexual discrimination of the early 1970s. The phrase, "the Vietnam War", has taken on the meaning of and will probably forever symbolize a warning against hasty, overcommitment of deadly force and the waste of human lives and resources in a situation without clearly defined objectives or national interests. The people, places, events, and, most importantly, the underlying philosophical theories and principles which brought about these changes can all be traced directly to The Sixties.

The Dream Is Alive

There are additional signs that the dreams and aspirations and the philosophical themes which give rational force to those dreams are still reaching out to us from The Sixties. Even given the rampant, crass commercialization of rock music, it has still demonstrated a kind of social consciousness which is dreadfully lacking among other major media. Early on, there was *The Concert for Bangla Desh.* This is a three-album set from a live concert at Madison Square Garden on August 1st, 1971, featuring Eric Clapton, Bob Dylan, George Harrison, Billy Preston, Leon Russell, Ringo Starr, Ravi Shankar, and others. Produced by George Harrison and Phil Spector, this "collector's item" comes in a boxed set which features the haunting black and white photograph of a starving child on the cover—probably not a very smart marketing strategy by today's standards. On the back of the program notes, which feature a serious social history of Bangla Desh, is a photocopy of a check made out to the United Nations Children's Fund for Relief to Refugee Children of Bangla Desh for the amount of $243,418.50.

In 1979, there were five consecutive nights of benefit concerts from September 19th–23rd at Madison Square Garden for MUSE (Musicians United for Safe Energy). The recordings from these concerts were collected in the double album, *No Nukes,* which features the likes of The Doobie Brothers, John Hall, Bonnie Raitt, James Taylor, Carly Simon, Crosby, Stills, and Nash, Jackson Browne, Chaka Khan, Poco, Tom Petty and the Heartbreakers, Bruce Springsteen, and the E Street Band. The program notes include serious anti-nuclear and safe energy sermonettes from the performers as well as a diagrammed article on the effects of radiation by a Nobel Prize-winning biologist. Proceeds of the concert and albums went to MUSE.

The collective social consciousness of rock music has continued into the 1980s and 1990s. In 1984, Bob Geldof of the Boomtown Rats organized Band Aid, a concert featuring 36 different artists for relief of the famine in Ethiopia. Performers included Phil Collins, U-2, Duran Duran, Culture Club, Kool and the Gang, Status Quo, and Wham! The song, "Do They Know It's Christmas?", written by Geldof and Midge Ure of Ultravox, hit Number One that year in Britain. In 1985 Geldof organized and produced Live Aid, a marathon, 16-hour concert in London and Philadelphia featuring most of the big names in rock music—old and new alike—including Queen, Madonna, and U-2. In 1986, Geldof was knighted by Queen Elizabeth II, and nominated for the Nobel Peace Prize.

"We Are the World", written by Michael Jackson and Lionel Richie, was the theme song of the 1985 USA for Africa relief project and became a Number One hit in the United States. The recording featured 46 different performers, and the proceeds went to the relief and economic development in Africa and to help feed the homeless in the United States.

Also in 1985, to help relieve the plight of the small farmer, Willie Nelson produced his Farm Aid I concerts, a series which reportedly produced $10 million in funds for farmers.[23] The Farm Aid concerts have now replaced Nelson's annual Fourth of July Picnic in Texas.

1989 saw the production of the environmentally sensitive *Greenpeace Rainbow Warriors* album. In 1990, Sting performed a benefit concert for the Rainforest Foundation with Paul Simon, Bruce Springsteen, Herbie Hancock, Jackson Browne, Don Henley, and newcomers Bruce Hornsby and Branford Marsalis, playing together at one time. The Earth Day 1991 Concert in Foxboro, Massachusetts, featured artists as diverse as Willie Nelson and 10,000 Maniacs.

So there is quite a bit of evidence that the influence and substance of the dreams of The Sixties live on, and besides, it's not really time yet for the dawning of the Age of Aquarius. The aging and greying children of The Sixties can continue to

"Dream On", as the Righteous Brothers sang in 1974 and Aerosmith sang in 1976. As Steven Tyler puts it in "Dream On",

> *Every time that I look in the mirror*
> *All these lines in my face getting clearer*

we must

> *Dream on. Dream on.*
> *Dream on. Dream on.*
> *Dream until your dreams come true.*

We continue to be reminded from time to time not to lose our dreams by the music: "Dream (Hold onto Your Dream)," Irene Cara sang in 1984 and, as Wilson Phillips sang in 1991, the "Dream Is Still Alive". The dreams from The Sixties and the philosophical themes which give substance to those dreams and the music which gives voice to those dreams are what remain.

The spirit of The Sixties lives in whatever dreams, hopes and aspirations we and our children and our grandchildren have for the future. No one captured this spirit any more succinctly or represented it personally any more than did Robert Kennedy: "Some men see things as they are and say, 'Why?' I dream things that never were and say, 'Why not?' "

Meanwhile we're just waiting for the chorus to come around again.

Notes

1. A Long, Strange Trip: From Rock 'n' Roll to Rock Music

1. For detailed discussions of early rock 'n' roll see Charles Hamm, *Yesterdays: Popular Song in America* (New York: Norton, 1979), Chapter 15; Don J. Hibbard and Carol Kaleialoha, *The Role of Rock* (Englewood Cliffs: Prentice-Hall, 1983), Chapter 2; Linda Martin and Kerry Seagrave, *Anti-Rock: the Opposition to Rock 'n' Roll* (Hamden, CT: Archon Books, 1984); and David R. Shumway, "Rock & Roll as a Cultural Practice" in *Present Tense: Rock & Roll and Culture,* edited by Anthony DeCurtis (Durham, NC: Duke University Press, 1992).

2. See, for example, Hibbard and Kaleialoha, *ibid.,* pp. 7–8.

3. See Joel Whitburn, *Top 40 Hits,* Fifth Edition (New York: Billboard Books, 1992), pp. 365–66.

4. *Ibid.,* p. 279.

5. *Ibid.,* pp. 652–54.

6. The version of the "Ballad of Davy Crockett" by Tennessee Ernie Ford only made it to the Number Five slot. Thus, for several weeks in March and April 1955, both of these versions of the "Ballad of Davy Crockett" were on the Top 40 charts. Ford's "Sixteen Tons", however, did reach Number One in 1955. See *ibid.,* p. 179.

7. *Ibid.,* pp. 652–54.

8. See Hamm, *ibid.,* p. 411–14.

9. Whitburn, *ibid.,* p. 153.

10. For a more thorough treatment of Dylan's impact on rock music see *The New Rolling Stone Record Guide,* edited by Dave Marsh and John Swenson (New York: Rolling Stone Press, 1979) pp. 153ff.

11. This was also a period of immense turmoil within the music industry. For discussions of the conflict between ASCAP (The American Society of Composers, Authors, and Publishers) and BMI (Broadcast Music Incorporated) see Hamm, *ibid.,* pp. 389 and 401ff. Also see Martin and Segrave, *ibid.,* Chapter 2.

12. Throughout this discussion of The Sixties, as well as the discussions which follow later about the philosophical themes which occur in the lyrics of particular songs, I do not try to distinguish between American,

English and Western European cultures. This book is written from a uniquely American perspective, but *many* of the most important rock groups whose works I discuss are British. Sorting out the reciprocal influences between Great Britain and the United States during this period—in terms of both music and social and political influences— would be a book in itself.

13.   You don't believe me? How about Russia's downing of the U-2 spy plane, the beginning of the Peace Corps, the March at Selma, the murders of Goodman, Schwerner, and Chaney, the murders of Medgar Evers and Malcolm X, the Free Speech Movement, LBJ's decision not to seek re-election, Woodstock, the moon landing, My Lai, the Charles Manson murders, and the breakup of the Beatles?

14.   I am not the first writer to attempt an answer. See, for example, Paul Williams, "What the Sixties Had That the Eighties Don't Have", *The Penguin Book of Rock and Roll Writing*, edited by Clinton Heylin (London: Viking, 1992), pp. 116–123.

15.   See *ibid.*, p. 116ff.

16.   The entire movie "The Graduate" can be seen as an allegory of life in The Sixties for the younger generation. Benjamin is simply a young man trying to make his way into manhood—dealing with the identity crisis of moving from childhood into an adult's world. Despondent, he gets laid and falls in love, but, as we all know, not by and with the same person. Mrs. Robinson represents everything evil about the older generation. She is seductive and alluring—providing the promise of and even the fulfillment of forbidden pleasure and satisfaction. She also embodies the power to manipulate and corrupt which threatens to use him and spit him out and ruin his life in the process. The rest of the story is a tale of Benjamin trying to find his future and happiness and values and how he will live his life *against and in contrast with* the adult world. So he flails about, like a bull in a china shop, desperately trying to make his own way. At the movie's end, as he symbolically rejects god and community, family and friends, he sets out to make his life and find his happiness with another man's wife—lovers on the run from the rest of society. The ending is uncertain rather than conventionally "happy".

17.   See Allen J. Matusow, *The Unraveling of America* (New York: Harper and Row, 1984), pp. 280ff.; Tom Wolfe, *The Electric Kool-Aid Acid Test* (New York: Bantam, 1968).

18.   See Dave Barry's syndicated column of Sunday, January 24th, 1993.

19.   If culture is defined so broadly that any learned behavior transmitted by imitation counts, then 'culture' includes much behavior of non-human animals, including much birdsong and some food-gathering behavior of primates. See, for example, John T. Bonner, *The Evolution of Culture in Animals* (Princeton: Princeton University Press, 1980). But the scope for cultural development in human populations greatly exceeds that among

non-humans, and almost every moment of our daily lives is dramatically different from what it could have been without thousands of years of cultural evolution.

20. While there are some important differences between American and English cultures, and while I discuss many English groups along with American groups, I do not think that whatever differences exist between the two cultures prohibit treating them as a single culture for the purposes of this book. But I treat British songs entirely from the American point of view and only insofar as they were widely-known in the U.S. For example, the Beatles had several successive hits in Britain while completely unknown in the U.S., then all these songs became popular in the U.S. simultaneously.

2. Stranger in a Strange Land: Alienation in Rock Music

1. For a detailed examination of the role of the New Left in the Sixties, see Todd Gitlin, *The Sixties: Years of Hope, Days of Rage* (New York: Bantam, 1987).
2. Allen J. Matusow, *The Unraveling of America* (New York: Harper and Row, 1984).
3. Luke 12:20.
4. In the cases of both "A Day in the Life" and "Richard Cory" we are not given enough details about the lives of the men involved to know the reasons for their unhappiness and the causes of their suicides. I admit that both of these songs might be understood and interpreted as examples of a more general, existential despair.
5. It's hard to know these days if the pun and the humor need to be explained. The 'Lennon' in the lyrics of the song is John Lennon, but the pun is on V.I. *Lenin* (1870–1924), the Marxist who founded the Bolshevik Party in Russia and led the October Revolution of 1917 which brought the Bolsheviks (later known as the Communist Party) to power in Russia.
6. In the "Name the Best Rock Album of All Time" contest, this is certainly one of my contenders for top spot. I discuss this album later in this chapter.
7. Matthew 16:26.
8. This album also contains a tribute song to Angela Davis ("Angela") and a call to arms to the women of the world by Ono ("Sisters, O Sisters") in which women are urged to "stand up" and "fight" for "freedom" in order "to build a new world."
9. Matusow, *ibid.*, Chapter 5.

10. *Ibid.*, pp. 149–150. For the actual text of the Gulf of Tonkin Resolution, see *Major Problems in American History Since 1945*, edited by Robert Griffith (Lexington, MA: Heath, 1992), pp. 406–07.
11. See Matusow, *ibid.*, pp. 153ff. and James Deakin, *Lyndon Johnson's Credibility Gap* (Washington, DC: Public Affairs Press, 1968).
12. See Matusow, *ibid.*, p. 150 and Austin, *The President's War*, Chapter 10.
13. Jean-Jacques Rousseau, *The Social Contract*, 1762.
14. In the liner notes to the double CD *2400 Fulton Street* (the address in San Francisco of the large victorian mansion where the members of Jefferson Airplane lived during most of their careers together), Marty Balin disavows any revolutionary intent. He says that he got the word 'Volunteers' from the side of a garbage truck and that Paul Kantner added the line "Got a Revolution. Got to revolution."
15. This is another strong candidate, for my money, for the best rock album ever produced.
16. For quite some time, "2001" was the favorite movie of many people to see while stoned. This was before "Rocky Horror Picture Show" (1975).
17. Although I have never seen any official industry numbers, the "button business" was big from the mid-1960s to the mid-1970s. "Everyone" wore buttons in order to publicly identify themselves with different political movements ("Stop the War") as well as more abstract ideologies ("Question Authority").
18. The Moody Blues also make other philosophical references in their songs. For example, in the song, "In the Beginning" from *On the Threshold of a Dream* (1969), Graeme Edge makes clever use of René Descartes's well-known maxim, "I think, therefore I am." In the song, which pitches individual existence against some kind of Hal-like computer of society, the line goes, I think: "I think, therefore, I am—I think." See my discussion in Chapter 5 below.
19. For Townshend's own explanation of some of the themes of *Tommy* and his influence by Meher Baba, see his *Rolling Stone* interview, July 12th, 1969.

3. Bridge Over Troubled Water: The Greening of Rock Music

1. See Aristotle, *Nicomachean Ethics*, Book VIII, A., 3.
2. *Ibid.*
3. James Taylor's version of "You've Got a Friend" was actually more successful than King's. It reached Number One in 1971.
4. E.M. Forster, *Two Cheers for Democracy*, "What I Believe".
5. Harvey Cox, *The Secular City* (New York: Macmillan, 1965).

6. *Ibid.*, p. 38.
7. *Ibid.*, p. 47.
8. *Ibid.*, p. 81.
9. Bishop John A.T. Robinson, *Honest to God* (Philadelphia: The Westminster Press, 1963), Chapters 5 and 7.
10. Approximately the same period saw the beginning and the growth and development of several similar "self-help" organizations, such as Save the Children and Oxfam.
11. Matthew 25:35–36.
12. Charles A. Reich, *The Greening of America* (New York: Bantam, 1970).
13. William H. Whyte, *The Organization Man* (New York: Simon and Schuster, 1956).
14. See Reich, *ibid.*, Chapter 6, "The Lost Self".
15. See Reich, *ibid.*, and Whyte, *ibid.*, Chapters 25 and 26.
16. For a discussion of various such attempts, see Peyton E. Richter, *Utopias: Social Ideals and Communal Experiments* (Boston: Holbrook Press, 1971). For criticisms of utopias, see Peyton E. Richter, *Utopia/Dystopia?* (Cambridge: Schenkman, 1975).
17. Ralph Waldo Emerson, *Essays: Second Series*, Politics. As an added note, Emerson is the first person, to my knowledge, to have the expression "keep cool" with anything close to the new "hip" meaning which this expression acquired in the 1950s and 1960s.
18. See Lewis Mumford, "Two Kinds of Utopia", in Richter, *Utopias, ibid.*, pp. 29–42.
19. *Ibid.*, p. 37.
20. I assume that 'Baba' reflects the influence of Meher Baba upon Townshend. See Townshend's interview in *Rolling Stone*, July 12th, 1969.

4. Sex, Drugs, and Rock 'n' Roll

1. Herbert Marcuse, *One-Dimensional Man* (Boston: Beacon Press, 1964), pp. 4–5, 245.
2. Horace, *Epodes*, II, xi, last stanza.
3. Aesop, "The Ant and the Grasshopper".
4. Joel Whitburn, *Top 40 Hits*, Fifth Edition (New York: Billboard Books, 1992), p. 367.
5. Vance Packard, *The Hidden Persuaders* (New York: Pocket Books, 1957).
6. Marcuse, *One-Dimensional Man*, pp. 56ff.
7. Some women experience health problems as a result of their use of birth control pills, and there was, and still is, a genuine feminist issue about women's health and some forms of birth control.

8. There has been some controversy over whether this is a uniquely male view of sex. Surveys have indicated that more women than men tend to associate sex with the desire for a permanent, loving relationship. Is a *carpe diem* view of sexual pleasure an exclusively masculine view of sex? It is unlikely that we will ever reach unanimity on an answer to this question. There seems to be little evidence that whatever differences there are between men and women are to accounted for in biological terms—in terms of genetics or hormones. Certainly some women are as promiscuous as some men, and some men are as monogamous as some women. The differences between men and women are to accounted for mainly in terms of socialized sex roles, and these certainly change from time to time. The period of The Sixties was a time when these sex roles were in a state of flux, and many women showed a greatly increased interest in casual sex.

9. Whitburn, *op. cit.*, p. 550.

10. *Ibid.*, p. 581.

11. *Ibid.*, pp. 601 and 525.

12. Theodore Roszak, *The Making of a Counter Culture* (Garden City, NY: Anchor Books, 1969), p. 155.

13. The science fiction stories of Philip K. Dick, which attracted a passionate cult following in the 1960s, are strongly influenced by his involvement in the drug culture. Such novels as *Eye in the Sky, The Three Stigmata of Palmer Eldritch, Ubik, A Maze of Death,* and *Time Out Of Joint* explore the weakened sense of reality and the subjectivity of different persons' constructions of reality. His later novel, *A Scanner Darkly,* looks back bitterly on the drug life-style as a tragic blunder. "Eye in the Sky" was also the title of a hit song (Number Three in 1982) by the Alan Parsons Project (written by Eric Woolfson and Alan Parsons):

> I am the Eye in the Sky
> Looking at you.
> I can read your mind.
> I am the Maker of Rules
> Dealing with Fools.
> I can cheat you blind.

14. Dennis Coon, *Introduction to Psychology: Exploration and Application,* Fifth Edition, (New York: West, 1977), pp. 160–61.

15. See *ibid.*, p. 161 and A.E. Reif, "The Causes of Cancer", *American Scientist*, Vol. 69, 1981, pp. 437–447.

16. Pamphlet entitled "Facts About Cigarette Smoking", published by the American Lung Association, 1990.

17. *Ibid.*
18. Hoyt Axton was a performer whose best-known songs were recorded by other artists, as is the case here. His "hits" include "Greenback Dollar" by the Kingston Trio, and "Joy to the World" and "Never Been to Spain" by Three Dog Night. His mother, Mae Axton, wrote "Heartbreak Hotel".
19. Steppenwolf took its name from the novel of the same name by Hermann Hesse. The song, "The Pusher", runs an incredible 21 minutes and 36 seconds. The album *Early Steppenwolf* was actually made when the group was still known as The Sparrow. See Dafydd Rhees and Luke Crampton, *Rock Movers and Shakers* (New York: Billboard Books, 1991), p. 502.
20. 'Snow' was a common underground designation for both cocaine and heroin. A 'snowbird' was a heavy user of either drug.
21. Aldous Huxley, *Doors of Perception* and *Heaven and Hell* (New York: Harper and Row, 1963).
22. *Ibid.*, p. 73.
23. *Ibid.*, p. 78.
24. *Ibid.*, p. 79.
25. See Robert Nozick, *Anarchy, State, and Utopia* (New York: Basic Books, 1974), pp. 42–43. Thanks to George Harris for suggesting the use of this example here.
26. *Ibid.*, p. 43.
27. Since this is the sort of thing that may confirm the reader's worst suspicions about philosophy, I should point out that hardly any philosophers, and none of any note, have been solipsists, or have even entertained solipsism as a serious candidate for truth. But knowing something for practical purposes and being able to prove it rigorously are two different things, and just as people knew for thousands of years that 2 + 2 = 4, but only made serious attempts to prove it in the last century or so, philosophers have sometimes found the exercise of refuting solipsism (without simultaneously "proving too much" by recommending complete credulity) a stimulating challenge.
28. Whitburn, *op. cit.*, p. 514.
29. *Ibid.*, p. 574.
30. *Ibid.*, p. 528.
31. *Ibid.*, p. 75.
32. The Beatles, 1967.
33. In William James, *Pragmatism and Other Essays* (New York: Washington Square Press, 1963).
34. See, for example, H.K. Beecher, *Measurement of Subjective Responses: Quantitative Effects of Drugs* (New York: Oxford University Press, 1959).
35. See *Schopenhauer Selections*, edited by DeWitt H. Parker (New York: Charles Scribner's Sons, 1928), pp. 175ff.

5. Keep on Trucking: A Majority of One

1. Joel Whitburn, *The Billboard Book of Top 40 Hits* (New York: Billboard Books, 1992), p. 569.
2. *Ibid.*, p. 518.
3. Whitburn, *ibid.*, p. 153.
4. Charles A. Reich, *The Greening of America* (New York: Bantam Books, 1970), pp. 241–43.
5. *Ibid.*, p. 518.
6. Whitburn, *ibid.*, p. 598.
7. *Ibid.*
8. Jean-Paul Sartre, *Being and Nothingness* (New York: Philosophical Library, 1956), p. 237.
9. *Ibid.*
10. Whitburn, *ibid.*, p. 418.
11. Although this song is known as Frank Sinatra's theme song, Elvis's recording in 1977 reached a higher position on the charts than Sinatra's 1969 version had. See Whitburn, *ibid.*, p. 586.
12. See William Golding, *Lord of the Flies* (New York: Capricorn Books, 1954), p. 190.
13. Whitburn, *ibid.*, p. 138.
14. From "Do Not Go Gentle into That Good Night", by Dylan Thomas (1914–1953).
15. Of course there were many others, including, Hoot Gibson, Ken Maynard, Tom Mix, Tex Ritter, and Bob Steele in the 1930s and 1940s, and Rex Allen, William Boyd, Johnny Mack Brown, William "Wild Bill" Elliott, Allen "Rocky" Lane, and Whip Wilson in the 1950s. See Alan G. Barbour, *The Thrill of It All* (New York: Collier, 1971).
16. Whitburn, *ibid.*, p. 23.
17. Whitburn, *ibid.*, p. 119.
18. Greil Marcus, *Mystery Train* (New York: Dutton, 1975). See the chapter entitled "Sly Stone: The Myth of Staggerlee".
19. Marcus, *ibid.*, p. 66.
20. *Ibid.*, p. 67.
21. Whitburn, *ibid.*, p. 569.
22. John Rawls, *A Theory of Justice* (Cambridge: Harvard University Press, 1971).
23. Robert Nozick, *Anarchy, State, and Utopia* (New York: Basic Books, 1974).
24. But, of course, if the paradise belongs to someone else, then he or she has the right to do with it as he or she will.
25. Nozick, *ibid.*, pp. 93–95.
26. *Ibid.*, p. 95.
27. *Ibid.*, Chapter 7, Section I, pp. 150–182.
28. *Ibid.*, p. 169. One of America's leading philosophers, Nozick has written

no further works of *political* philosophy since *Anarchy, State, and Utopia,* though he has made clear in passing remarks that he no longer fully accepts the position he advanced there. Others do, however. See, for instance, Jan Narveson, *The Libertarian Idea* (Philadelphia: Temple University Press, 1988).

29. The New Left arose after the Soviet invasion of Hungary in 1956. Numerous individuals who had been Soviet sympathisers ceased to be so, yet still sought social change upon broadly Marxist lines.
30. Henry David Thoreau, *Walden* (New York: Norton, 1966), p. 215.

6. Brother Love's Traveling Salvation Show: The Theology of Rock

1. See Michael Bane, "Fahrenheit 250: Florida Minister, Flock, Fire Rock", *Rolling Stone,* February 12th, 1976.
2. See Tom Zito, "Is Rock Unrighteous?" *Rolling Stone,* February 19th, 1981.
3. John Sippel, "'Demonic' Messages Are Focus of California Proposal", *Billboard,* May 15th, 1982. Linda Martin and Kerry Seagrave, *Anti-Rock: The Opposition to Rock and Roll* (Hamden, CT: Archon Books, 1988), p. 288.
4. Bill Holland, "'Demonic' Message Bill Is Introduced in Congress", *Billboard,* July 10th, 1982 and Martin and Seagrave, *ibid.,* p. 289.
5. Dave Marsh, "Goulish Beatlemania", *Rolling Stone,* January 22, 1981, p. 29.
6. Carlos Castañeda, *The Teachings of Don Juan* (New York: Ballentine, 1968).
7. Hermann Hesse, *Siddhartha* (New York: Bantam, 1951). This is the same Hermann Hesse who wrote the book *Steppenwolf* from which the group took its name. For a history of Buddhism in the United States, see Rick Fields, *How the Swans Came to the Lake* (Boston: Shambhala, 1986).
8. Joel Whitburn, *The Billboard Book of Top 40 Hits* (New York: Billboard Books, 1992), p. 591.
9. Dafydd Rees and Luke Crampton, *Rock Movers and Shakers* (New York: Billboard Books, 1991), p. 460.
10. John B. Noss, *Man's Religions,* Fifth Edition, (New York: Macmillan, 1974), p. 536.
11. *Ibid.*
12. See, for example, Peter Lemesurier, *Gospel of the Stars* (Longmead, England: Element Books, 1990), p. 55.
13. *Ibid.,* p. 60.

14. Whitburn, *ibid.*, p. 613.
15. Whitburn, *ibid.*, p. 537.
16. Noss, *ibid.*, p. 44.
17. See *Understanding the New Testament,* Third Edition, by Howard Clark Kee, Franklin W. Young, and Karlfried Froehlich (Englewood Cliffs: Prentice-Hall, 1957), pp. 399ff.
18. There is much dispute about who the author of *Revelation* actually was. For discussion of this issue, see *Understanding the New Testament, ibid.,* p. 401.
19. See Noss, *ibid.*, pp. 404 and 407.
20. *The Koran Interpreted,* A.J. Arberry (London: Allen and Unwin, 1955) LXXXI. 2–14, (Vol. II, p. 326).
21. Noss, *ibid.*, p. 208.
22. Dafydd Rhees and Luke Crampton, *Rock Movers and Shakers* (New York: Billboard Books, 1991), p. 230.
23. *Ibid.*
24. Actual passages are much too numerous to cite completely here, but compare Psalms 90:4; Matthew 26:40–41; Luke 13:35; I Corinthians 16:13.
25. Ezekiel 33:1–9.
26. Revelation 6:8.
27. See, for example, Psalms 72:6 and Hosea 6:3.
28. Whitburn, *ibid.*, p. 306. A song has really touched a nerve if another song is written purely as a rejoinder, and all the more so if that other song is similarly a hit. "The Dawn of Correction" by The Spokesmen reached Number 36 in the same year (and the "Correction" foreseen was harsh and nasty).
29. See, for example, Matthew 24:36–44.
30. Matthew 24:36.
31. Matthew 24:44.
32. See Dee Brown, *Bury My Heart at Wounded Knee* (New York: Washington Square Press, 1970), p. 406.
33. *Ibid.*, p. 390.
34. *Ibid.*, p. 408.
35. *Ibid.*, p. 411.
36. See Noss *ibid.*, pp. 397ff.
37. It is tempting to carry the analysis of the metaphor of wooden ships too far. With the connection of wooden ships to music, it is tempting to think that perhaps the wooden ships are the guitars which provide the melodies which can transport us to some new, distant land. Perhaps. But the image soon breaks down. If this metaphor were to be consistent with the theme of being saved by turning to something simple and natural for our salvation, then it seems, both the guitars and the music would have to be simple and natural, i. e., *acoustic.* And the music of Jefferson Airplane was anything but.

38. Amos 1 and 2.
39. Matthew 19:24.

7. Too Old to Rock 'n' Roll, Too Young to Die

1. This line and variations on it are commonly attributed to various sources. One of the earliest and most reliable is to the hoodlum character played by John Derek in the movie, "Knock on Any Door", 1949, starring Humphrey Bogart.
2. Dave Marsh, *Before I Get Old: The Story of The Who* (New York: St. Martin's Press, 1983).
3. It is significant and ironic that this is the only song by the Grateful Dead ever to break into the Top 40 during the entire existence of the band. The simple explanation is the greying of the "Deadheads"—both real and imagined.
4. Charles A. Reich, *The Greening of America* (New York: Bantam, 1970), p. 379.
5. *Ibid.*, p. 380.
6. *Ibid.*, pp. 380–81.
7. Todd Gitlin, *The Sixties: Years of Hope, Days of Rage* (New York: Bantam, 1987).
8. *Ibid.*, p. 433.
9. *Rolling Stone Magazine*, January 21, 1971, p. 41.
10. Joe McGinniss, *The Selling of the President 1968* (New York: Pocket Books, 1969).
11. Don J. Hibbard and Carol Kaleialoha, *The Role of Rock* (Englewood Cliffs, NJ: Prentice-Hall, 1983), p. 135.
12. See Dafydd Rees and Luke Crampton, *Rock Movers and Shakers* (New York: Billboard Books, 1991), p. 580.
13. Marshall McLuhan and Quentin Fiore, *The Medium is the Massage* (New York: Simon and Schuster, 1967).
14. Television is the only other likely candidate for such a claim, but at least in the early years of television, it did not have the partisan message and underlying dominant philosophical themes which I have identified for rock music.
15. Dave Marsh, "Goulish Beatlemania", *Rolling Stone*, January 22nd, 1981, p. 29.
16. Alan Light, "Bob Dylan", in *The Rolling Stone Illustrated History of Rock & Roll*, edited by Anthony DeCurtis and James Henke (New York: Random House, 1976), p. 308.
17. See, "What the Sixties Had that the Eighties Don't Have," by Paul Williams in *The Penguin Book of Rock & Roll Writing*, edited by Clinton

Heylin (New York: Viking, 1992), pp. 116ff. This piece is excerpted from Williams's book, *The Map*.

18. *Ibid.*, p. 117.
19. *Ibid.*
20. At the time of this writing, *The Sound of the City* is unfortunately out of print. "Five Styles of Rock and Roll" excerpted from the book is included in *The Penguin Book of Rock and Roll Writing* (New York: Viking, 1992), pp. 6–22.
21. *Ibid.*, pp. 6–7.
22. *Ibid.*
23. See Dafydd Rees and Luke Crampton, *Rock Movers and Shakers* (New York: Billboard Books, 1991), p. 358.

Bibliography

Adorno, Theodor, W. "On Popular Music". *Studies in Philosophy and Science,* Vol. 9, No. 1, 1949.

Aldridge, John W. *In the Country of the Young.* New York: Harper and Row, 1969.

Arberry, A.J. *The Koran Interpreted.* London: Allen and Unwin, 1955.

Aristotle, *The Nicomachean Ethics.* Translated by W.D. Ross. New York: Oxford University Press, 1980.

Atcheson, Richard. *The Bearded Lady.* New York: John Day, 1971.

Austin, Anthony. *The President's War.* Philadelphia: Lippincott, 1971.

Baggelaar, Kristin and Minton, Donald. *Folk Music: More Than a Song.* New York: Crowell, 1976.

Belz, Carl. *The Story of Rock.* New York: Oxford University Press, 1972.

Bonner, John T. *The Evolution of Culture in Animals.* Princeton: Princeton University Press, 1980.

Booth, Mark W. *American Popular Music: A Reference Guide.* Westport, CN: Greenwood Press, 1983.

Bowie, Norman and Simon, Robert L., eds. *The Individual and the Political Order.* Englewood Cliffs: Prentice-Hall, 1977.

Brown, Dee. *Bury My Heart at Wounded Knee.* New York: Washington Square Press, 1970.

Carson, Rachel. *Silent Spring.* Boston: Houghton Mifflin, 1962.

Castañeda, Carlos. *The Teachings of Don Juan.* New York: Ballentine, 1968.

Chapple, Steve and Garofalo, Reebe. *Rock n Roll is Here to Pay: The History and Politics of the Music Industry.* Chicago: Nelson-Hall, 1977.

Christgau, Robert. *Any Old Way You Choose It.* Baltimore: Penguin, 1973.

Cohn, Nik. *Rock From the Beginning.* New York: Pocket Books, 1969.

Cox, Harvey. *The Secular City.* New York: Macmillan, 1965.

Davies, Hunter. *The Beatles.* New York: Dell, 1968.

Davis, Phillip E. *Moral Duty and Legal Responsibility.* New York: Appleton-Century-Crofts, 1966.

Deakin, James. *Lyndon Johnson's Credibility Gap.* Washington, DC: Public Affairs Press, 1968.

De Curtis, Anthony, ed. *Present Tense: Rock and Roll and Culture.* Durham, NC: Duke University Press, 1992.

De Curtis, Anthony, and Henke, James. *The Rolling Stone Illustrated History of Rock and Roll.* New York: Random House, 1976.

Denisoff, R. Serge, and Peterson, Richard A. *The Sounds of Social Change.* Chicago: Rand McNally, 1972.

De Ropp, Robert S. *Drugs and the Mind.* Delacorte Press, 1957.

Dick, Philip K. *Eye in the Sky.* New York: Berkeley, 1958.

——. *Time Out of Joint.* Boston: Hall, 1959.

——. *The Man in the High Castle.* New York: Berkeley, 1962.

——. *The Three Stigmata of Palmer Eldritch.* New York: Berkeley, 1964.

——. *Ubik.* New York: Berkeley, 1969.

——. *A Maze of Death.* New York: Berkeley, 1972.

——. *A Scanner Darkly.* New York: New American Library, 1978.

Edelstein, Andrew J. *The Pop Sixties.* New York: World Almanac Publications, 1985.

Eisen, Jonathan. *The Age of Rock.* New York: Vintage, 1969.

——. *The Age of Rock 2.* New York: Vintage, 1970.

Elliott, Brad. *Surf's Up! The Beach Boys on Record 1961–81.* Ann Arbor, MI: Popular Culture, Ink, 1984.

Ellul, Jacques. *The Technological Society.* New York: Knopf, 1965.

Emerson, Ralph Waldo. *Essays: First and Second Series.* New York: Vintage, 1990.

Erlich, Paul R. *The Population Bomb.* New York: Ballantine, 1968.

Fields, Rick. *How The Swans Came to the Lake: A History of Buddhism in the United States.* Boston: Shambhala, 1986.

Fong-Torres, Ben, ed. *The Rolling Stone Rock 'n' Roll Reader.* New York: Bantam, 1974.

Freud, Sigmund. *Civilization and Its Discontents.* Garden City, NY: Doubleday, 1958.

Gillett, Charles. *The Sound of the City.* New York: Outerbridge and Dienstfrey, 1970.

Gitlin, Todd. *The Sixties: Years of Hope, Days of Rage.* New York: Bantam Books, 1987.

Gleason, Ralph. *Jefferson Airplane and the San Francisco Sound.* New York: Ballentine, 1969.

Golding, William. *Lord of the Flies.* New York: Capricorn Books, 1954.

Goldstein, Richard. *The Poetry of Rock.* New York: Bantam, 1969.

Goodman, Paul. *Growing Up Absurd.* New York: Random House, 1956.

Gottlieb, Annie. *Do You Believe In Magic?* New York: Times Books, 1987.

Gould, James A. and Truitt, Willis H. ed. *Political Ideologies*. New York: Macmillan, 1973.

Griffith, Robert. *Major Problems in American History Since 1945*. Lexington, MA: Heath, 1992.

Hamm, Charles. *Yesterdays: Popular Song in America*. New York: Norton, 1979.

Hardy, Phil and Laing, Dave. *The Faber Companion to 20th-Century Popular Music*. Boston: Faber and Faber, 1990.

———. *The Encyclopedia of Rock*. New York: Schirmer, 1987.

Held, Virginia, Nielsen, Kai, and Parsons, Charles, ed. *Philosophy and Political Action*. New York: Oxford University Press, 1972.

Heller, Joseph. *Catch-22*. New York: Dell, 1951.

Herbst, Peter, ed. *Rolling Stone Interviews, 1967–1980: Talking With the Legends of Rock and Roll*. New York: St. Martin's Press, 1981.

Hesse, Hermann. *Siddhartha*. New York: Bantam, 1951.

———. *Steppenwolf*. New York: Bantam, 1983.

Heylin, Clinton. *The Penguin Book of Rock and Roll Writing*. New York: Viking, 1992.

Hibbard, Don J., and Kaleialoha, Carol. *The Role of Rock*. Englewood Cliffs: Prentice-Hall, 1983.

Hobbes, Thomas. *The Leviathan,* edited by Michael Oakeshott. New York: Collier, 1962.

Hopkins, Jerry. *The Story of Rock*. New York: Signet, 1963.

Horowitz, David, Lerner, Michael, and Pyes, Chris. *Counterculture and Revolution*. New York: Random House, 1972.

Hotchner, A.E. *Blown Away*. New York: Simon and Schuster, 1990.

Huxley, Aldous. *Doors of Perception and Heaven and Hell*. New York: Harper and Row, 1954.

Jahn, Michael. *Rock*. New York: Quadrangle, 1973.

James, William. *Pragmatism and Other Essays*. New York: Washington Square Press, 1963.

Jasper, Tony. *Understanding Pop*. London: CCM Press, 1972.

Josephson, Eric and Mary, ed. *Man Alone*. New York: Dell, 1962.

Kee, Howard Clark, Young, Franklin W., and Froehlich, Karlfried. *Understanding the New Testament,* Third Edition. Englewood Cliffs: Prentice-Hall, 1957.

Keniston, Kenneth. *The Uncommitted*. New York: Dell, 1962.

Kerouac, Jack. *On The Road*. New York: Viking, 1959.

Kesey, Ken. *One Flew Over the Cuckoo's Nest*. New York: Signet, 1962.

Keyes, Ken, Jr. *The Hundredth Monkey*. Coos Bay, OR: Vision Books, 1982.

Laforse, Martin W., and Drake, James A. *Popular Culture and American Life.* Chicago: Nelson Hall, 1981.

Landau, Jon. *It's Too Late to Stop Now.* San Francisco: Straight Arrow Books, 1972.

Leary, Timothy. *The Politics of Ecstasy.* New York: Putnam, 1968.

Lemesurier, Peter. *Gospel of the Stars.* Shaftesbury, England: Element Books, 1990.

Levine, Lawrence W. *High Brow/Low Brow.* Cambridge: Harvard University Press, 1988.

Logan, Nick and Woffinden, Bob. *Illustrated History of Rock.* New York: Harmony, 1977.

Lothstein, Arthur. *"All We are Saying . . .": The Philosophy of the New Left.* New York: Capricorn, 1970.

Lydon, Michael. "Rock for Sale", *Ramparts,* June, 1969.

Machiavelli, *The Prince and Other Works.* New York: Hendricks House, 1941.

Macken, Bob, Fornatale, Peter, and Ayers, Bill. *Rock Music Source Book.* Garden City, NY: Doubleday, 1980.

Madden, Edward. *Civil Disobedience and Moral Law.* Seattle: University of Washington Press, 1968.

Malcolm, Henry. *Generation of Narcissus.* Boston: Little Brown, 1971.

Marcus, Greil. *Rock and Roll Will Stand.* Boston: Beacon Press, 1969.

———. *Mystery Train.* New York: Dutton, 1975.

Marcuse, Herbert. *Eros and Civilization.* Boston: Beacon Press, 1955.

———. *One-Dimensional Man.* Boston: Beacon Press, 1964.

Marsh, Dave. *Born to Run.* New York: Dell, 1981.

———. *Before I Get Old.* New York: St. Martin's Press, 1983.

———. *Glory Days.* New York: Dell, 1991.

———. *The Heart of Rock and Roll.* Markham, Ontario: New American Library, 1989.

Marsh, Dave, and Swenson, John. *The New Rolling Stone Record Guide.* New York: Rolling Stone Press, 1979.

Marshall Cavendish Illustrated History of Popular Music. Freeport Long Island, NY: Marshall Cavendish Corporation. Annual.

Martin, Linda, and Segrave, Kerry. *Anti-Rock: The Opposition to Rock 'n' Roll.* Hamden, CT: Archon Books, 1988.

Marx, Leo. *The Machine in the Garden.* New York: Oxford University Press, 1964.

Matusow, Allen J. *The Unraveling of America.* New York: Harper Torchbooks, 1984.

McGinnis, Joe. *The Selling of the President 1968.* New York: Pocket Books, 1969.

McLuhan, Marshall. *Understanding Media: The Extensions of Man.* New York: McGraw-Hill, 1964.

McLuhan, Marshall, and Fiore, Quentin. *The Medium is the Massage.* New York: Simon and Schuster, 1967.

Mellers, Wilfried. *Twilight of the Gods: The Music of the Beatles.* New York: Viking, 1973.

Miller, Jim. *The Rolling Stone Illustrated History of Rock and Roll.* New York: Rolling Stone Press, 1976.

Milne, Tom, ed. *The Time Out Film Guide* Second Edition. New York: Penguin, 1989.

Mukerji, Chandra, and Schudson, Michael. *Rethinking Popular Culture.* Berkeley: University of California Press, 1991.

Murchland, Bernard, ed. *The Meaning of the Death of God.* New York: Vintage, 1967.

Narveson, Jan. *The Libertarian Idea.* Philadelphia: Temple University Press, 1988.

Nite, Norm. *Rock On: The Illustrated Encyclopedia of Rock 'n' Roll,* Three Volumes. New York: Harper and Row, 1982.

Noss, John B. *Man's Religions.* New York: Macmillan, 1974.

Nozick, Robert. *Anarchy, State, and Utopia.* New York: Basic Books, 1974.

Orwell, George. *Nineteen Eighty-Four.* New York: New American Library, 1984 [1948].

Packard, Vance. *The Hidden Persuaders.* New York: Pocket Books, 1957.

Pareles, John, and Romanowski, Patricia, eds. *The Rolling Stone Encyclopedia of Rock and Roll.* New York: Rolling Stone Press, 1983.

Parrinder, Geoffrey. *World Religions: From Ancient History to the Present.* New York: Facts on File Publications, 1971.

Pichaske, David. *A Generation in Motion: Popular Music and Culture in the Sixties.* New York: Schirmer Books, 1979.

———. *The Poetry of Rock: the Golden Years.* Peoria, IL: Ellis Press, 1981.

Pious, Richard M., *Civil Rights and Liberties in the 1970's.* New York: Random House, 1973.

Quinn, Edward and Dolan, Paul J., *The Sense of the Sixties.* New York: The Free Press, 1968.

Rawls, John. *A Theory of Justice.* Cambridge, MA: Harvard University Press, 1971.

Rees, Dafydd, and Crampton, Luke, eds. *Rock Movers and Shakers.* New York: Billboard Books, 1991.

Reich, Charles A. *The Greening of America.* New York: Bantam, 1970.

Richter, Peyton E., ed. *Utopias.* Boston: Holbrook Press, 1971.

Richter, Peyton E., ed. *Utopia/Dystopia?* Cambridge, MA: Schenkman Publishing Company, 1975.

Robinson, James A.T. *Honest to God.* Philadelphia: Westminster Press, 1963.

Roszak, Theodore. *The Making of a Counter Culture.* New York: Doubleday, 1968.

Rousseau, Jean-Jacques. *The Social Contract and Discourses,* translated by G.D.H. Cole. London: Everyman's Library, 1913.

Roxon, Lillian. *The Encyclopedia of Rock.* New York: Universal Library, 1970.

Salinger, J.D. *The Catcher in the Rye.* New York: Bantam, 1951.

Sander, Ellen. *Trips: Rock Life in the Sixties.* New York: Scribner, 1973.

Sartre, Jean-Paul. *Being and Nothingness.* New York: Philosophical Library, 1956.

Scheurer, Timothy E. *Born in the U.S.A.: The Myth of America in Popular Music from Colonial Times to the Present.* Jackson: University of Mississippi Press, 1991.

Somma, Robert, ed. *No One Waved Goodbye.* New York: Outerbridge and Dienstfrey, 1971.

Spinner, Stephanie, ed. *Rock is Beautiful.* New York: Dell, 1970.

Taylor, Gordon Rattray. *The Doomsday Book.* Greenwich, CT: Fawcett, 1970.

Teich, Albert H., ed. *Technology and Man's Future.* New York: St. Martin's Press, 1977.

Thompson, Elizabeth, and Gutman, David, ed. *The Dylan Companion.* London: Macmillan, 1990.

Thoreau, Henry David. *Walden and Civil Disobedience,* edited by Owen Thomas. New York, Norton, 1966.

Tolkien, J.R.R. *The Lord of the Rings.* Boston: Houghton Mifflin, 1974.

Vahanian, Gabriel. *The Death of God.* New York: George Braziller, 1957.

Ward, Ed, Stokes, Geoffrey, and Tucker, Ken, ed. *Rock of Ages.* New York: Rolling Stone Press, 1986.

Watts, Alan. *The Joyous Cosmology.* New York: Pantheon Press, 1962.

Weiner, Rex, and Stillman, Deanne. *Woodstock Census.* New York: Viking, 1979.

Whitburn, Joel. *Billboard Book of Top 40 Hits.* New York: Billboard Books, 1992.

————. *Billboard's Top One Thousand.* Milwaukee: Leonard, 1986.

Whyte, William H., Jr., *The Organization Man.* New York: Simon and Schuster, 1956.

Williams, Paul. *Outlaw Blues.* New York: Dutton, 1969.

Williams, Raymond. *Problems in Materialism and Culture.* London: Verso, 1980.

Wolfe, Burton. *The Hippies.* New York: Signet, 1968.

Wolfe, Tom. *The Electric Kool-Aid Acid Test.* New York: Farrar, Straus, and Giroux, 1968.

Index

Titles of songs appear in quotation marks. Titles of albums as well as books appear in italics.